KEY ISSUES IN SECONDARY EDUCATION
2ND EDITION

Key Issues in Secondary Education

Introductory Readings

Second Edition

Edited by
John Beck & Mary Earl

continuum
LONDON • NEW YORK

Continuum

The Tower Building
11 York Road
London SE1 7NX

15 East 26th Street
New York
NY 10010

First published 2000
Reprinted 2001
This edition 2003

British Library Cataloguing-in-Publication Data
A catalogue record for this book is available from the British Library.

ISBN 0–8264–6129–8 (paperback)

Typeset by BookEns Ltd, Royston, Herts.
Printed and bound in Great Britain by MPG Books Ltd, Bodmin, Cornwall

Contents

About the Contributors

Madeleine Arnot is Reader in Sociology of Education and Fellow of Jesus College at the University of Cambridge. She has an international reputation for her expertise in the field of gender, race and class relations in education and for work promoting equality policies and citizenship education. She directed a project for the Office for Standards in Education on *Recent Research on Gender and Educational Performance* (1998) and for the Equal Opportunities Commission on *Educational Reforms and Gender Equality in Schools.* Her recent books include: *Feminism and Social Justice in Education* (edited with K. Weiler, Falmer Press, l993); *Closing the Gender Gap* (with G. Weiner and M. David, Polity Press, 1999); *Challenging Democracy: International perspectives on gender, education and citizenship* (edited with J. Dillabough, Routledge/Falmer 2000) and *Reproducing Gender? Essays on educational theory and feminist politics* (Routledge/Falmer 2002).

John Beck teaches sociology of education and curriculum and professional studies. He is Education Team Chair in the University of Cambridge Faculty of Education and a fellow of Homerton College. His research interests include citizenship education and personal and social education. He is author of *Morality and Citizenship in Education* (Cassell 1998) and (with John Ahier and Rob Moore) *Graduate Citizens? Issues of Citizenship and Higher Education* (Routledge/Falmer 2003).

Gabrielle Cliff Hodges is a lecturer in the University of Cambridge Faculty of Education where she is secondary course manager and co-ordinator of the secondary English and Drama PGCE course. Recent publications include chapters about speaking and listening and poetry in *Learning to Teach English in the Secondary School* (1997) and about reading in *Where Texts and Children Meet* (2000) and *Issues in English Teaching* (2000). She is also co-editor of *Tales, Tellers and Texts* (1999). From 1996 to 1998 she was Chair of the National Association for the Teaching of English.

Mary Earl is Lecturer in Religious Studies in the University of Cambridge Faculty of Education. She was formerly Head of RE at a Hertfordshire comprehensive school and then at a Cambridgeshire Sixth Form College. She has also worked both at school and higher education level as a trainer and consultant in PSHE areas of the curriculum. Research interests include A-level teaching of world religions; spirituality and psychology; and narrative and the development of values. Recent publications include 'Narrative and the development of values' in E. Bearne (ed.) *Language Across the Secondary Curriculum* (Routledge 1990) and 'Shadow and spirituality' *International Journal of Children's Spirituality*, 6, 3, 2001.

Philip Gardner is Senior Lecturer in Education at the University of Cambridge and a Fellow of St Edmund's College. He has written widely on the history of education and, with Peter Cunningham, has co-directed a sequence of major oral history research projects investigating the teaching profession in the twentieth century.

Ruth Joyce OBE is Home Office Blueprint Manager and is in charge of the Drug Prevention Unit of the Home Office Drug Prevention Office. She was previously Head of Education for Prevention at SCODA (the Standing Conference on Drug Abuse) and, before that, Drug Education Advisor for Cambridgeshire LEA.

Ruth Kershner is a lecturer in the Faculty of Education, University of Cambridge, with particular interests in the fields of educational psychology, special educational needs, learning difficulties, intelligence and assessment. She has previously worked as a teacher and child care worker. She has recently carried out research projects on pupils' and teachers' views of the classroom environment and on strategies for raising boys' achievement in special schools. A recent publication, co-authored with Roland Chaplain, is *Understanding Special Educational Needs*: *A teacher's guide to effective school-based research* (David Fulton 2001).

Terence H. McLaughlin is Professor of Philosophy at the University of London Institute of Education and a Fellow of St Edmund's College, Cambridge. He specializes in philosophy of education and has published widely on many aspects of the field. He has taught English and been Head of Year and Head of Sixth Form in two comprehensive schools and is currently Chair of the Philosophy of Education Society of Great Britain. He has recently edited (with Mark Halstead) *Education in Morality* (1999), a collection of papers on philosophical aspects of moral education.

John Raffan is a lecturer in the University of Cambridge Faculty of Education with particular responsibility for Science/Chemistry Education. He has been involved with curriculum development and evaluation for several large-scale national projects and with assessment as an examiner for Awarding Bodies and as a consultant with the Qualifications and Curriculum Authority (QCA) and its predecessors. His recent publications include: 'School-based assessment: principles and practice' in *School-Based Assessment and Equivalence of Qualifications* (ACEAB 2001) and 'Assessment for certification using non-traditional modes: an analysis of case studies and a review of recent literature' in *Empowering Teachers and Learners in Classroom Assessment* (ACEAB in press).

Michael J. Reiss is Professor of Science Education and Head of the School of Mathematics, Science and Technology at the Institute of Education, University of London, a priest of the Church of England and an accredited counsellor. He was a member of the Cambridgeshire LEA Working Group that produced the County's Sex Education Guidelines in 1992 and has acted as a consultant on sex education and/or values to a number of governments and organizations. He is the editor of the journal *Sex Education*. Recent publications in the field of sex education include: M. J. Reiss, and S. A. Mabud (eds) *Sex Education and Religion*, (The Islamic Academy 1998); and J. M. Halstead and M. J. Reiss *Values in Sex Education: From Principles to Practice*, Routledge/Falmer (2003).

Martyn Rouse is a teacher and researcher in the field of special educational needs and inclusion at the University of Cambridge Faculty of Education. He has undertaken commissioned research for international agencies such as UNICEF and for local authorities into the development of inclusive schools in the UK. Recently he carried out research on the impact of school reform on the education of children with special needs for the US Department of Education in association with a consortium of US universities. Other research interests include the evaluation of special education policies and the assessment of students with special needs. He is currently co-ordinating a Department for International Development project on inclusion with the Kenyan Ministry of Education and Kenyatta University. He has published extensively on a wide range of issues in the areas of special educational needs and inclusive education. Recent publications include: *Special Education and School Reform in Britain and the United States* (with M. McLaughlin) (Routledge 2000); 'Inclusive practice in secondary classrooms: lessons learned' (with L. Florian), *Cambridge Journal of Education*, 31, 3, (2000) 399–412; 'Inclusive practice in secondary schools' (with L. Florian), in R. Rose and I. Grosvenor (eds) *Doing Research In Special Education* (David Fulton, 2001).

Kenneth Ruthven taught in Scotland and England before joining the University of Cambridge Faculty of Education where he is Reader in Education. His contribution to this book reflects his particular interest in the part that assessment plays in the teaching and learning of mathematics, which is discussed more fully in his recent writing on 'Assessment in mathematics education' in L. Haggarty (ed.) *Teaching Mathematics in Secondary Schools* (Routledge/Falmer, 2002) pp. 176–91.

Jacqui Stanford is Economic and Social Research Council (ESRC) Fellow at University of Cambridge. She is currently researching teacher vulnerability in multicultural settings.

Christine Tubb lectures in Education Studies in the University of Cambridge Faculty of Education; she is also a member of Homerton College. She teaches philosophy of education and also contributes to curriculum and professional studies courses for both undergraduate and PGCE students. Her research interests include moral and values education, and she is particularly interested in the morality of war and just war theory.

Rex Walford is a Fellow of Wolfson College, Cambridge, and a past Head of the Department of Education in the University of Cambridge. He has particular interests in experiential learning in classrooms and has written several books about gaming and simulation techniques. His most recent book, *Geography In British Schools 1850–2000* has won the Silver Award of the Geographical Association, and he was awarded the OBE in the Millennium Honours List for 'contributions to geographical scholarship'. He is a recent winner of a Pilkington Prize, Cambridge University's award for outstanding teaching.

Angela Webster is Senior Manager/Head of Key Stage 4 and Professional Tutor for initial teacher education and training at Parkside Community College, Cambridge, and a former Head of Geography at schools in Cambridgeshire and Sheffield. Recently seconded to Homerton College as Secondary Subject Lecturer for Geography, she has written extensively on teaching styles and enquiry-based learning, and on issues of assessment in geography.

Michael Younger is Director of PGCE Courses within the University of Cambridge Faculty of Education and is a fellow of Homerton College. He has co-authored – with Molly Warrington – a series of papers on perspectives on the gender gap in primary and secondary schools in England and Wales, the most recent of which have been published in the *British Educational Research Journal*, 28, 3 (2002), *Gender and Education*, 12, 4 (2000) and the *British Journal of Sociology of Education*, 20, 3 (1999). He is currently Co-Director of a ten-term DFES sponsored project on Raising Boys' Achievement, working with 50 secondary and primary schools in different parts of England.

Introduction

This book mainly concerns the work of secondary schools, although this focus cannot be separated from many questions of much wider educational concern. The book is primarily addressed to teachers in training and to those in their induction year, though the topics it discusses are of significance to all who teach in secondary education. Teacher training has undergone extensive reform in recent years, much of it, rightly, focused upon raising the quality of subject teaching. Subject teaching, however, is far from being the whole of teaching or education. All who work in schools share a set of wider concerns and responsibilities – having to do with the education of the whole child or young person. Although discussion of these broader dimensions of education can all too easily become either platitudinous or else polarized (often around false dichotomies), the issues involved are of central importance – both for schools and for society as a whole.

The book originated as an 'in-house' set of readings written for initial teacher training students taking the secondary PGCE in the Faculty of Education in the University of Cambridge. Like most such courses, this PGCE programme contains a substantial element of general Professional Studies taken by all trainees alongside their main subject work. The main aim of such courses, and of this book, is to introduce student teachers to a range of issues which are of decisive importance in the general professional development of all teachers of the 11–19 age phase, irrespective of their subject specialisms. Some of these issues are mainly *cognitive* matters – for example the nature and development of intelligence, or different learning styles and how they relate to teaching styles. Other topics, however, are more obviously *value-related* and have to do with the personal, moral, spiritual, social and political development of young people. Many of these overtly value-related issues are also ones which central government and its agencies now *require* teacher training institutions to include within initial teacher education. For example, Standard 1.8 of the 'Standards for the

Award of Qualified Teacher Status' requires those awarded QTS to demonstrate that 'they are aware of, and work within, the statutory frameworks relating to teachers' responsibilities' (DfES and TTA 2002, p. 6). This requires teachers to know about their statutory duties and rights in relation to a whole swathe of legislation bearing on education, including for example: The Children Act 1989, The Race Relations Act 1976 as amended in 2000 to contain laws against discrimination on grounds of sex, race and disability, duties to promote educational and social inclusion, the Human Rights Act 1998, and so on.[1] There are, in addition, government guidance documents on areas such as citizenship, sex and relationship education, drug education, and so forth.

It is important to recognize that not only are many of the specific *issues* identified here ones which involve significant controversy but also that the whole idea that schools should seek to get formally involved in matters of this kind is itself controversial. However, education is through and through a value-laden enterprise. Value issues and value choices cannot be eliminated and it is better not to evade them, for example by pretending that they do not exist. What is important, therefore, is to recognize this reality and try to equip those engaged in education to properly understand the complexity of the task they are engaged in – not only in these contested areas of personal, moral, social, spiritual and political education, but also in relation to the apparently more 'everyday' issues of subject teaching, assessment, the ways in which language is used in the classroom, relating to parents and their concerns, etc. These apparently more straightforward aspects of education are indeed in some respects mainly technical or practical but, beneath even the most mundane, value issues and questions of value priorities lurk.

What this book seeks to do is to link issues of 'theory' to these highly practical questions and dilemmas which teachers face every day of their lives. The contributors, in addition to being specialists in their various academic fields, are also, in most cases, qualified teachers who have direct experience of working regularly with trainees and alongside mentors and other staff in a wide range of schools. The 'tone' of different articles varies. In some cases, particularly where the issues under discussion have a directly practical and 'chalk-face' relevance, authors address the reader in a direct and personal way. On other topics, particularly those which deal with broader issues of educational policy or primarily with conceptual issues, the tone is more 'academic'. Nevertheless, in all cases all of us who have contributed to this book have tried to write in a way which is clear and accessible but without over-simplifying the complexity of the issues or the value problems they pose.

We have taken the opportunity, in preparing this second edition of *Key Issues in Secondary Education*, to include two completely new chapters – one by Ruth Kershner on the nature and measurement of intelligence, and one by Jacqui Stanford on issues of race and racism in school and society. Other chapters have been revised more or less radically for the second edition. Those which deal mainly with issues of principle and justification have, in most cases, stood the test of time and have required relatively little change.

Those addressing the rapidly changing world of educational policy and innovation, on the other hand, have been substantially rewritten to take account of recent developments and current debates.

The lay out of the book is, hopefully, self-explanatory. Part One deals with certain 'macro' issues: secondary schooling in England and Wales and its recent history, the school curriculum as a whole, and monitoring and assessment; this is followed by the new chapter on intelligence; also discussed are two key aspects of classroom teaching and learning – teaching and learning *styles*, and the use of language in classrooms and across the curriculum. Part Two focuses upon the school as a caring community and issues of educational opportunity – within the broader context of locality and environmental concerns. The topics included are pastoral care and the role of the tutor, children with special educational needs, equal opportunities in relation to social class and gender, issues of race and racism in school and society, the school and the community, and finally and in one sense most inclusively, environmental education. The third and final section is centred on subjects in which questions of values and controversiality are particularly prominent, including questions about approaches to *teaching* about controversial issues in schools. The topics covered are: values and controversial issues, moral education, citizenship and citizenship education, sex education and drug education. In all the areas discussed, the writers have taken account of recent research, the latest available policy initiatives and directives, and the likely shape of future programmes of initial teacher training, professional induction and Continuing Professional Development priorities.

NOTES

1. A very useful and frequently updated summary of these legal responsibilities affecting schools and individual teachers is *The Bristol Guide* (see Bibliography).

Part I

Schools, Curriculum and Classrooms: Issues of Teaching and Learning

Chapter 1

The Secondary School

PHILIP GARDNER

INTRODUCTION

What shapes the sequence of daily events that go on in any of the 5,000 or so secondary schools dotted all over England and Wales?

One obvious answer would be that the character of such events flows from the people who spend their everyday lives in the schools – the teachers and the pupils. Another answer might be to examine the influence of those with an immediate or direct interest in the life of a school – parents, governors, neighbouring businesses and the local community in general. Yet another would be to concentrate on those responsible for funding, administering and regulating the work of schools – central and local government, charities and the churches.

In one way or another each of these groups exerts important effects upon the secondary school. Often, these effects may be short-lived; they make up the ceaseless daily round of the here and now and may fade and be soon forgotten. Sometimes, however, actions may have a deeper or more enduring significance. When this happens, their consequences become sedimented into patterns of routine practice over a long period. In other words, the consequences of some actions have an impact which extends well beyond their own time. What is done today may continue to shape the life of the secondary school many years hence.

This means that those who work in the secondary schools of the future will fully understand their professional and academic lives only to the degree that they understand something of decisions that were taken years before. The same applies to us. To understand the nature of the institutions within which we work, we have to know something of how they came to be as they are. In other words, we have to know something of our educational history (DfEE, 1997, p. 10).

Some events in the evolution of the secondary school have had a particularly extensive force. In the nature of things, such events tend to take the form of legislative action or executive decisions implemented by central government. Major pieces of educational legislation can exert a pervasive influence over an entire educational generation and might even be seen as emblematic of the dominating educational interests and priorities of a particular historical period. We might take three such legislative turning points as critical markers in the historical development of the modern secondary school; they are the Education Acts of 1988, 1944 and 1902.

Before we do this, however, it is important to remember that, despite the many changes which have marked the development of the secondary school over the years, there is much that remains stubbornly familiar about patterns of daily life in schools. This is because of the powerful institutional and situational constraints which schools themselves, at least in the form we have known them throughout the whole of the twentieth century, exert upon teachers and pupils. Such constraints mean that some things are extra-ordinarily hard to change, and that many of the sights and sounds of the modern secondary school – classrooms with the teacher standing at the front; crowded, noisy corridors; regular assemblies; periodic bells; piles of books and paperwork – would all be quite intelligible to the schoolgirl and schoolboy memories of our grandparents.

We should also recognize that beneath the apparently clear-cut nomen-clature of 'secondary' schooling there lies a multitude of different institutional forms, each with a distinctive and often complex history. Among many others, we might, for example, trace the historical development of single-sex schools, co-educational schools, voluntary schools associated with religious denominations, comprehensive schools, grammar schools, city technology colleges, grant-maintained schools, special schools, technical schools, secondary modern schools, middle schools, private schools (including the confusingly named 'public' schools), residential schools and experimental schools of various kinds.

The educational patchwork which is represented by such a diverse list of types of school could be simplified by dividing them into two broad groups – the private and the public. At the beginning of the twentieth century, the former was much larger than the latter; at the close of the century, the position was reversed. The twentieth century, in other words, saw the progressive reformation of secondary schooling by successive governments as a principally public service. In consequence, it is with publicly provided schools – attended by more than 90 per cent of the nation's young people – that our discussion is chiefly concerned.

The current New Labour government envisages three basic categories of publicly funded schools for the future. These are community schools (schools maintained by the local education authority (LEA) which also employs their staff and owns their premises); aided schools (religious schools employing their own staff, owning their own premises and contributing at least 15 per cent towards their own capital spending); and foundation schools (schools, including existing grant-maintained schools, employing their own staff and owning their own premises, but with their capital costs met wholly from public funds).

THE 1988 EDUCATION ACT AND AFTER

The Education Reform Act of 1988 has shaped – and will continue to shape – the educational generations of the late twentieth and early twenty-first centuries. Like all seminal pieces of legislation, the importance of the Act lay not just in its substantive provisions but in the degree to which its underlying principles reflected the state of wider social attitudes and aspirations. For example, a belief in the values of the market, together with an emphasis on deregulation, public accountability and the paramount interests of the consumer can all be seen as having a significant influence upon the construction of the Act. Such views were often expressed in the general perception that schools had to be opened up to new and broader influences and shaken out of the grip of a teaching profession that was characterized as looking inward to its own interests, and backwards to allegedly ineffective and unchallenging traditions of professional practice. This approach saw education as having been in some sense captured by its producers – that is, the teachers – who had ultimately failed to respond to the interests of educational consumers, whether conceived as school students, parents or the nation as a whole. In order to address this concern, the 1988 Act invoked revolutionary new provisions in which novel institutional freedoms were combined with unprecedented control from the centre.

The first great achievement of the 1988 Act was to penetrate the traditional heart of the secondary teacher's professional autonomy through its specification of a national curriculum and associated attainment targets. Secondly, the Act endeavoured to give more freedom to the governors and headteachers of individual schools, particularly in terms of the disposition of devolved school finances and opportunities for seeking grant-maintained status outside the ambit of the LEA. In doing so, it marked an important and continuing trend in the shift of the balance of power in education away from the local education authorities. Thirdly, the Act sought to make parental choices in the selection of a school, and parental voices in the day-to-day running of that school, more prominent. Fourthly, it endeavoured to make that which went on in schools more visible to the world outside the school gates. As a consequence, public accountability has become a paramount concern. Among other things, this has led to the publication of examination results and other information in the form of school league tables, and to the establishment in 1992 of more formalized and judgemental procedures for the regular inspection of every school by the Office for Standards in Education (Ofsted) along with sweeping new powers to deal with schools perceived to be failing.

In the years since the passing of the Act, there have been some important modifications to this immensely ambitious programme. Most notably, as a result of the recommendations of the Dearing Report of 1993, the size of the statutory national curriculum has been considerably slimmed. However, the cardinal principle that it is the legitimate business of the elected government to control the commanding heights of the curriculum is now an established one and periodic curricular innovations from the centre – most recently the addition of citizenship to the national curriculum – can continue to be anticipated by the teachers of the twenty-first century. More generally, it would be fair to say that the broad policy direction established by the Act in other areas of secondary school life has been maintained and often augmented by successive governments since its passing. The Act and subsequent legislation has created a new discursive landscape for secondary schools in which terms such as 'excellence', 'standards', 'partnership', 'leadership', 'performance', 'effectiveness', 'accountability' and 'moderniza-tion' have become towering features. Under the influence of such terms, many secondary schools have begun to re-think the nature of their educational mission, the quality of their relationship with their local communities and the extent of their accountability to the many parties with a legitimate interest in the outcomes of what they do. Where these pervasive shifts will lead in terms of the future shape of the education system is uncertain, but the appetite for modernization is clearly not restricted to central government alone. While many secondary teachers might originally have regarded the passing of the 1988 Act with some trepidation, more than a decade later, the continuing, unrelenting accent upon change – some of it until recently, unthinkable – has for others evinced a more receptive and optimistic mood. The teaching profession has in this respect adapted, as it has always had to do, to the requirements of the policy context within which it operates.

One of the most important trends to emerge in the modernized educational landscape of the twenty-first century has been a heightened emphasis upon diversity or flexibility in the provision of secondary education. Diversity, however, is an immensely problematical concept when applied to an educational system which has historically been marked by a high degree of segmentation, status differentiation and unequal provision. For those with memories reaching back to the mid-twentieth century, such an emphasis may raise images of an earlier period in which diversity in education could amount to little more than a euphemism for profound structural inequalities in the provision of secondary schooling. Politicians are well aware of the strength of such historical associations and the current New Labour administration has sought to distance its support for diversity from any association of this kind. The words of its 1997 White Paper, *Excellence in Schools* were instructive in this respect, offering an implicit critique of the inequalities of the pre-1988 period.

> We are not going back to the days of the 11-plus; but neither are we prepared to stand still and defend the failings of across-the-board mixed ability teaching.... We intend to modernise comprehensive education to create inclusive schooling which provides a broad, flexible and motivating education that recognises the different talents of all children and delivers excellence for everyone. (DfEE, 1997, p. 38)

In other words, from the perspective of the present administration, diversity and flexibility are seen as key strategies commensurate with the achievement of both equality of opportunity and economic effectiveness in a globalized economy. Moreover, they are not seen to threaten that principle of parity of esteem between different forms of educational provision which underpinned much of the educational debate of the immediate postwar decades. Rather, the product of strategies of diversity and flexibility is presented in terms of finding more effective and appropriate ways of safeguarding a wide range of learning outcomes across different groups of students and, in so doing, allowing each individual to achieve their full potential. The related notion that successful educational arrangements and practices at the local level might be identified, formalized and generalized across the teaching profession has important consequences for pedagogy and for teacher autonomy. Just as the national curriculum has codified that which is to be taught, pedagogical styles and approaches are now seen by many as amenable to a similar degree of formalization and standardization. In this view, effective teaching practices may be identified through focused research and disseminated within the teaching profession as commended practical pedagogies, alongside associated organizational innovations such as 'target-grouping', 'fast-tracking', 'accel-erated learning' (DfEE, 1997, p. 39), each derived from a general suspicion of mixed-ability teaching. The celebration of diversity and flexibility finds expression in other ways too, including moves towards written agreements or contracts between home and school, and the launching of innovative programmes of learning activities outside school hours.

All of these changes have been seen to call forth a new type of teaching force and this has led to further reforms centred upon the reshaping of programmes of teacher training as a more school-based activity; the inception of specialist training for prospective headteachers and co-ordinators of special educational needs provision; the creation of a new grade of Advanced Skills Teacher; the proposed reformation of career structures for classroom teachers; and the inauguration in 1998 of Educational Action Zones and, a year later, of the Excellence in Cities programme. Action Zones are based upon a recurring set of organizational themes in which small groups or 'families' of local secondary schools work together with feeder primaries, local parents, business interests and local education authorities (DfEE, 1997, pp. 39–41).

A further part of the move towards diversity and away from a single model of schooling – an idea which, in the recent past, was exemplified in the comprehensive school movement of the 1960s and 1970s – has been the encouragement given to individual schools to play to their perceived strengths and to develop their own distinctive educational identities. Historically, this may come to be seen as the single most important shift in secondary schooling for more than a generation. It reconfigures the old three-way partnership between the centre, the LEAs and the schools themselves which dominated the twentieth century. In its place comes the celebration of diversity and enhanced administrative independence for individual schools, with the central state offering financial incentives and other encouragement to those institutions which are most prepared, in the name of the driving up standards, to experiment, to innovate and to inspire the local educational culture around them. This is the model in which the dynamic benefits of diversity are managed and encouraged from the centre, in which individual schools are set free to develop a distinctive ethos, in which successful institutions are rewarded and admired as flagship examples of outstanding local practice from which other nearby schools may learn through example and emulation. At the heart of this process stands the notion of 'earned autonomy' for individual schools. The freedoms for those institutions which achieve this status include a substantial release from precisely the legislative and administrative machinery which, for more than a decade, has been the primary motor of educational change. Now a new, more devolved impetus is sought. In the words of the current Secretary of State for Education:

> The freedom to innovate means challenging those aspects of legislation that have become a block to progress and performance improvement. That is why the recent Education Act 2002 established a 'Power to Innovate' which is one of the most radical and far-reaching powers available to Government – it enables me as Secretary of State to exempt educational legislation that is standing in the way of common sense and in the way of schools wanting to innovate and to achieve the very best for the children in their care. (DfES, 2002b)

The operationalization of the agenda of diversity has generated new categories of school which raise question marks against the future of the comprehensive school as it has been known in the past. 'Beacon' schools nominated by the Department for Education and Skills receive additional funding in return for sharing 'the secrets of their success' thereby helping 'to raise standards in other schools, particularly in inner city areas.' (DfEE, 1998) From 2000, City Academies, effectively publicly funded independent schools, began to appear and were noted by a government minister as 'leading the reforms that will radically improve secondary education in this country' (DfES, 2002a). Numerically far more significant is the ongoing expansion of the specialist schools programme, inherited in 1997 from the previous Conservative administration. Fifteen hundred institutions are now projected to be designated as specialist schools by 2006, together with a smaller complement of new advanced specialist schools. By the end of the decade specialist schools, majoring in one of seven specified curriculum areas, may well have generated – as the government hopes – a new atmosphere of optimism, initiative and achievement both within their own walls and within the communities that they serve. But what of the schools which do not or cannot satisfy the necessary qualification for specialist school status? How will they come to be perceived? What will be their place in the new system? The danger here is that the weight of an educational history in which different school labels have always been seen to signal hierarchy and exclusion may be hard to avoid. This certainly proved to be the case for the tripartite system which emerged from the Education Act of 1944.

THE 1944 EDUCATION ACT AND AFTER

The 1944 Act – unlike its successor of 1988 – was forged in a period of strong national consensus and laid the foundation for the complex post-war settlement in secondary education. This period was principally dominated by the problem, not of nuancing the character of secondary education or ensuring its effectiveness, but of achieving an equitable experience of secondary schooling for all children – and not just a privileged minority – as a basic social principle. The 1944 Education Act was the culmination of the appeal, led by the radical writer R.H. Tawney, for – to use his great slogan – 'secondary education for all' which had begun to gather momentum from the 1920s.

The 1944 Act sought to end a great structural divide in educational provision which had its roots in the nineteenth century. This divide, echoing the sharp class divisions of British society, meant that much of the schooling provided in the interwar period continued to take place in hierarchically separated settings. Broadly, this meant that the majority of secondary school places available were filled by middle-class children, with most working-class children restricted to separate elementary schools throughout their entire school lives. The 1944 Act sought to end this segregation between the elementary and secondary sectors. It provided that elementary (now renamed primary) schooling and secondary schooling should be fused as a sequential unity of experience for all children. For the first time, every child in the nation was entitled to a secondary education as a right. In a post-war atmosphere marked by a sense of the collective sacrifice of a democratic citizenry in a just war, such a settlement was widely welcomed. But the sense of social justice and equality of opportunity in education went beyond the provision of a secondary school place for all. The 1944 Act also abolished the right of publicly provided secondary schools to charge some of their pupils fees. This closed the pre-war loophole whereby wealthier parents had been able to buy places at local grammar schools for sons or daughters who had failed the competitive entry examination. The provisions of the Act meant not only that secondary schooling was now free to all, but that the allocation of a school place rested upon demonstrated individual merit and not on the ability to pay.

For two decades, the 1944 settlement enjoyed a honeymoon period – what historians have referred to as the 'period of consensus'. But it was not long before problems were looming. Free and universal secondary schooling was now a reality, but the new question was – what sort of secondary schooling and for whom? Post-war thinking did not favour the notion of a common secondary school in which all children, regardless of ability or social background, might mix and share the same range of educational opportunities. This was because educational opinion was dominated by the view – inherited from the interwar years – that children's intellectual ability and academic potential was substantially innate. This assumption of fixed intelligence led many to the related position that children could be categorized at a relatively early age into scientifically identifiable types based upon distinctive educational aptitudes and measured 'intelligence' (see Chapter 4 in this volume). On this view, the creation of common secondary schools was seen not merely as a futile exercise but a potentially damaging one in which innate ability and educational provision would be mis-matched.

A more appropriate solution was seen to be the establishment of differentiated and institutionally separate forms of school to cater for 'different' categories of ability and aptitude. After 1944, most local authorities set up systems of secondary schooling designed to cater for three categories of student which were popularly understood as the bookish, the handy and the average. In most localities it was assumed that this categorization could be effectively achieved through competitive examination for primary school pupils at the age of 11+. Upon the results of such examinations, pupils were allocated to the type of school which was deemed to be most appropriate to their demonstrated aptitude and 'ability'. The acceptance of this three-way division led to a post-war structure of schooling which became widely known as the tripartite system. The corresponding grades of school for each of the three groups were grammar schools, offering an academically based education leading on to university and the professions; technical schools, providing an education which prepared students for skilled manual and technical occupations; and secondary modern schools, offering a basic all-round education which was seen as sufficient for the needs of the generality of the nation's future workforce. As such, the courses of study offered by the secondary modern schools – in which the majority of the school population in the immediate post-war decades came to be educated – were not designed to lead to any form of external qualification. By contrast, grammar school courses culminated in the award of high status GCE (General Certificate of Education) certificates at Ordinary and Advanced level. It was not until 1965 that the less prestigious CSE (Certificate of Secondary Education) was inaugurated as an appropriate qualification for secondary modern students.

The distinction between the GCE and the CSE was symbolic of the most intractable problem which weighed on the post-war tripartite system. Despite the insistence by local and national politicians that each type of school should enjoy 'parity of esteem', this was never achieved. The dispersal of the nation's children into three effectively stratified levels of secondary schooling seemed to many to look back to the old hierarchical social inequalities of the interwar years and not forward to a more just post-war society. Instead of each level of schooling achieving a common respect, the technical and secondary modern schools were overshadowed by the perceived superiority of the grammar schools and the celebration of the academic curriculum they followed.

By the 1960s, the failure to achieve parity of esteem had massively undermined the tripartite system. Moreover, it was increasingly questioned whether children's educational ability could be definitively measured at the relatively early age of 11. Many frustrated parents came to believe that their children had been wrongly allocated to a form of schooling which was restricting their potential and from which there was no easy escape. There was a growing recognition that success in the 11 + examination was not, as had been once thought, a simple, meritocratic reflection of innate ability but the product of a complex cocktail of factors in which home background, social class, gender and ethnicity all played their part, alongside individual aptitude. As a result, a new language of deprivation began to give voice to these concerns. This was a discourse which seemed to indicate that there was a social as well as an educational role for the secondary school. In this view, segregation by type of school could be seen as not only educationally invalid but also as damaging to the fabric of a democratic society itself. A form of common schooling increasingly commended itself for its potential to ensure the mixing of diverse social classes and ethnic groupings as well as for its promise to secure greater educational opportunity for individual students.

For many – and by no means only those on the political left – the answer to all these concerns lay in the spread of the comprehensive school movement. As a result, national reorganization along comprehensive lines moved to the top of the political agenda and in 1965, the then Labour government issued the landmark Circular 10/65, inviting LEAs to draw up plans for comprehensive reorganization with the ultimate long-term goal of achieving 'the complete elimination of selection and separatism in secondary education' (Gordon, *et al.* 1991, p. 190).

By the mid-1980s, the vast majority of pupils in the state sector were being educated in undifferentiated comprehensive schools. In the reorganization process, most secondary modern schools and, more controversially, very many traditional selective grammar schools disappeared in programmes of local amalgamation and reformation.

In 1970, Brian Simon and Caroline Benn had published an optimistic account of the progress to date of the comprehensive movement under the celebratory title *Halfway There*. The 'there' to which Simon and Benn looked forward has not turned out quite as they hoped or expected. In itself, this constitutes an important historical lesson. As Simon himself has pointed out on many occasions, all legislative and administrative interventions have unanticipated consequences, and in this respect educational policy has proved no exception to the rule. The comprehensive school is still with us in great numbers, as are its many supporters, but neither its practical nor its moral hegemony carry quite the same assurance as they once did. Moreover, some have seen New Labour's enthusiasm for increasing numbers of specialist schools as evidence of an end of commitment to the comprehensive principle (see Chapter 2).

THE 1902 EDUCATION ACT AND AFTER

The 1902 Act restructured the administration of education at the local level through the establishment of Local Education Authorities – LEAs – which were required to take over responsibility for all levels of public educational provision in a locality. Before this point, the school boards – the Victorian forerunners of the LEAs – had had control only over the elementary sector of schooling. The widened role of the new LEAs marked an important stage in the complex and often combative history of relationship between local initiative and central prescription in the provision of public education which, like the even longer running educational struggle between the churches and the state, has been played out over the course of the twentieth century.

Under their new powers, many LEAs set about establishing their own secondary schools – the first publicly funded schools of this type. In most respects, the new LEA secondary schools modelled themselves on the older elite private sector secondary schools with all the appurtenances associated with such institutions – house systems, elaborate uniforms, team sports, honours boards, prefects, and so on. One important difference though was that – chiefly as a result of cost pressures – many of the new schools tended to be co-educational in place of the established tradition of single-sex schooling.

In terms of their curriculum, the new secondary schools were required by central government to offer a course of study which, as has often been pointed out, was strikingly similar to that outlined in the national curriculum specification of 1988, with the earlier formulation stipulating English, Mathematics, Science, Foreign Languages, Geography, History, Drawing, Physical Exercise and Manual Work or Housewifery (Aldrich, 1996).

Another very important feature of these new maintained secondary schools was that, though they charged fees for most of their intake, a proportion of free places were set aside for able pupils from the public elementary school sector to begin their climb up the educational ladder. These scholarship places were to be awarded on the basis of competitive examination, usually at 11 + . Those who were not able to set foot on the ladder – more often as a consequence of poverty than lack of ability – were destined to remain in their lowly elementary schools until the statutory school leaving age of 14. (The minimum school leaving age was raised to 15 in 1947 and 16 in 1972, where it currently remains.) The explicitly hierarchical and segmented character of the national educational system as it had evolved in the nineteenth century was therefore not fundamentally confronted. By the end of the First World War in 1918, however, the assumptions underlying that older system were increasingly challenged, both on the moral grounds of social justice and on the instrumental grounds of the massive national wastage of human capital represented by unequal access to educational opportunities. Four years later, Tawney's *Secondary Education for All* gave voice to these concerns and signalled the future direction of the development of secondary schooling.

CONCLUSION

How might we conclude this brief survey of the evolution of the secondary school in the twentieth century? In the first place we should note that secondary schooling is no longer the privilege of a select and wealthy few as it was at the beginning of the century. In the second, we should record that issues involving the principle of a common as against a differentiated experience of secondary schooling have been at the centre of educational debate for most of this period. Thirdly, we should recognize that, from the earliest years of the century, there has been a persistent tension between, on the one hand, demands for educational equality of opportunity in secondary schooling and, on the other, the emphasis on the efficient use of the nation's human capital. Fourthly we should remind ourselves that, as for example in the case of the curriculum, continuity as well as change remains an important explanatory concept in understanding our educational history. Finally, we should note that the pervasive notion of differentiation in our national education system – now often expressed in the less controversial language of 'flexibility' – remains as central a policy issue at the close of the twentieth century, as it was at its opening. The degree to which this principle can be seen to express itself within a context of genuine equality of opportunity rather than deep structural or institutional inequalities will be one of the major educational stories of the next century.

Chapter 2

The School Curriculum, The National Curriculum and New Labour Reforms

JOHN BECK

WHAT IS MEANT BY 'CURRICULUM'?

In thinking in general terms about the school curriculum it may be useful initially to consider the following three issues:

The scope of 'curriculum'

Several writers on the curriculum have distinguished between the overt and the 'hidden' curriculum. The latter term has been used to refer to various aspects of *how* schools transmit the knowledge which is part of the formal curriculum: for example, how pupils are grouped for learning (setting, mixed-ability, etc.), how different forms of achievement are recognized (or not), the character of the school's pastoral system – all conveying messages about what the school really values and does not value (see, for example, Hargreaves 1982). Various 'structural' features of schooling can also convey unintended messages – for example, the existence of business sponsorship in some types of school, the effects of a 'faith' ethos, etc. In what follows, the emphasis will mainly be on the overt curriculum but it is always important to be aware of the complex inter-relationships between the formal and hidden curriculum – for example: do similar principles underlie both or are there discrepancies or contradictions?

The content of the curriculum

In terms of its contents, any curriculum is a *selection* from all the worthwhile knowledge which schooling could potentially transmit. This implies that questions about *priorities* are inseparable from curriculum design. An important issue, therefore, is to identify the *principles* that have been salient in shaping any particular curriculum. Five such principles which have historically been significant are:

- children's and students' own interests and choices
- economic relevance
- vocational relevance
- shaping national identity and allegiance
- a humanistic conception of liberal education, emphasizing the value of knowledge and understanding for its own sake

Linked to these underlying principles is the question of whether the curriculum should be similar for all pupils or whether it should differ for different 'types' of pupil – and if so, on what basis and from what age.

The structure of the curriculum

Curriculum structure has to do, at a fairly abstract level, with the nature of the elements that make up the curriculum and their relationship to one another. Within the National Curriculum, for example, the fundamental 'elements' are a set of discrete subjects, each separately timetabled and often taught by specialist teachers. However, in the 1960s and 1970s, many innovative comprehensive schools organized their curricula within broad Faculty structures such as Integrated Humanities, planning content around inter-disciplinary topics like 'war', 'the developing world', 'the family', etc. 'Progressive' or *child-centred* education typically involves structures that are even more flexible – for example, where pupil *choice* strongly influences what shall be learned, how much time shall be devoted to it, etc. Here, the 'elements' of the curriculum may be pupil-chosen topics.

A key variable, therefore, is the definition and strength of the *boundaries* between the different elements. According to sociologist Basil Bernstein, *strong* boundaries indicate strong authority relationships – both in the structuring and transmission of knowledge and often in pedagogic relations too. Where boundaries are *weak*, authority relationships may be less secure and more open to change, and there is likely to be scope for learners to exercise greater control over what is learned, how, and at what pace (see Berstein 2000, Introduction and chapter 1). But the 'bottom line' is that *all* forms of curriculum structure contain *some* set of principles which shape the selection and sequencing of knowledge and the pacing of learning. And for this reason, it is not sensible to draw too sharp a distinction between curriculum structure and curriculum content. Often, common principles shape both together – and also shape 'pedagogy' – i.e. the form of the teaching–learning relationship.

Another important aspect of curriculum 'structure' concerns the relationship between curriculum as specified nationally – e.g. in National Curriculum Programmes of Study – and curriculum as interpreted in individual schools and classrooms. This is sometimes referred to as the 'delivery' of the curriculum –

but it's worth noticing that the very use of a term like 'delivery' itself contains significant messages, not least about *control* and where it is located.

THE CONTROL OF THE CURRICULUM

Because what children learn in school influences the attitudes and beliefs of future generations, the content of the curriculum is often *contested*, especially in contemporary democratic societies which are politically and culturally pluralistic. A range of 'key players' compete or co-operate to influence what is selected for transmission as 'educational knowledge'. Among the most important of these are: politicians, state bureaucrats, 'think tanks', employers' organizations, trade unions, religious groups, the media, parents, and, of course, teachers themselves. All these groups and sub-groups have particular (some would say 'vested') interests – but each frequently assumes that there is a natural correspondence between its own aims and 'the national interest' or 'society's needs'. This being so, there is often good reason to be sceptical about those who engage in 'needs talk' – those who confidently assert that 'society' or 'our children' *need* this or that. Educational 'needs', we should remember, do not simply 'exist' in the same sense as basic biological needs. Almost invariably, 'needs talk' conceals hidden value judgements. But even if we accept this last point, all of the groups mentioned can reasonably claim to have some degree of *legitimate* interest in the curriculum. However, the extent to which the views of any one category, parents for example, should outweigh the views of others, opens up questions of formidable complexity. And given the value-laden nature of most decisions about the curriculum, such questions cannot be neatly settled by any simple appeal to reason or to evidence: equally reasonable and equally intelligent people using the same evidence may reach very different conclusions.

   In many countries, including England and Wales since 1988, it is, of course, *government* which determines the basic structure and content of the curriculum in state schools. However, it is far from universally agreed that such state control is desirable. First, it is factually the case that affluent parents can bypass the 'national' curriculum by sending their children to a range of independent schools. More fundamentally, various commentators, especially but not only on the political right, see great dangers in government control over educational knowledge. Some of these critics argue that parents' and students' interests would be better served by creating an 'educational marketplace', in which parents as *consumers* could choose the kind of education they wanted for their children without 'interference' by the state (see, for example, Tooley 2000).

THE INTRODUCTION OF A NATIONAL CURRICULUM IN ENGLAND AND WALES: DIFFERING RATIONALES

For many decades, from the mid-1920s until 1988, there was very limited direct state prescription of curriculum structure or content in England and

Wales. Support for the *idea* of a 'common core' curriculum began to be politically canvassed from the mid-1970s when a Labour government Green Paper tentatively asked whether 'there should be a "core" or "protected" part' of the curriculum common to all schools, perhaps comprising English, maths, science and maybe a foreign language (DES 1977). From this hesitant beginning, there is a huge leap to the extensive and highly prescriptive National Curriculum of Core, Foundation and Basic subjects introduced by Kenneth Baker in 1988. Moreover, even at the time, some within the government and many more outside it did *not* support so centralized, extensive and prescriptive an approach. Margaret Thatcher herself later expressed serious reservations:

> ... the national curriculum ... the most important centralising measure – soon ran into difficulties. I never envisaged that we would end up with the bureaucracy and the thicket of prescriptive measure that eventually emerged. I wanted the DES to concentrate on establishing a basic syllabus for English, mathematics and science with simple tests to show what pupils knew. (Thatcher 1993, p. 593)

In the light of this, it is worth emphasizing that the simple fact of there now being a National Curriculum in England and Wales does not in itself constitute a *justification*. Justification, after all, has to do with the quality of the *arguments* that can be advanced – both for and against. We turn now, therefore, to examine some of the justifications that have been offered for a compulsory, common curriculum for all the nation's children (or, more often, for all those in state schools).

Curriculum entitlement

One important justification was advanced by some of those who successfully advocated the introduction of *comprehensive* schooling. The establishment of a national system of unselective comprehensive secondary schools in the 1960s and 1970s, they argued, itself implied that such schools should provide broadly similar curricular experiences for all their pupils. One key argument here related to equality of educational opportunity. All pupils in such schools, it was contended, should have a common curriculum *entitlement*.

> Pupils should be entitled to the same opportunities wherever they go to school .... A national curriculum will help to raise standards of attainment by ... ensuring that all pupils, regardless of sex, ethnic origin and geographical location, have access to broadly the same good and relevant curriculum. (DES 1987 pp. 3–4)

Part of the justification here is to rule out *arbitrary* sources of unequal opportunity – and that clearly *is* important. Two reservations, however, immediately arise. First, it is not self-evident that equality of opportunity always implies *sameness* for all. This is very clear if we consider children with special needs, who often require significantly *unequal* provision (e.g. learning support) if anything like equal opportunities are to be provided for them. Secondly, even if one broadly accepts the common entitlement argument, it is, at best, incomplete. There are certain fundamental questions which the notion of entitlement does not itself address. Most importantly, it provides no answers to the question 'entitlement to what?' and why?': what, for example, might *constitute* 'the same good and relevant curriculum' referred to above?

'Standards', continuity and progression

Among the arguments which were probably most powerful in winning support for a national curriculum in England and Wales were those relating to continuity and progression. A prime concern here was to eliminate what Sir Keith Joseph memorably called 'curriculum clutter' – the tendency endemic in a decentralized system, for children to repeat similar content in different years and with different teachers (the 'not dinosaurs again, miss!' syndrome). More seriously, there is obviously a legitimate concern that children's learning is clearly sequenced and logically ordered, that it builds on prior achievements and that it avoids unnecessary repetition. A properly planned and quite highly prescriptive national curriculum is one effective way, at least at the 'macro' level, of achieving these aims. It is, however, not the *only* way. Much *less* prescriptive approaches can achieve continuity and progression for individual students as long as children's work and development is carefully monitored and guided.

The *'standards'* agenda was probably of even greater significance in gaining support for the National Curriculum than were concerns about continuity and progression. A main reason is that 'standards' were and are closely linked to a core preoccupation of recent governments – the need to demonstrate that attainment in subjects relevant to economic performance is high and is rising. In a world which, it is claimed, is increasingly *globalized*, the need to be able to score highly in international league tables of educational performance is seen as key to attracting and retaining *inward investment*, especially by multi-national companies. Furthermore, the rise of the 'knowledge economy' is taken to reinforce such arguments powerfully. Both these developments are, indeed, increasingly presented as unarguable *imperatives*. For example, a New Labour publication of 1998 asserted: 'we are in a new age – the age of information and global competition . . . . We have no choice but to prepare for this new age', adding later, 'young people need to have high level skills for this complex new world of global markets and competition' (DfEE 1998, pp. 9 and 20)). A highly prescriptive national curriculum linked to a strong and centralized system for assessing and reporting achievement is, of course, key to demonstrating in clear and accountable ways, what is happening to 'standards'. It is no surprise therefore that New Labour has not fundamentally changed either the basic structure of the National Curriculum nor the system of assessment that is its essential counterpart. Tony Blair's mantra 'education, education, education' at the time of the 1997 General Election, is symbolic of the extent to which both main political parties in the UK have 'bought in' to such highly *instrumental* views of education.

There are two essential points to note here. The first is simply to notice just how *strongly* instrumental this approach to education is. The term 'instrumental' here simply means that education is seen less as an end in itself, something worthwhile pursued for its own sake; instead, education is viewed mainly as a means to *extrinsic* ends – in this case the need to sustain a competitive economy in a new world order. Although such instrumental views are strongly supported by politicians, by many in the media and by many parents anxious about their children's economic futures, it does not follow that there is an unassailable case for so strongly instrumental a view of education as that which is now being promoted. (The arguments discussed in the next two sections, for example, will suggest other priorities.) The second key point is that despite the force and influence of the rhetoric about 'unstoppable globalization', again, there are respected theorists who are sceptical about and critical of these tendencies:

> Many commentators have ... pointed to the way globalisation is used to promote only one future, and how globalisation and its assumed impact on education is 'ideologically packaged' (Carnoy 2000). Such rhetoric is used to justify only a particular set of policies, the apparently practical common-sense politics of fitting the nation to global reality, and modernising the economy to fit the new situation. There is, in such visions, no place for citizens to stand back and protect themselves collectively from the demands of global change. (Ahier, Beck and Moore 2003 p. 90)

Many *environmentalists*, of course, have similarly highlighted the (ironically) 'global' risks to the environment that headlong pursuit of economic globalization may entail.

Liberal education for all: promoting rational autonomy

A quite different approach to justifying a broad, common curriculum is that offered by certain liberal philosophers of education, many of whom were associated with the University of London Institute of Education in the 1960s and 1970s (see, for example, Hirst and Peters 1970, Bailey 1984). These writers argued that pupils of all abilities – and not just an academic minority – should be offered a broad liberal education. A key aim of this particular kind of liberal education is the development of *rational autonomy*. All young people should receive an education designed to help them to become more capable of making their *own reasoned* decisions about what might, for them, constitute 'the good life'. Liberal education would do this by developing in young people both a respect for reasoning and evidence, and a capacity to employ rational thought and argument to interrogate the world around them. The disposition to ask: 'what's the evidence for that?', to seek reasoned justifications and to reach justifiable conclusions based on relevant evidence is therefore central to this particular conception of liberal education.

Such reasoning, however, cannot take place in a vacuum. To think *seriously* about such matters requires that young people acquire the kinds of knowledge and understanding relevant for these purposes. Exactly what forms of knowledge and understanding should have highest priority within this kind of liberal education has been (and continues to be) the subject of debate. But there is broad agreement that it is desirable that young people should understand the physical, non-human world (through mathematics and the natural sciences) and also the human world of society and culture – including their own place within it. *Moral* reasoning and understanding are also seen as central – not least because thinking seriously about what one ought and ought not to do, and why, is an essential element of individual moral agency and autonomy.

According to the philosophers of 'the London School' therefore, children and young people should be offered a curriculum which is broad and balanced in the sense that it includes, in addition to mathematics, science and technology, humanistic, aesthetic, social, political and moral education as vitally important elements (not tokenistic 'add-ons'). And crucially, in the light of the discussion in the second section above, the primary *purpose* of being initiated into all these different forms of knowledge and understanding is *not* that they will help to pay the rent or create a prosperous economy – though they may in fact do so. It is that such an education is worthwhile for its own sake and that it is indispensable if young people are to have any chance of growing up to be seriously thoughtful and autonomous individuals, capable of exercising their own judgement and able to play an active role as democratic citizens.

What was most genuinely radical about this approach to liberal education was the contention that it should be offered to *all* the nation's children. Previously, it was widely accepted that only an academic minority (such as those who went to grammar and independent schools) could cope with a curriculum of this kind – and that it was better to provide 'less able' pupils with something less intellectually demanding and/or more vocationally relevant.

The *right kind* of national curriculum, therefore, is something which most philosophers in this group might broadly be expected to support. The 1988 National Curriculum arguably met their specification in some ways and to some extent, though far from perfectly. However, having the right kind of curriculum *content* is only part of the story. What is truly essential is that teachers understand and share the underlying aims and objectives of liberal education – and that they do so *autonomously*. This, of course, is a tall order – and it carries major implications for the education of teachers themselves and for teacher accountability. As Charles Bailey so clearly pointed out, liberal educators 'cannot be held accountable for not satisfying aims, or not achieving objectives which are themselves inimical to the purposes of liberal education' (*op. cit.*, p. 236).

Neo-conservative versions of liberal education

During the educational debates which surrounded the introduction of the National Curriculum, however, other voices argued strongly for a somewhat *different* kind of liberal education. They too wanted to provide all children with a broad curriculum whose purposes were not merely economic or vocational. But their basic agenda was one of *cultural restoration*, with a strong emphasis on nationhood, the nation's cultural heritage, orthodox Christian doctrine and morality, and 'family values'. As they saw it, Britain in the 1960s, 1970s and 1980s had experienced a dangerous decline in both educational and moral standards, and British culture was being undermined by 'an increasing politicisation of the curriculum', resulting in indoctrination into 'anti-racism, anti-sexism, peace education … and even heterosexism' (Hillgate Group 1986, p. 6). Writers of this *neo-conservative* persuasion included many of the contributors to a series of polemical 'Black Papers on Education' published between 1969 and 1977 (see Cox and Dyson 1969) and also the members of the Hillgate Group in the 1980s (see, for example, Scruton 1987). The often baleful tone of these polemics is caught in the following quotation from Dr Edward Norman, then Dean of Peterhouse College, Cambridge:

> the values of this country are under threat; society discloses advanced symptoms of moral collapse …. a great moral chaos will accumulate within a few decades if the whole absurdity is allowed to go on that long. (Norman 1977, p. 103)

There was similarly intense contestation *within* each subject area of the curriculum. In History, for example, there was heated debate between supporters of the so-called 'New History' with its emphasis on world history, historical enquiry, empathy, etc. and traditionalists like Deuchar who contended that 'school history had tried 'deliberately to deny British children the legitimate pride in themselves and their cultural heritage which is their birthright' and that 'our civilisation is threatened not only by cultures with different attitudes and values, but by destructive tendencies within ourselves' (Deuchar 1989, pp. 13–14 quoted in Phillips 1998, p. 36).

Such neo-conservative writers, then, generally supported the introduction of a national curriculum based on 'a settled range of proven subjects', with an emphasis on the cultural heritage of 'the British people' and on 'traditional values'. Some of them, however, had reservations about such a curriculum being state controlled:

> the best way to guarantee the continuance of a sound curriculum is not – or at least not initially – through state control …. Until a stable

consensus emerges, the attempt to impose a national curriculum by law will be construed as yet another exercise in arbitrary state control .... While a legal guarantee of the curriculum (on the West German model) may be eventually desirable, it can be provided only against the background of a new consensus. (Hillgate Group 1986, p. 7)

Others of a broadly neo-conservative persuasion, including the then Secretary of State for Education Kenneth Baker, were happier to use the device of a state-imposed curriculum as part of the restorationist project. They were not unsuccessful. The inclusion of RE as a Basic Subject with at least 50 per cent of the available time devoted to Christianity, a stronger emphasis on British art and literature, more space given to British history and geography, were among their achievements. In all these respects, therefore, neo-conservatives were influential in establishing a version of a national curriculum which was academic rather than vocational, quite broad in its subject range, and which emphasized a sense of national belonging.

However, it is important to highlight an important difference between the underlying educational *aims* of neo-conservatives, on the one hand, and those of liberal philosophers like Peters or Bailey, on the other. While the latter are committed to intellectual *openness* – to widening pupils' intellectual horizons so that they may become more rationally autonomous – the former are, to varying degrees, concerned to promote a kind of *closure* – to socialize children into the acceptance of a set of more specific and pre-selected beliefs and values – arguably constructed around a highly selective, conservative, and idealized version of the nation's past. The verdict of one left-wing commentator was:

> at the very moment when the so-called material basis of the old English identity is disappearing over the horizon .... Thatcherism brings Englishness into ... a narrower but firmer definition than it ever had before. (Hall 1991, p. 25)

COMMONALITY, CHOICE AND MARKET FORCES: TENSIONS AFFECTING THE NATIONAL CURRICULUM AND SECONDARY EDUCATION SINCE 1988

During the years of the Thatcher and Major governments (1979–97) discussions about the National Curriculum were caught up in the wider tensions that existed between two significantly different strands of New Right ideology – those of *neo-conservatism* and *neo-liberalism*. As we have seen, neo-conservatives were preoccupied with reinstating a particular version of 'British culture' in the face of what they saw as subversive, immoral and alien tendencies which were undermining 'traditional' beliefs and values – and at least some neo-conservatives were not averse to using strengthened state control to achieve their goals. The neo-liberal project, on the other hand, was concerned with 'rolling back the state', in the sense of dismantling state provision of education, health, housing, etc. and replacing it with privatized and marketized provision. According to neo-liberals, the only effective way to make services like education or health care really responsive to clients' concerns is to replace monopolistic state provision with free market competition. A much canvassed idea in education, for example, was that of educational 'vouchers' which parents could use to purchase the sort of education which *they*, and not self-styled educational 'experts', wanted for their children. Empowering the consumer, partly at least as a way of *disempowering* 'producers' (i.e. professionals within the public sector) is therefore central to the neo-liberal project.

But as many commentators have pointed out, these two tendencies within the New Right in many ways pulled in opposite directions. We have seen already that members of the Hillgate Group expressed significant reservations about a state-imposed curriculum. And for *radical* neo-liberals, state control was complete anathema. According to Sheila Lawlor (1994), for example, 'the National Curriculum has become the organ for enforcing an educational consensus on all and crushing dissent by the weight of the law'. Even more fundamentally, as writers like David Marquand have pointed out, it is precisely market forces – especially when their reach is globally extended, which are most damaging to those things which neo-conservatives cherish:

> The global market place ... is cold and hard; in a profound sense it is also subversive. It uproots communities, disrupts families, mocks faiths and erodes the ties of place and history. It has created a demotic global culture, contemptuous of tradition, hostile to established hierarchies and relativist in morality. (1995)

A key part of the political achievement of 'Thatcherism' was that successive Tory governments managed to *combine* these antithetical agendas in a way that was both popular and politically potent even though it was ideologically 'impure'. Within education (and across the public sector), a *strengthened* role for the central state was combined not with 'pure' marketization but with the creation of 'quasi-markets', i.e. arrangements which set organizations which were still publicly owned into *competition* with one another.

- In terms of increased centralization, all schools were required to 'deliver' the National Curriculum and to administer centrally set national tests. All schools were also subjected to recurrent Ofsted inspections and teachers were regularly appraised. Teacher training was controlled through the imposition of national standards for ITT, combined with inspection.
- But at the same time, government created an 'educational marketplace' in which schools competed with one another for customers and in which income depended on recruitment. Performance indicators such as league tables of results, enabled parents to become more informed choosers. Government also widened choice for some by creating new types of

schools – grant maintained schools and city technology colleges for example – and established the Assisted Places Scheme which provided funding for less affluent pupils to take up places in the independent sector.

These measures, therefore, combined commonality of provision in some respects with an emphasis on widening choice and promoting diversity in others.

The coming to power of New Labour from 1997 did relatively little to change the fundamentals of this potent if partially contradictory policy mix. Whitty, surveying Labour's first term, has said:

> many of New Labour's changes to the Conservative agenda were largely cosmetic. In some of its manifestations, New labour's so-called Third Way looked remarkably similar to quasi-markets. The central thrust of the policies was probably closer to that of the Conservative agenda than to Labour's traditional approach . ... The main elements of the reforms of the 1980s and 1990s remained in place. (2002, p. 127)

More specifically, under New Labour, two main tendencies have operated to reshape the curriculum: the first is intensified instrumentalism; the second is increased differentiation between different types of schools. Both have tended to reduce the commonality, breadth and balance of the common curriculum introduced by the 1988 Education Reform Act.

Intensified instrumentalism has increasingly subordinated education to perceived economic imperatives, in order, as Education Secretary David Blunkett put it in 1998, 'to support and work with [industry] for skilling and re-skilling for what Tony Blair has described as the best economic policy we have – education' (quoted in Ball 1999, p. 201). The most conspicuous examples of such directly instrumental interventions have, of course, been the Literacy Strategy introduced from 1998 and the Numeracy Strategy which was 'rolled out' a year later. A key (and generally successful) aim of both was to raise Britain's position in international numeracy and literacy league tables. Both initiatives, though technically non-statutory, represent a degree of government intervention into the curriculum which is unprecedented in recent times, in that they in effect closely prescribe not only day-by-day curriculum content but also the approved pedagogic means of 'delivery'. Symptomatically, government and its agencies have repeatedly claimed that these interventions are 'research-based' and 'disseminate proven best practice' (e.g. Barber and Sebba 1999, p. 186). Critics have taken leave to doubt whether, in so complex an enterprise as developing children's abilities in literacy or numeracy, it is possible to identify uncontroversially 'best practice', let alone 'proven' best practice. But over-confidence is the handmaiden of instrumentalism and technicism. The strengthened focus on 'the basics' was facilitated by so-called 'new arrangements for curriculum flexibility' introduced in 1998. This allowed primary schools to partially 'disregard' the Statutory Orders for the six Foundation Subjects, thus inevitably changing the balance of the curriculum and reinforcing the message about which areas 'really mattered'. The specification of literacy and numeracy 'targets' for individual schools further narrowed the focus. Richards (1999), with only some overstatement, warned that the outcome could be a 'neo-elementary' primary curriculum, with a new 'core' of English, mathematics and science (supported by ICT) squeezing out other subjects.

Increasing instrumentalism reinforced by a resurgence of vocationalism has also driven successive changes to the curriculum at Key Stage 4. Few would question that the post-1988 National Curriculum suffered from content overload. This was largely a consequence of allowing too much influence to subject enthusiasts in the original subject working parties. Nevertheless, the aim of preserving substantial curriculum breadth was a cardinal (if always contested) feature of the original KS4 National Curriculum. A succession of initiatives has radically eroded this common element, permitting in its place various kinds of specialization and greater choice for individual students. The effect of the 1993 Dearing Report with its proposals for academic, prevocational and vocational 'pathways' and its shrinking of the requirements for breadth, was, according to former Chief HMI Eric Bolton (1994), to 'deconstruct the National Curriculum'. The shape of *New Labour* policies for the 14–19 age range was set out in a 2002 Green Paper (DfES). Employing the rhetoric of 'life-long learning', 'flexibility' and 'world class technical and vocational education', it proposed a radical restructuring of 16-19 education with the key cut-off point in terms of a broad common curriculum occurring at age 14. Post-14, it opened up possibilities of students following increasingly diversified routes, some mainly vocational, some combining academic and vocational subjects, some purely academic, and it sought to raise the status of vocational subjects, e.g. by introducing A2 level assessment. From Year 10, all students would follow a reduced core curriculum of English, maths, science and ICT; some would take GCSEs at age 15 and others might 'skip' GCSEs and move directly on to AS and A2 level courses. The details of these proposals are perhaps less important than the broad thrust (especially as there may be unforeseen changes – for instance, the introduction of a British baccalaureate). But the overall principles guiding the direction of change are quite clear: 'relevance', utility, choice and earlier specialization.

This leads us, finally, to examine the other major imperative behind recent New Labour reforms: increased institutional and curricular specialization. Although Labour rapidly abolished the Assisted Places Scheme, in other ways it has extended the Conservatives' enthusiasm for 'specialist schools'. On top of the tripartite division into Community, Foundation and Faith schools introduced by the 1998 Schools Standards and Framework Act, New Labour has encouraged the creation of more and more 'specialist' schools – i.e. comprehensive schools with a distinctive curricular emphasis. In the Major years, the Conservatives had already developed a Specialist Schools Programme which included Technology Colleges and Language Colleges, further extended to include Sports and Arts Colleges by 1996. New Labour's

1997 White Paper 'Excellence in Schools' indicated more expansion, leading to proposals in 2002 to increase the number of specialist schools from the 181 which existed in May 1997 to at least 1,500 by 2005. The developing agenda has also seen the creation (from 2002) of City Academies – schools mainly in inner city areas offering diverse kinds of specialism – for instance, Bexley Business Academy and Compton Enterprise and Sports Academy, both in London. Education Secretary Estelle Morris described the government's approach as offering 'greater consumer choice', asserting that 'this greater diversity is good for pupils and parents and will ensure there is more choice and innovation within the school system' (Morris 2002, p. 7).

'Excellence in Schools' symptomatically described this whole process as 'modernizing the comprehensive principle'. But 'modernising', it is worth noting, is an instance of what Bill Readings has called 'de-referentialization', i.e. using terms having virtually no intrinsic meaning but which sound good and can be mobilized to promote and legitimize initiatives favoured by politicians or corporate managers (Readings 1996, see also Beck 1999). In his speech to the Labour Party Conference 2002, Tony Blair was ready to be rather more explicit about what such 'modernizing' involved:

> In education we need to move to the *post-comprehensive era*, where schools keep the comprehensive principle of equality of opportunity but where we open the system to new and different ways of education built round the needs of the individual child [my italics].

The term 'post-comprehensive' had been 'spun' for some time in the days preceding the speech – alongside slogans like 'we need an end to the 'one size fits all' mass production public service'. The Prime Minster's speech highlighted the associated 'need' to widen consumer choice: 'why shouldn't there be a range of schools for parents to choose from ... [all] offering excellent routes into university and skilled employment?' (ibid.) *Critics* of these 'radical' new directions would argue that such a policy may be internally contradictory – carrying grave risks of further *undermining* equality of opportunity as well as eroding common curriculum entitlement. First, the specialist emphasis of different specialist schools leads to increased curriculum differentiation, in terms of both overt and hidden curriculum effects. For instance, Bexley Business Academy planned to fit the National Curriculum into four days a week, leaving Fridays to be devoted to business skills including practical experience in its purpose-built mini stock exchange (Bloom 2002). Secondly, specialist schools differ from mainstream comprehensives (notoriously dubbed 'bog-standard' comprehensives by Tony Blair's spin-doctor-in-chief Alistair Campbell), in that they are in many cases better funded and are allowed to *select* a proportion of their pupils on the basis of aptitude in the designated specialism (something which is extraordinarily difficult to assess reliably). As Roy Hattersley, a consistent critic of these policies warned in 2002:

Specialist schools and city academies, with massive extra resources, will be rated more highly in the public mind than ordinary comprehensives. And more and more of them will exercise their option to select a percentage of their pupils.

It is, here, important not to fall into the trap of thinking that the old comprehensive school system was extensively egalitarian: there is clear evidence that locality and social class differences meant that some schools were significantly 'more equal than others'. Nevertheless, it is difficult to see how the emerging new system will not widen inequality even further – for example, by enabling more affluent and 'aspirational' parents to secure greater relative advantage for their own children.

Chapter 3

Monitoring and Assessment

JOHN RAFFAN AND
KENNETH RUTHVEN

INTRODUCTION

Every area of Education raises philosophical and practical issues and probably none more so than assessment. We all know how it feels to be assessed, to have our work marked, to sit tests and examinations and to read reports on our attainments and progress. But do we agree that it was all 'fair'? Was it helpful to us and to our teachers? As every teacher has a major professional role in assessment, teachers need to appreciate and manage both its possibilities and limitations.

The title for this chapter is drawn from Section 3 of the document *Qualifying to Teach* (DfES and TTA 2002).

- 'Monitoring' means keeping in touch with your pupils' learning, the difficulties that they are experiencing and the progress that they are making. The term also summarizes the various procedures used by any organization responsible for education, from schools to local and national government, to check on standards and progress. (The term 'audit' is also used in this latter connection.)
- 'Assessment' refers to any process which gives information about pupils' learning. Informal classroom processes include observing pupils tackling a task, questioning them about their work, looking at their written recording of their work, or listening in on their discussion. More formal processes include testing and setting assignments for marking, and the national system of tests and examinations. Assessment processes usually include the stages of *recording* and *reporting* and also have an important role in *accountability*.
- 'Recording' means maintaining up-to-date records of the classroom experience and achievement of individual pupils, relating these systematically to the agreed curriculum and assessment framework laid down by

the National Curriculum or the corresponding requirements of upper secondary courses and qualifications.

- 'Reporting' means preparing a summary overview of the performance of individual pupils. Intended both for official purposes and to advise pupils and their parents, pupil reports must relate achievement to the standards defined by national frameworks for curriculum and assessment, but also convey this and broader information about the pupils' learning in a way that pupils and parents can understand.

- 'Accountability' refers to the important part that formal assessment plays in evaluating the performance not just of pupils but also of their teachers and schools. Through the processes of recording and reporting, teachers and schools demonstrate their seriousness of purpose – and their success – in promoting pupils' learning. The results of public examinations for schools are usually published in local newspapers and, more controversially, scores based on these results, are calculated to provide national and local 'league tables'.

PURPOSES OF ASSESSMENT

Much of the debate about assessment, whether at national or at school level, is concerned with 'How?' questions, with techniques of testing and interpretation and reporting of results. There is another debate, usually less public but hardly less important, about the 'Why?' questions, the nature of assessment and its purposes.

Analysis of thinking and performance

Assessment can give insights into very specific aspects of the thinking and performance of pupils. How are they thinking about a particular situation? Where and why is skilled performance on some task breaking down? Using assessment to ask and answer such questions improves the information available to the teacher and makes it possible to identify and address learning difficulties.

Feedback to pupils, teachers and parents

Feedback should be the most important use of assessment. The procedures may range from informal 'impressions' to formal written tests but the main purpose is to keep pupils and teachers informed about progress and achievements during the course. This is known as *formative* assessment, as it guides the ongoing processes of teaching and learning and is integral to these processes. Formative assessment is in contrast to *summative* assessment which attempts to summarize and evaluate the outcomes of pupils' performance at the end of a course of study but is unlikely to help change their performance.

Motivation

Most learners find that the feedback on their performance, gained from assessment, is motivating. The prospect of a test or examination also usually concentrates minds and acts as an incentive to both pupils and teachers, but using this external stimulus of assessment does raise the issue of how far it may become an instrument of coercion in work or behaviour. The inclusion of a wider range of evidence in a Record of Achievement can help to raise pupils' self-esteem and motivation.

Prediction and selection

Assessment of pupils' present attainments gives teachers evidence which they use to attempt predictions about future performance and progress. When this is undertaken at the end of a course of study, typically in summative, end-of-year tests, the predictions often lead to selection. Within a school there is usually some form of assessment before pupils are assigned to 'ability groups' in sets, bands or streams. Selection is also probably the major outcome of the public examinations system, as the results play an important part in the recruitment to further and higher education, and to employment.

Monitoring and maintaining standards

Assessments may lead to the award of qualifications, such as public examination grades, university degrees or awards from professional bodies. These should provide reasonable guarantees that successful candidates have achieved acceptable standards; we are unlikely, for example, to have any confidence in the competence of an unqualified medical doctor or engineer. The demanding specifications in the standards for the award of qualified teacher status are intended, in part, to improve the professional capabilities and status of teachers. Analysis of data gathered from National Curriculum tests allows national monitoring of standards of pupil performance at the different Key Stages.

Controlling the content of the curriculum and teaching styles

For many teachers, this is a somewhat undesirable side effect, rather than a main purpose of assessment. There is no doubt, however, that the techniques and frequency of assessment and examinations do profoundly affect both the content of the curriculum and how it is taught. (This is discussed further in a later section of this chapter on 'Impact')

FORMATIVE ASSESSMENT AND EFFECTIVE TEACHING

Research into the use of formative assessment in classroom settings has confirmed the important contribution that it can make to effective teaching and learning. Informal classroom assessment offers immediate information to support important teaching functions. It provides timely evidence to guide teachers' interventions in support of pupils' learning, and their management of the ongoing lesson. Formative assessment helps teachers to match the planning of future lessons more effectively to the learning characteristics and needs of particular groups of pupils. It also provides the basis from which teachers can give pupils constructive oral and written feedback, and helps them set appropriate targets for the development of their work.

The research we have mentioned also indicated approaches to assessment which are particularly helpful and unhelpful. Black and Wiliam (1998) surveyed 600 research studies from across the world, conducted at levels from nursery school to university undergraduate, and in subjects from mathematics to PE. These studies indicate that teacher assessment which diagnoses pupils' difficulties and provides constructive feedback leads to significant learning gains, particularly for lower-attaining pupils. The effect is to reduce the spread of attainment in a group while at the same time raising performance overall, so tackling what is often seen as an intractable – and inevitable – problem of a 'tail' of underachievement and consequent alienation. The most modest improvement found in these studies raises the performance of the average pupil to the level previously achieved by only one in three. In Britain, improvement on this scale would push GCSE performance up by between one and two grades per subject.

So what exactly are teachers doing in classrooms where formative assessment produces such remarkable effects? Black and Wiliam's 1998 survey identified five factors seemingly crucial for successful learning, and a further five that hinder it.

Standards are raised by:

- regular classroom testing and the use of results to adjust teaching and learning rather than for competitive grading
- enhanced feedback between teacher and pupils which may be oral or in the form of written comments on work
- the active involvement of all pupils
- careful attention to the motivation and self-esteem of pupils, encouraging them to believe that they can learn what is being taught
- time allowed for self-assessment by pupils, discussion in groups and dialogue between teacher and pupils

Standards are not raised by:

- tests which encourage rote and superficial learning, even when teachers claim they wish to develop understanding
- failure by teachers to discuss and review testing methods between themselves
- over-emphasis on the giving of marks and grades at the expense of useful advice to learners

- approaches which compare pupils in a way which persuades them that the purpose is competition rather than personal improvement, and which demotivate some pupils
- feedback, testing and record-keeping which serves a managerial rather than a learning function

In a further study on learning gains produced by enhanced formative assessment (Black *et al.* 2002) the research team reported in more detail on the positive effects of:

- careful framing of teachers' questions to encourage active participation by pupils
- increasing 'wait time' after questions to give pupils time to think and contribute
- comments on written tasks which identify what has been done well and what still needs improvement
- making the criteria for evaluating any learning achievements transparent to the pupils
- teaching pupils the habits and skills of collaboration in peer-assessment
- encouraging pupils to keep in mind the aims of their work and assess their own progress to meet these aims
- the formative use of summative tests

ISSUES OF VALIDITY, RELIABILITY, PRACTICABILITY AND IMPACT OF ASSESSMENT

Validity

Validity in assessment requires that the procedures actually test what the assessors intend. This may seem self-evident but achieving validity is often difficult. Among several types of validity, the variety which most concerns teachers as assessors is *content validity*. It requires that assessment procedures should be well matched to the actual content and objectives of the taught course, covering as much as possible of the specification or syllabus and not going beyond it. Validity would be limited, for example, if an assessment system was established for a course of study with a substantial practical or oral content (for example, in the sciences, languages or art) without giving the candidates opportunities to show their competencies in practical or oral activities. If candidates for an examination were not familiar with particular styles of questions, such as multiple choice or essay, a paper containing these questions would lack validity.

Assessors try to ensure high content validity for any test or examination by arranging that the objectives and content of the taught course be sampled as fully as possible. It helps to draw up a *specification grid*; an example for an examination in Humanities is shown in Table 3.1.

Table 3.1: A specification grid

Objectives	%	Culture and beliefs 50%	Co-operation and conflict 25%	Resources and conservation 25%
Recall	30	10	10	10
Interpretation	30	20	5	5
Analysis	20	10	5	5
Application	10	5	2.5	2.5
Evaluation	10	5	2.5	2.5

The grid shows the skills and abilities (objectives) in the first column and, in the other column headings, the main content topics to be tested. Percentages of marks are allocated to each objective and content section; these are known as the 'weightings'. For example: the 'interpretation' of topics concerning 'Culture and Beliefs' has a 20 per cent weighting in the test. Public examination specifications (syllabuses) always publish the weightings for assessment objectives, skills and abilities to be examined and much use is made of specification grids by examiners to ensure high validity.

Reliability

In general terms, reliability is about the consistency of assessment procedures. There is probably more public concern about reliability of test and examination scores than any other aspect of assessment as assessment systems rely upon an assumption that competent assessors would all award the same mark to the same piece of work. In practice this is notoriously difficult to achieve. Reliability of marking can be affected by many personal factors, for example; the assessor, whether a teacher with a set of test responses or an examiner with examination scripts, may not give each script the same amount of attention or may be influenced by poor handwriting. There is always a concern about how representative, how generalizable and how dependable is any result – as the pupils/candidates, for a variety of personal reasons, may not have performed reliably to their predicted standard at the time of the test.

Awarding Bodies (Examination Boards) are the guardians of reliability for national examinations and much of the fee income they receive is allocated to:

- co-ordination meetings where examiners approve a mark scheme for a paper and agree the standards of answers expected
- moderation procedures where marks from different examiners are checked for consistency
- possible multiple marking of the same scripts
- statistical techniques for monitoring sources of unreliability in test papers and the treatment of results

Despite these careful and expensive procedures, almost every year there are reports about apparent inconsistencies in the marking and grading in national examinations. The reliability of grading for A Levels, for example, was so severely questioned in 2002 that the Secretary of State for Education had to arrange a special inquiry conducted by a former Chief Inspector (DfES 2002).

Practicability

All assessment incurs costs in time, effort and finance and, in the case of national tests and examinations, the costs of trying to ensure that they are valid and reliable can be very high. Anyone involved with assessment systems must establish some form of time and financial controls.

Formative assessment has positive effects on learning and teachers are generally willing to accept the time and effort involved in testing, marking and processing of results. Summative assessment, however, often raises more problems of practicability with obvious examples in the assessment of 'coursework', oral proficiency in languages and practical performance in the arts and sciences. To what extent might it be practicable and cost-effective to employ external examiners to ensure consistency in coursework assessment across a large number of examination centres? Would it be practicable to provide candidates with word processors in examinations, as many are able to use a keyboard quickly but cannot produce their best performance in handwriting?

Impact

Assessment has a profound effect upon teaching and learning. Indeed, as mentioned above, effective learning (and hence teaching) could hardly proceed without the feedback that assessment provides.

We must also recognize the impact of assessment in instances where its procedures may actually control the teaching and learning and perhaps distort the original intentions of the designed course. The history of education is full of concerns about teachers 'teaching to the test'; most recently this has been raised in the case of the tests used to monitor standards achieved under the National Curriculum. Other national testing procedures have produced an examination-led curriculum in the later years of secondary education, with specifications (syllabuses) from the Awarding Bodies determining the content and, to some extent, even the style of teaching and learning.

It is an issue for debate in education as to whether this impact of assessment upon the curriculum is an unintended side-effect rather than deliberate policy. Indeed, educational policy-makers tend to make statements such as:

> The assessment process itself should not determine what is to be taught and learned. (National Curriculum Task Group on Assessment and Testing 1987)

Many practitioners and observers who experience the realities of the educational system will, however, recognize the pragmatic assertion of J. D. Rowntree (1977)

If we wish to discover the truth about an educational system, we must look into its assessment procedures. What student qualities and achievements are actively valued and rewarded by the system? ... The spirit and style of student assessment defines the *de facto* curriculum.

Arguments can become quite lively over the impact and advantages and disadvantages of external and internal modes of assessment and these are outlined in the following section.

ISSUES OF ASSESSMENT MODES

Comparisons of external and internal (teacher) assessment

External assessment occurs when an external organization, typically an Awarding Body (Examination Board), specifies all of the conditions of assessment, from the objectives and content to the setting of examination papers, and organizes the marking and processing of results.

Internal assessment (now more officially recognized as 'teacher assessment') is provided by teachers who organize the course of study and commonly includes, for example, assessment of coursework essays, projects, practical and oral assignments. In the case of public examinations, internal (teacher) assessment is guided by specifications from the Awarding Bodies. Teachers are responsible for most of the setting of assessment tasks and marking the work produced; the Awarding Bodies provide a framework for approval of assessment procedures and moderation of the marks and teachers' judgements.

Advantages of an external assessment mode

- It provides assessment procedures unaffected by personal relationships between teachers and pupils.
- It reduces the possibility of conflict for a teacher between their roles as a teacher and as an assessor.
- It supports reliability of assessment by providing for uniformity of practice and standards, with all pupils being assessed upon common qualities by common criteria.
- It supports practicability of assessment by concentrating resources and expertise for setting and marking.
- It provides an independent assessment whose results are more likely to be accepted by the 'users' of examination results such as employers and admissions officers in universities.

- It enables the assessment procedures in, for example, practical activities to exert an influence on the nature of the work carried out in schools.

Disadvantages of an external assessment mode

These are largely in terms of *reducing the validity* of the assessment.

- Assessment techniques are limited to those which can be administered by an external agency such as an Awarding Body.
- The assessment is limited to the outcomes of work under examination conditions and does not include a consideration of the quality of performance as it happens.
- The number of occasions upon which the assessment can take place is limited by administrative considerations.
- The assessment may narrow the teaching objectives to those which can be assessed in external mode; for example, it may restrict the types of practical and other coursework carried out in schools.

Advantages of an internal (teacher) assessment mode

These are largely in terms of *enhancement of the validity* of the assessment.

- It requires teachers to think about assessment in terms of the educational and assessment objectives of their courses.
- It makes possible the development of assessment procedures which are suited to the facilities available in particular schools and which are closely related to the courses devised by those schools.
- The dangers of untypical failure or success are reduced, by providing assessment possibilities on a number of occasions.
- It enables pupils to be assessed during their performance, for example while undertaking practical tasks, as well as upon the outcomes.

Disadvantages of an internal (teacher) assessment mode

- With many different teachers acting as assessors, reliability of assessment is more difficult to achieve and comparisons of standards between school and school are possibly less reliable.
- Teachers are often concerned about their role as assessor affecting relationships with pupils.
- It can place a severe strain upon teachers in terms of time, effort and expertise.
- It is likely to be more subjective, certainly less objective, than an external mode and the 'users' may be less confident about the validity and reliability of the results.

ISSUES OF COMPARISONS OF PERFORMANCE: CRITERION- AND NORM-REFERENCING

Many tests are designed to show whether or not a candidate has become sufficiently competent to perform at a pre-determined and stated level. Familiar examples of these 'mastery' and 'can-do' tests include the driving test and graded examinations in music or languages. The tests have explicit criteria for success and the individual candidate either satisfies the criteria or should undertake more practice and re-enter. This type of assessment is said to be *criterion-referenced*.

In criterion-referenced assessment there is no intention to compare the performance of individual candidates. This is in contrast to *norm-referenced* assessment procedures which are intended to be discriminating and to distinguish between higher and lower achievers in a group of individuals who have undertaken a course. For norm-referenced procedures a test would contain questions across a range of difficulty and the candidates' marks would be widely spread. The results should allow the assessors to compare the performances of candidates against each other and the 'norm' for the class or age group.

Teachers have to interpret the marks and grades gained from assessment to pupils, parents, employers and admissions officers in further and higher education. It is essential that they distinguish between marks and grades achieved through criterion-referenced or norm-referenced assessments.

National Curriculum standardized assessment tests (familiarly called 'SATs') are criterion-referenced tests, as criteria are published in 'level descriptions' for performance at each attainment level. They are intended to help teachers to monitor their pupils' progress against national standards and to allow the government, through the Qualifications and Curriculum Authority (QCA), to undertake national monitoring of schools' performance.

Some years ago public examinations were mainly designed to discriminate and paper setters were criticized if the results produced a narrow, rather than a broad range of marks. GCSE examinations are now supposed to be much more criterion-referenced, with performance criteria published for each grade in all subjects. These criteria are intended to be helpful for teachers and pupils, so that they know clearly what they have to teach or learn for success in the examinations and we should not be surprised that grades at GCSE have improved over the years. Instead of welcoming this improvement, however, as more candidates achieve higher standards, many hostile voices are raised in the media each year, complaining about 'grade inflation' and that the examinations must have been too easy. There is no evidence that examination questions have become easier and the critics may not be aware of assessment grades based on standardized criteria. They would probably be more content with the deliberately discriminating, norm-referenced examinations of earlier times.

Another effect of using more criterion-referencing in examinations is a change in the perception of pass and fail grades. People who, by now, ought to know better, persist in asking applicants 'How many GCSE passes do you have?' rather than 'What grades have you achieved?' Grades A–C are all too often referred to as 'passes', with the implication that D and below are 'fail' grades. This is probably because statistics on the numbers of A–C grades are published each year for individual schools. Pass and fail, however, should be related to the level of grades required for particular purposes. The skills and abilities needed to achieve a D grade at GCSE may be entirely suitable for appointment to a large number of jobs or for admission to many courses, for example in Further Education.

ISSUES OF REPORTING GRADES

Apart from interpreting grades as achieved under criterion- or norm-referencing, there is the issue of the single grade itself. Grades are usually awarded as a result of tests designed to reveal candidates' proficiency and competence in a variety of skills, knowledge and understanding. In a well-designed test it should be possible to attribute marks for success in attaining particular objectives such as knowledge and understanding of the content of a syllabus, or practical skills, or the ability to write a coherent essay. Then, recording the marks and grades achieved under the different objectives, rather than aggregating them into a single grade, should surely reveal a fuller and clearer picture of the candidate's capabilities? There have been requests over the years for more detailed recording of achievement in specified skills and abilities and many schools do use internal 'profile' reports and records of achievement. Regrettably there has not yet been sufficient incentive for the Awarding Bodies to unpack the grades they award in each subject and to reveal the underlying patterns of achievement. Providing a profile of achievements within subjects in public examinations would, of course, cost more, but the gains would be a much better informed and realistic discussions with the pupils, parents and other 'users' than is possible using the relatively uninformative single grade for each subject.

ISSUES ON CHOOSING TECHNIQUES OF ASSESSMENT

An extensive range of techniques is available for assessment. These are the means through which pupils/candidates try to demonstrate what they 'know, understand and can do'. The choices for assessors are shown in Table 3.2.

An *objective question* or *item* is assumed to have only one correct answer. There is a special vocabulary for multiple-choice items. Here is an example of an item from a test used for university entrance:

Choose the word or phrase that is most nearly opposite in meaning to the word INFERNAL.

(a) exquisite (b) frigid (c) ephemeral (d) mortal (e) celestial

Table 3.2: Choices for assessors

Techniques	Examples
Objective tests	Multiple-choice items
	Adding single words to gaps in sentences
Short answer questions	Structured questions
Extended writing	Essays
	Accounts of experience, e.g. in practical work
Comprehension exercises	Questions based on a substantial portion of text; may include précis task
Projects and extended assignments	Use of databases, questionnaires, surveys, field-work
Practical work and performance	Based on work in laboratory or studio; includes short 'can-do' tests for particular skills
Oral assessment	Mainly in languages including English; often in other subjects as part of project assessment

- The section containing the information and instruction or question at the beginning is known as the *stem*.
- The *alternative* answers are divided into the single correct answer, known as the *key*, with the others described as *distractors*. (In the item above, the key is (e).)

Objective items are at their most valid in assessment requiring factual recall and rule-governed reasoning. Many questions may be answered in a fairly short time and the appropriate objectives and content of a section of a syllabus or course can be well covered. Their validity is much lower for testing higher cognitive abilities (such as analysis, synthesis or judgement), as these abilities may not be effectively revealed in the exercise of choosing from a list of predetermined answers. The practicability of multiple-choice items is also somewhat limited, as setters are often challenged to find up to four plausible distractors. Awarding Bodies have to keep large banks of multiple-choice items for use and reuse. The great strength of objective items, however, is their high reliability as there is rarely disagreement about the answers. This commends them to assessment systems in many countries where reliability and ease of marking is of particular concern.

The major issue in the use of all of the other techniques is that of reliability. As soon as an opinion is required about a candidate's answer, there is the possibility of different marks being awarded by different assessors. This issue of subjectivity and reliability is understandably raised most often in the more creative areas such as English essays or performance in Drama, Art or Music but also occurs in assessment of investigative and project work in other subjects. Assessors, particularly in the Awarding Bodies, try to improve reliability by insisting upon detailed marking schemes and criteria for grades, using more than one marker for each script and a variety of moderation techniques. There have to be compromises with practicability, however, as all improvements towards reliability incur time and financial costs.

Validity is also an issue for examination papers consisting of essays. Only a limited sample of course content may be covered by essay questions in even a 2–3 hour paper. There is concern too that gender bias may affect the validity of assessment styles as, for example, females tend to achieve higher standards in questions requiring extended answers and males tend to perform more successfully in objective items.

Assessors in different subjects recognize that there are these issues of validity, reliability, practicability and bias in designing tests and examinations and usually make sensible compromises by choosing a suitably mixed variety of techniques.

FURTHER INFORMATION

Relevant and recent information about developments in national assessment may be found in the websites of the main institutions involved in public examinations.

The Qualifications and Curriculum Authority (QCA) was established in 1997 to advise the Secretary of State for Education on all aspects of the school curriculum and as a regulatory body for public examinations and publicly funded qualifications. The QCA website is http://www.qca.org.uk

The Awarding Bodies (formed by mergers of the older Examination Boards and Vocational Bodies) in England are:

- Assessment and Qualifications Alliance (AQA) at http://www.aqa.org.uk/
- Edexcel at http://www.edexcel.org.uk/
- Oxford, Cambridge and RSA Examinations (OCR) at http://www.ocr.org.uk/

In Northern Ireland: the regulatory and awarding body is:

- Council for the Curriculum, Examinations and Assessment (CCEA) at http://www.ccea.org.uk/

In Scotland the regulatory and awarding body is:

- Scottish Qualifications Authority (SQA) at http://www.sqa.org.uk/

In Wales:

- the regulatory body is ACCAC at http:// www.accac.org.uk/
- the awarding body is the Welsh Joint Education Committee (WJEC) at http://www.wjec.co.uk/

Chapter 4

Intelligence

RUTH KERSHNER

INTRODUCTION

If you had the chance to choose one of the following, would you rather be:

a) richer?
b) more intelligent?
c) taller?
d) more attractive?

In answering, you might think that you could maximize this opportunity if you could only think through all the connections and possibilities. For instance, would greater intelligence automatically lead to greater wealth? Do taller people tend to be more intelligent? Does being rich and intelligent make you more attractive? However, as a probable veteran of fairy tales with a catch, you might also be wary of the pitfalls. If you choose (d), would you end up as more attractive to frogs alone? If (b), do you know what is meant by 'intelligence': is it quick thinking, adaptability, good judgement, general knowledge, or something else?

This chapter focuses on the concept of intelligence and its educational meaning. It is not intended to replicate the many overviews already in existence (e.g. Sternberg's (2000) *Handbook of Intelligence* has 677 densely written pages!). Instead attention will be given to three questions. First, what do our beliefs about intelligence say about us? Secondly, in understanding intelligence are we identifying differences between people or between cultural values and practices? Thirdly, is the concept of intelligence useful in education?

WHAT DO OUR BELIEFS ABOUT INTELLIGENCE SAY ABOUT US?

'Brainy crow upsets pecking order'
Betty the New Caledonian crow made a tool from a piece of garden wire

and used it to hook a tasty morsel of meat out of a tube too deep for her beak. The experiment once again raises questions about the uniqueness of human intelligence ... The young bird had never before seen garden wire ...

Professor Kacelnik of Oxford University said:
It would be wrong to think there is only one kind of intelligence, and it has to be the one we happen to possess ... Animals have the abilities they need for the circumstances in which they evolved, and we suspect that these animals are exceedingly clever – if you want to use the word – for the problems they usually face. (*Guardian*, 9 August 2002)

Intelligence is a topic which must be approached with caution. There is little consensus about exactly what intelligence is, never mind whether it is valuable as either a predictor of educational success or an appropriate aim of education. Yet intelligence is clearly something that it is possible to have a conversation about. It is generally understood to be a good thing on the whole, although not sufficient in itself for a successful and happy life. In general terms it is seen as a significant, unique and valuable factor in human experience and evolution, although in discussing the actual meaning of intelligence there might be disagreements about whether we value it above other qualities such as empathy or sense of humour, or about what it means to be an intelligent footballer or musician (or cat), and about whether children can be taught to be more intelligent.

The study of intelligence is not just of academic interest to students of animal behaviour, psychology, philosophy, history and sociology. The concept of 'intelligence' has been, and remains, educationally and politically controversial for a number of reasons. One of the most important is that the traditional assessment of intellectual ability using IQ tests or other assessments of abstract reasoning has commonly been followed by consequences that have real impact on the lives of individual children and young people such as secondary school placement at 11, setting for certain subjects, or transfer to a special school. More generally, there continues to be fierce debate about the view that psychological measurements of intelligence can explain or predict the likely or maximum performance of individuals in particular social groups (e.g. race, gender or social class) with associated implications for expectations and equality of opportunity. Also, recent advances in genetic research have revived the eugenic possibility of selecting or 'designing' babies to have certain characteristics including, it has been suggested (and disputed), aspects of behaviour, personality and intellectual ability.

These social and educational applications of the concept of intelligence are underpinned by complex assumptions about the validity of IQ tests, about the similarities and differences within and between social groups, and the relationships between genes and behaviour. One of the problems in getting to grips with these assumptions is that modern theories of intelligence are located at different levels of analysis (Davidson and Downing 2000). While some researchers focus on biological differences in neural efficiency or speed of information-processing to explain intellectual differences, others concentrate on mapping the hierarchical connections between general and specific cognitive processes such as memory, comprehension and problem solving. Another field of research goes beyond the individual person to develop contextual models of cultural variability in definitions of intelligent behaviour. There are also complex systems models which combine all three of these biological, cognitive and contextual levels of analysis usually incorporating some sort of interactive view of the intellectual development of individuals in different environments.

As Davidson and Downing remark, each type of theoretical model 'provides a different answer to the questions of what it means for someone to be intelligent or for one person to be more intelligent than another' (*ibid.*, p. 47). This is one reason why research on different aspects of intelligence still retains its interest and momentum after many years of research, and when put like this it has the advantage of providing entry points for people with different areas of expertise in science, biology, history, creative arts, etc. However, the questions asked and the assumptions made about intelligence can reveal certain interests and purposes which may go beyond mere curiosity. This is most obvious when direct links are made to social and political thought as seen in early nativist ideas about biologically determined human differences which are mirrored in the social order, such as Plato's categorization of citizens into 'gold' rulers, 'silver' auxiliaries and 'brass' craftsmen (Gould 1996, p. 51). Fictional accounts of biological determinism and social predestination can be powerful and memorable, as in Huxley's (1932) *Brave New World* where a peaceful stratified society depends on the intellectual differences created in the Hatchery and Conditioning Centre.

Current concerns about the negative influence on children's intelligence of environmental pollution, economic deprivation and social class are not necessarily deterministic in the same way but, as Gould points out, there is a continuing danger that the more simplistic beliefs about social differences in intellectual ability can recur in line with currently fashionable political dogmas or preconceptions:

> What argument against social change could be more chillingly effective than the claim that established orders, with some groups on top and others at the bottom, exist as an accurate reflection of the innate and unchangeable intellectual capacities of people so ranked? (1996, p. 28)

This is particularly relevant to education, with its history of selection and differential achievement and its limited financial resources. In their critical discussion of the links between intelligence testing and special education, Thomas and Loxley (2001) suggest that certain 'ways of knowing' about children, including ideas about intrinsic differences in intelligence and ability, can be unintentionally created out of the (mis)application of the philosophies, science and social beliefs in play at the time. Moreover, beliefs about the nature of children's intellectual ability can become an important part of one's social and professional identity, particularly when a teacher or parent trying to act consistently is faced every day with differences in children's behaviour, learning and educational attainment (Mugny and Carugati 1989). So if there is a view that, say, a certain early education programme failed because of the intrinsic intellectual limitations of the disadvantaged groups targeted, or that exam performance primarily reflects pupils' varying intellectual abilities rather than factors like teaching quality or resources, then clearly the underlying beliefs about intelligence and the technology of testing need to be explored.

UNDERSTANDING INTELLIGENCE: INDIVIDUAL DIFFERENCES OR CULTURAL VALUES AND PRACTICES?

Individual differences – the psychometric approach

There has been a long-standing belief that intelligence is a measurable personal quality which expresses one's intellectual power or capacity for learning. In considering the sources of this influential idea about individual differences in intelligence, most psychology texts look back to the end of the nineteenth century as the starting point of scientific and specifically psychological approaches to understanding intelligence. Even the most simply informative accounts of the various ideas and theories put forward cannot fail to convey the intellectual investments, the passionate arguments and the practical significance of these endeavours to understand the structure, heritability and measurement of mental abilities. Reference is commonly made to the work of researchers such as Galton, Binet, Spearman, Terman, Thurstone, Guilford, Cattell, Burt, Eysenck, Jensen, Wechsler and several others in western Europe and North America who contributed in different ways to the development of the *psychometric* approach to understanding intelligence and the use of IQ (intelligence quotient) tests. Psychometric models assume that people have different levels or amounts of mental ability which can be measured by the use of a standardized test in which one person's score is compared to the typical performance of a large sample of people of the same age. Fundamental beliefs about the causes of these individual differences may vary in the weight given to genetic and environmental factors ('nature vs. nurture'), although most people now acknowledge that the influences of these two aspects of life cannot be separately quantified (Richardson 1998).

  Certain key assumptions are central to the testing procedures with which the psychometric approach is associated. These are

- that intellectual ability (whether general or specific) is distributed between people in a 'bell-shaped' pattern so that most have an average amount, and a roughly even number are found on either side of the mean with few at the high and low extremes (this is the 'normal distribution' in statistical terms and it occurs in the distribution of physical characteristics such as height)

- that the ability can be measured by a test in which the questions and activities reliably call on the cognitive processes which are of interest, such as reasoning, problem-solving, memory, etc.
- that in measuring the ability one is somehow getting at an underlying characteristic which explains or predicts an individual's performance in another activity such as reading, general educational attainment, job success, and even social position

On this basis, for the last hundred years, psychometric tests of intelligence have been extensively used in selection procedures for the military services, employment and educational placement.

These psychometric assumptions have been extensively attacked in recent years (e.g. Gould 1996, Howe 1997, Richardson 1999). For instance, it has been noted that the test items (questions and instructions) are selected to spread out the typical scores in a normally distributed numerical scale, but it makes little sense to claim that twice the IQ score means twice as intelligent (unlike height, for example, where the comparison is mathematically clear and uncontroversial). It is impossible to assess general intellectual power or 'pure' cognitive abilities such as memory without the influence of factors like reading, previous learning and cultural knowledge. Also, the statistical technique of factor analysis which underlies most psychometric approaches uses correlations to indicate connections between test results, but the naming of underlying cognitive abilities is entirely down to the theoretical view of the researcher. Furthermore, it is well known and even expected that the person taking the test is motivated, alert and eager to do well; in this sense the tests are aiming to identify 'maximum performance' rather than 'typical response' (Cronbach 1990, p. 37).

Perhaps the most controversial psychometric assumption is that test results can explain or predict other successes, or give a measure of one's future potential for learning and achievement. Many people accept that tests can provide a useful description of a person's performance and that there is commonly a statistical correlation between IQ test performance and, say, school achievement. Difficulties arise, however, when a correlation is assumed to indicate that IQ causes or explains school achievement. What if the quantity and quality of school experience itself increases IQ? Ceci (1996) argues exactly this from his analysis of studies which have looked at the effects of school attendance, length of schooling, early education, cultural and geographical differences and intergenerational changes in school experience. Ceci points out that, at a cognitive level, the school curriculum tends to enhance children's perceptual abilities, concept formation, memory and other cognitive skills, exactly those skills which are examined in IQ tests in a form which resembles many worksheet-type school activities.

At a more personal level, it has been found that children with initially the same measured IQ score often respond differently to teaching. These differences in 'learning ability' were noted by Vygotsky in his discussion of the 'zone of proximal development', defined as the 'distance between the actual developmental level as determined by independent problem solving and the level of potential development as determined through problem solving under adult guidance or in collaboration with more capable peers' (1978/1935, p. 86). Vygotsky's ideas about social influences on learning and cognitive development prompted the development of a wide range of techniques for the 'dynamic assessment' of children, in which it is assumed that the person doing the assessing is not just there to record what a child can do, but also to intervene in order to see whether and how the child can learn (Lidz and Elliott 2000). Many new dynamic tests have been developed and published in recent years by psychologists working in clinical, educational and research settings. Some of these tests are formal and quantified (e.g. counting the number and type of prompts given to a child) while others take a more qualitative responsive approach to judging a child's learning ability or potential. Dynamic approaches to assessment are particularly relevant in school, where teachers inevitably adjust their expectations in accordance with their observations of how different pupils respond to teaching over a period of time. Some teachers of children with learning difficulties regularly incorporate short-term assessments, often focusing on the pupils' progress towards targets in very focused tasks. However, the dynamic assessment of learning ability differs from other superficially similar procedures in that it is not just a measure of a pupil's responses to teaching over time, but also of the quality of the teacher's input and skills in mediating learning and cognitive development.

While some people would reject any sort of 'intelligence' testing as fundamentally flawed, others have continued in the attempt to explain its use in education (e.g. Black 1998) or to show how it is possible to employ alternative statistical techniques such as the Rasch models for measuring cognitive abilities (Styles 1999). In the end one's decision to test or not depends on the purpose of doing so, and purposes vary in both research and education. The informed testing of cognitive abilities still has its place in many schools, and it is used by teachers, educational psychologists and other professionals such as learning support teachers for purposes ranging from screening and baseline setting to the assessment of specific difficulties in learning. However, the technology of testing for certain purposes in school has to some extent been separated from many teachers' alternative and often broader views of the nature of intelligence. For example, the notion of 'multiple intelligences' has become popular, and it is to this and other complex models of intelligence which we now turn.

Complex and cultural views of intelligence

Complex theories of intelligence all take account of the ways in which individuals and groups of people live their lives in different social and cultural contexts. It is assumed that people have goals, desires and needs which are fulfilled to a greater or lesser extent at different times, and that behaving 'intelligently' in one context will not necessarily be seen as such elsewhere. Different emphases are placed on the relevance of thinking skills, communication, social behaviour, emotions, effort, creativity, judgement and practical skill.

This section includes outlines of the theories of Sternberg, Ceci and Gardner as well as the general sociocultural model of 'distributed intelligence'. Reference will also be made to the growing interest in the links between intellectual development and other factors such as motivation, emotion and personality. (For reviews of these and other influential modern theories of intelligence the reader is referred to Anderson 1999, Gardner *et al.* 1996, Sternberg 2000).

Sternberg's (1985) *triarchic* theory refers to three interrelated aspects of intelligence.

- the *internal* skills of information processing, which include the cognitive components of knowledge acquisition, lower-order mental processes such as the encoding of key information in a problem, and higher-order 'metacomponents' which guide and regulate the problem-solving process
- the *experiential* aspects of intelligence which allow individuals both to cope with novelty and to increase intellectual efficiency by automatizing basic procedures like sight word reading
- the *external* or practical application of intellectual skills to real-world problems. This involves adapting to the environment and, when appropriate, selecting and shaping the environment to fit one's needs and aims

According to Sternberg, a person is not necessarily equally skilled in all three of these aspects of intelligence, which explains the familiar observation that performance in solving abstract problems in a traditional IQ test will not necessarily match a person's skill in solving day-to-day practical problems.

Ceci's (1996) *bioecological* framework also has three elements, but his emphasis is more on the importance of knowledge and activity in different contexts. Ceci proposes that:

- intelligence involves 'multiple cognitive potentials', partly genetically determined – i.e. not just one underlying intellectual power or capacity
- the context, including motivational forces, social and physical factors, cultural values and the task content and structure – is important in both the development and the testing of intelligence
- knowledge and cognitive abilities are inseparable and intertwined, so that cognitive processes such as memory and problem-solving draw on the knowledge base, which is then altered in turn

Ceci also takes a developmental perspective, assuming that the timing of key experiences in life will significantly influence intellectual growth.

Gardner (1993) formulated an equally complex theory of intelligence, which he defines as 'the ability to solve problems, or to create products, that are valued within one or more cultural settings' (p. x). However, in contrast to the models of Sternberg and Ceci there has emerged one 'big idea' from Gardner's work which has been extensively taken up by educationalists. This is the notion of *multiple intelligences*. Gardner uses a range of evidence from studies in biology, medicine, psychology and anthropology to support his framework, which began as a set of seven intelligences (linguistic, musical, logical-mathematical, spatial, bodily-kinesthetic, interpersonal and intrapersonal) and which has since been extended to include two more (existential and naturalist) with possibly more in the future. Gardner suggests that the assessment of children's multiple intelligences is best done by observation in a range of purposeful activities in natural contexts where the children might be experts or novices according to their previous experience. The multiple intelligences framework has been seen both as a way of giving credit to people's varying strengths and interests, and as a way of structuring experience to promote learning, e.g. within the school curriculum (see Smith 1998). It has also been used to explain why certain pupils may find obstacles to learning in school, where literacy and numeracy are commonly given priority over other subjects.

Another view of intelligence which closely connects the child with the learning environment is *distributed intelligence*. This emerges from the sociocultural belief that education is a cultural practice in which meanings are created through the inseparable activity of mind and culture:

> The distinctive feature of human evolution is that mind evolved in a fashion that enables human beings to utilise the tools of culture. Without those tools, whether symbolic or material, man is not just a 'naked ape' but an empty abstraction.
> (Bruner 1996, p. 3)

Distributed intelligence includes not just the people involved in an activity, but also the cultural tools and artefacts we use all the time to help in remembering, communicating and solving problems. The tools are perceived to afford certain opportunities to use and develop knowledge. They may be physical, psychological or symbolic, such as computers, mnemonics, diagrams and language, and they are seen to carry or represent the intelligent activity of the people that have previously devised and used them. As with the other theories outlined above, the assumption is that intelligence is produced in specific purposeful activity, rather than 'possessed' to a certain 'level' by an individual person. The new uses of information and communications technologies in education bring the elements of distributed intelligence to the fore, in that pupils do not just learn *about* ICT, but also *with* and *through* the computers and other devices which make new forms of visualization, communication and computation possible (Pea 1993).

The final view of intelligence in this section touches on a new set of approaches which explicitly link intelligence with factors like motivation, emotion, alertness and curiosity. Some of these models extend the concept of intelligence well beyond its original focus on thinking, learning and the acquisition of knowledge, as in Goleman's (1996) *emotional intelligence*. Goleman builds on Gardner's work but claims that, while Gardner's 'intrapersonal' intelligence includes knowledge *about* emotions, the notion of emotional intelligence emphasizes the integrated role of feelings *in* the intelligences and indeed in all aspects of life.

Another example comes from Sternberg, who was mentioned earlier as the formulator of the triarchic theory of intelligence in the 1980s. He went on in subsequent years to incorporate views about personal preferences, social success and wisdom. For example, in the late 1990s he wrote about *thinking styles* defined as 'how we prefer to use the abilities we have' (1997, p. x). He does not reject the concept of ability of some sort, but says that

> constructs of social, practical and emotional intelligence, or of multiple intelligences, expand our notions of what people *can do* but the construct of style expands our notion of what people *prefer to do* – how they capitalise on the abilities they have. When your profile of thinking styles is a good match to an environment, you thrive. When it is a bad match, you suffer. (Sternberg 1997, p. x)

Sternberg describes his thinking styles using the metaphor of 'mental self-government'. He identifies thirteen styles, each linked to different aspects of thinking, and he matches different approaches to teaching and assessment with the relevant styles. So that, for example, he suggests that co-operative learning will suit pupils with an 'external' outgoing style rather than the 'internal' more introverted pupils. Classroom projects suit 'legislative' pupils who like to create their own rules rather than those with an 'executive' style who prefer to work within existing structures, or those with 'judicial' styles who are more interested in analysis and evaluation. The key point is whether the match between pupils' preferences, teachers' preferences and the demands of the school curriculum serve to extend or restrict pupils' educational opportunities and attainment.

IS THE CONCEPT OF INTELLIGENCE USEFUL IN EDUCATION?

As Gardner *et al.* note, the education system in different societies 'provides a window on how those societies think about the realm of the intellect' (1996, p. 247). This applies to the stated aims of education, the selection of students and the ways in which diversity between students is handled. So an emphasis in the curriculum on literacy, on decontextualized knowledge and on the use of symbol systems in subjects like mathematics is mirrored in the assessment procedures which are used to define school achievement and identify the more and less 'intelligent' pupils. Given the growing interest in complex and contextual theories of intelligence and the increasing precision in identifying how the brain works, it could be argued that a narrow concept of intelligence is now redundant. Even within a selective educational system, the educational emphasis would ideally be on how to help pupils to become 'more intelligent' (however defined) through improving teaching and learning rather than to leave things as they are. So in aiming to enhance pupils' intelligence we might refer mainly to theories of learning, such as Piaget's investigations of how knowledge develops through the child's accommodation to and assimilation of key aspects of the environment, or Vygotsky's model of the 'zone of proximal development' mentioned earlier in this chapter. Yet the effort that has been put into researching intelligence at biological, cognitive, contextual and cultural levels may still have some mileage in suggesting how best to intervene to promote and extend children's intelligence(s) and learning. In some of the examples below it can be seen how theories of *learning* are combined with this intention.

At the biological level, neural interventions to enhance or repair the functioning of the brain are still rare, except in cases of severe injury or abnormality. There are signs that indirect approaches through nutrition, physical exercise and even drugs are beginning to catch people's attention as a way of helping children to learn, particularly those with general or specific learning difficulties. However, this is a controversial area and there is still much research (and ethical thinking) to be done in this field (Grotzer and Perkins 2000).

In contrast it is now common practice for teachers to work at the cognitive level in developing teaching programmes which aim to improve pupils' cognitive skills and powers of reflection. The National Curriculum includes a 'thinking skills' element which identifies aspects of information processing, reasoning, enquiry, creativity and evaluation. It is possible to find an expression of these thinking skills within all the subjects of the curriculum (see the National Curriculum Online website: start at *www.nc.uk.net* and follow the links for skills in the 'Learning across the curriculum' section).

One of the original *thinking skills* programmes was devised by Feuerstein (1980), based on his clinical work with 'culturally deprived' pupils showing difficulties in learning and motivation in school. Feuerstein was concerned that the children's learning had not been mediated or scaffolded in the way that Vygotsky had argued was essential for learning. Feuerstein devised a programme of 'Instrumental Enrichment', which comprises a series of exercises calling on a range of perceptual and cognitive strategies such as scanning, memorizing, comparing and problem solving. A typical basic task would be to find the differences between two patterns; a more advanced task asks students to recreate complex patterns through the mental manipulation of coloured stencils. The job of the teacher is to mediate the child's learning by guiding them through each task, particularly addressing the aspects of thinking which are presenting obstacles to success. The deliberately abstract and 'content-free' exercises are then 'bridged' to real life when the child is asked, say, to think about when strategies like scanning and counting are important in daily tasks such as shopping. 'Instrumental enrichment', then, is a process of teaching and learning, conceptualized as 'cognitive modification' in that the child's thinking is stimulated and developed in a way that can be applied in the future. In this sense, the aim is for the child to become a more intelligent learner, and many would argue that there are similar benefits for the teacher who has learned these precise methods for assessing and guiding pupils whose progress in learning has persistently caused concern.

Thinking skills programmes for *all* pupils, which are more closely curriculum-related, are now finding their way into nurseries, primary and secondary schools. For example, Shayer and Adey (2002) developed an extensive programme of 'Cognitive Acceleration across the Curriculum' which moved on from its roots in secondary science and maths to include schemes for all ages in these subjects, the arts, design and technology. Cognitive Acceleration combines elements of Piaget's and Vygotsky's theories of learning, metacognition and the 'bridging' process seen above in Feuerstein's approach. Lessons will typically include elements of whole-class teaching and groupwork with a plenary intended to make the learning explicit. Shayer and Adey have made a point of presenting evidence that the programme promotes cognitive growth in ways which both persist over time and transfer to other subjects (e.g. in GCSE performance).

A more qualitative and generalized use of different theories of learning and intelligence is seen in the increasingly popular 'brain-based' Accelerated Learning framework of Smith (1998), which is aimed at enhancing pupils' motivation and achievement in education. The programme is based on the idea that intelligence is multiple, as Gardner argued, and that it is modifiable in school so that pupils can be taught to think and learn more effectively using a range of visual, auditory and kinesthetic techniques (VAK) such as mindmapping, visualization, debates, musical stimulation, physical activity and practical design and technology. Smith suggests that pupils' multiple intelligences can be activated and developed in a series of stages from initial stimulation, observation and modelling through to problem solving, understanding and finally the generalization of new learning in a wide variety of contexts. The learning strategies are made explicit to the pupils, so that they can become more engaged and independent learners in school and later life.

Programmes of cognitive acceleration and accelerated learning tend to focus on the development of individual pupils' thinking skills, although they assume a need for collaborative learning and curriculum changes in school. However, there are other programmes which emphasize the sociocultural context of learning as the *starting point* for influencing pupils' intellectual development. One example is the development of a 'community of learners' in which the principles are that expertise is distributed in the classsroom, pupils learn through research, and the ethos couples individual responsibility with sharing and respecting classmates. Familiar routines for participation are established (e.g. 'jigsaw' groupwork) and there is constant discussion and questioning to create a common understanding. Assessment is dynamic and participatory, with a particular emphasis on how well pupils can transfer their understanding to new situations (Brown *et al.* 1993). A concept of 'intelligence' may be less visible in such a classroom, but many of the principles discussed earlier in this chapter are evident.

CONCLUSION

In conclusion, it is hard to assess the usefulness in education of the concept of intelligence without returning to all the earlier debates about what it means. Perhaps the key point is to work out the links between our understanding of intelligence and the actions we take? So while any teacher may have a general interest in intelligence as a member of society, the professional responsibility might prompt different questions, such as: How does what I believe about intelligence affect my responses to my pupils? Is my understanding of intelligence complete and what can I do about any gaps and misconceptions? What power do I have to help pupils to develop the intellectual qualities and skills that are valued and useful? Less commonly asked by teachers is: How can I use my teaching experience and my own research to advance knowledge about intelligence and its relevance to education? The ongoing academic disputes which only rarely give explicit and up-to-date attention to current educational policy and practice demonstrate the importance of such a question.

Chapter 5

Classroom Teaching and Learning

REX WALFORD

INTRODUCTION

'Now what I want is Facts. Teach these boys and girls nothing but Facts. Facts alone are wanted in life. Plant nothing else and root out everything else …. Stick to Facts, sir!' That was the educational philosophy of Thomas Gradgrind, the schoolmaster in Charles Dickens's *Hard Times*, based on the belief that children's minds were akin to empty vessels. Mr M'Choakumchild, lately trained in one of the earliest of the teacher-training colleges, obediently followed Gradgrind's precepts and poured gallons of Facts into the waiting receptacles. Dickens observes wistfully (at the end of Chapter 2) 'Ah, rather overdone, M'Choakumchild. If he had only learnt a little less, how infinitely better he might have taught much more!' A danger which still has a message for any who undertake a contemporary postgraduate Initial Teacher Training course.

It is just possible that some new entrants approach a career in teaching in the twenty-first century believing the Gradgrind philosophy. If not, whatever subject they may teach, they have surely realized that it is necessary to have a grasp of some fundamental insights into the way in which children's minds develop and how they learn: and the most appropriate ways of matching teaching activities and situations to their needs, so that education takes place with common intent.

HOW DO CHILDREN'S MINDS DEVELOP?

The way in which children's minds develop has been a matter of speculation, investigation and theorizing for many decades. In the nineteenth century and at the start of the twentieth, the experimental work of *Friedrich Froebel* (1782–1852) and Maria Montessori (1870–1952) drew attention in different ways to the importance of providing activity and spontaneity in children's learning. Froebel, a German educationalist, was founder of the kindergarten system and his avowed aim was to allow the mind of the child to grow naturally and through activity; Montessori was the first woman in Italy to receive a medical degree but also an educationalist who developed a system of education based on spontaneity of expression and freedom from restraint. The views and practices of these pioneers were in stark contrast to the passive rote-learning of earlier times and they strongly influenced elementary (later to be called primary) educators, especially the American John Dewey (1859–1952) who saw the essence of education as children involved in constructive play and problem-solving. In later years, this has been characterized as 'enquiry' or 'discovery' learning, and its influence has stretched beyond primary education and into the secondary sector in almost all academic subjects.

Alongside this has been investigation into the way in which children develop their mental and specifically their cognitive faculties. For many years, the most eminent worker and writer in this sphere was Jean Piaget (1896–1980), a Swiss psychologist, whose development of a theory of 'stages of mental development' was based on a series of closely observed empirical experiments carried out under specialized conditions. Piaget's theory is not an overall theory of child development, still less a theory of education, but it linked cognitive development to a series of stages approximately related to age;

- 0–2 years *The sensory-motor period* when the infant is combining sensation and movement to construct an initial picture of the world
- 2–7 years *The pre-operational period* when the development of language enables mental structures to be transformed into symbolic ones, and concepts of past and future are formed
- 7–11 years *The period of concrete operations* when children can reason about particular events if they have particular observable examples to work from
- 11–adulthood *The period of formal operations* when there is the development and maturation of logical reasoning, and complex causal relationships can be deduced even if the relevant phenomena are not immediately observable

Piaget viewed the child as a solitary explorer, regarded language development as little more than a corollary of biologically based maturation, and assumed that the development of thought followed the same basic pattern in all children. His view of the stages of development was thus biologically based.

In more recent times, Piaget's theories have been challenged, notably by the American, *Jerome Bruner* (1915 –). Bruner's work suggested that even very young children could think in a sophisticated way. Some of his experiments suggested that even babies in their cradles were capable of making hypotheses (rather than reacting by instinct) *before* they were capable of language – a significant difference to Piaget's account. Bruner acknowledged that thinking is greatly enriched and facilitated by language but yet not, in essence, dependent on it. He consequently suggested the possibility of the 'acceleration' of the curriculum, in the belief that 'any topic can be taught to any child at any age' as long as it is presented in appropriate ways. Associated with this was the idea of the 'spiral curriculum': the notion that a curriculum for a subject or topic should centre around a set of key ideas which were revisited in successively more complex ways.

Like Piaget, however, Bruner also developed theories about stages, but stages of how we represent the environment to ourselves when we are learning. Bruner's stages were not tied to chronological age. Bruner's first stage is 'enactive representation' – in which certain commonly performed actions (eating, riding a bicycle) become automatic, through the development of a kind of 'memory bank' in relevant areas of the brain. The second stage is 'iconic representation' in which we use connected imagery (e.g. spatial patterns) to help us remember what we have experienced (e.g. the names of people in a group). The third stage is 'symbolic representation' in which the connection between underlying reality and representation is (and is understood to be) detached and arbitrary (e.g. a chemical formula, a map, a word), but we nevertheless understand the link, its meaning and accept it.

Piaget's ideas were also challenged by the Russian psychologist *Lev Vygotsky* (1896–1934), who developed theories about language in relation to children's thinking and of the importance of cultural and social factors in developing cognition. Vygotsky believed that even the youngest child is a *social* being and that it is through interaction with others that the child develops an understanding of self and a capacity for thought. Vygotsky's three key stages of 'development' were: instinct; learning by training (or reflex conditioning); and learning through the intellect. For Vygotsky, the relationship between teacher and learner, and between learners and other learners, was the key to promoting more effective learning. The area between what could, at a particular moment, be achieved by independent learning and what could be achieved with the help and guidance of the teacher (or other more experienced helper) he called 'the zone of proximal development'. He also believed that *language* played a vital part in the development of thought and was not merely a passive or automatic reflection of essentially non-linguistic thought processes. Thus talk and socializing were key factors in Vygotsky's principles of education.

Benjamin Bloom and his co-workers developed an 'educational taxonomy' in the 1970s which identified and sought to clarify what they called different 'domains' of learning – the cognitive (concerned with levels of intellectual learning), the affective (concerned with feelings and values) and the psycho-motor (concerned with physical skills, such as putting a ball in a netball net). Bloom's work has in practice been most used in relation to the cognitive domain and has led to a greater understanding for teachers of how to plan classroom tasks and also how to evaluate learning. His 'ladder' of cognitive attributes begins with 'remembering' and continues upwards with 'compre-hending' and 'application' (applying material in a new circumstances). These precede 'analysis', 'synthesis' and – at the top of the ladder – 'evaluation'. Teachers who design learning tasks with care find 'cuewords' which can indicate the level of thinking required from students. For example, 'Give an account of' is a straightforward task which requires mainly the remembering and comprehending of material ; ' Evaluate' is clearly a task requiring a higher level of thinking (one which will, in all probability, encompass all the other levels of thinking below it). 'Discuss' – a favourite enigmatic cueword of examiners at all levels – invites a student to choose which level of thinking they think is appropriate to the question in hand ... and then see if the examiners agree!

Following on from this, the work of *D. Kolb* and others, on the differing 'styles' in which individuals learn most comfortably, illuminates this area further. (Kolb identifies 'accommodators', 'divergers', 'convergers' and 'assimilators' as his main categories) – see his book *Experiential Learning* for further details.

We know that some people appear to be more *creative thinkers* than others; correspondingly some are better at puzzling through problems, using logic. For instance, consider these two tasks:

a) 'Brothers and sisters have I none, but that man's father is my father's son'. Who am I?
b) How many uses can you think of for a brick?

It is likely that you will be much more 'comfortable' with one than the other: perhaps those who are scientifically and mathematically inclined can solve the first problem easily; those who have studied in the creative subjects may find the second task more to their liking. *Edward de Bono* has written a number of popular and readable books which have illuminated the different ways in which people think (and don't think) and the ways in which more creative problem-solving might be encouraged and developed.

Good teachers take account of these differences in 'learning styles' in lesson-planning and teaching, ensuring that they do not set the same type of learning activity all the time, nor unduly value one type to the exclusion of all the others.

WHAT CONTENT SHOULD WE TEACH?

Keiran Egan has pointed out that schoolteachers need to know not only how children's minds work, but what is the most appropriate content and style to use at each stage of their development. His theory of educational development links both and identifies successively:

1. the 'mythic' stage (during which children respond best to stories)
2. the 'romantic' stage (during which pupils are keen to learn facts, and will absorb great amounts of information)
3. the 'philosophic' stage (during which children become interested in developing generalizations, and principles)

4. the 'ironic' stage (the sign of a 'mature' mind, during which the focus shifts to the exploration of those instances which do not obey the usual rules)

In Eggan's opinion, children who enter the secondary school have usually at least reached the second stage, though some may not progress much further. These stages are curiously named, but they may well, nevertheless, remind you of the interests and enthusiasms which you had at different stages of your own education. They are a pointer for the development of teaching materials and also for the setting of appropriate tasks in lessons and for homework. Egan's work reminds us too that what enthuses and interests an adult does not necessarily do the same for a 12-year-old, and that teachers need to both select and interpret subject material in different ways for different age-groups and ability groups. The advent of a closely specified National Curriculum removed some of the options from this debate but then this National Curriculum is still for the most part only a basic prescription and not an encompassing umbrella for learning or a detailed stipulation of pedagogy.

HOW DO WE MOTIVATE PUPILS SO THAT THEY LEARN EFFECTIVELY?

The pessimists in education (Mr Gradgrind prominent) argue that children must be coerced into educational tasks: that the rule of fear and competition is the only effective weapon for the schoolteacher to use. *John Holt* has eloquently recorded the results of such a system in *How Children Fail* (1969). The progressive diminution of the unquestioning acceptance of authority in society at large is a potent argument against this position, a diminution achieved, in large part, because of the fruits of education itself. 'Do it because I say so' has now only a limited effectiveness in most schools and that because of respect for the speaker, rather than fear. Such respect, increasingly, is earned rather than imposed.

The more significant debate in this area is between those who favour systems of extrinsic motivation, that is to say, providing a system of rewards and satisfactions as an 'external' response to good or successful work, and those who believe that intrinsic motivation is more powerful.

B. F. Skinner (1904–90) is the most celebrated proponent of extrinsic mechanisms of 'positive or negative reinforcement' and his 'behaviourism' led, *inter alia,* to the development of programmed learning (with its immediate feedback mechanisms) and also to schemes in which 'house points' or small privileges of various kinds are offered as a routine incentive to those who do well or work hard.

Psychologists like *J. McV. Hunt* (1969 and 1971) take the view that there is more virtue and more ultimate success in selecting and designing tasks so that there is a ready acquiescence from the learners – in other words, seeking to obtain the goodwill and co-operation of pupils so that they themselves are self-motivated to achieve without seeking extrinsic rewards. Many teachers see intrinsic motivation as a desirable goal but a key issue is whether *all* school learning can be made intrinsically interesting. Some would argue that pupils need to achieve certain goals (e.g. learning their tables) which cannot be made intrinsically appealing; others argue that there are always ways of 'dressing-up' material so that pupils will want to learn.

WHAT STRATEGIES AND METHODS SHOULD WE USE TO TEACH?

An understanding of learning and motivational insights needs to be buttressed with an understanding of pedagogy (i.e. teaching methods) and, a vital third part of the equation, a corresponding ability to perform well so that the chosen strategy successfully delivers the educational goods.

Early writers about education assumed a one-to-one relationship: Rousseau's *Emile* was postulated on a teacher with a single child, and this was a preferred style of education for the very rich until quite recently (the 'governess', the 'tutor'). As formal education became a mass-experience, however, the development of schools in which teachers had classes of dozens of pupils was inevitable, and rules of management and control developed. There has, however, long been a radical school of thought which argues that schooling should not be compulsory, and/or that it should be based on a negotiated rather than an imposed curriculum. Schools such as the independent Summerhill in Suffolk, originally run by A.S. Neill and his family, and the state-funded Countesthorpe College in Leicestershire (for a period in the 1960s and 1970s) sought to make this a convincing reality, but it has never been a model seriously followed by any but a handful of schools.

In the 1970s, the writings of *Ivan Illich and Paulo Freire* encouraged debate about 'de-schooling' and the merits of informal education beyond school buildings and in wider community settings. The current initiatives about lifelong learning and (for example) certain versions of the idea that the state should give everyone vouchers to spend on whatever education they wish when they wish, are offspring of this simmering debate about the appropriate nature of educational *institutions*.

A second strand of the debate (also manifest in the debate about selective and comprehensive schooling) relates to the *groupings* in which pupils are taught. The tripartite system (grammar, technical, secondary-modern) established by the 1944 Education Act (discussed in Chapter 1) was replaced by a gradual 'comprehensivization' of schools in the 1970s and 1980s, and there grew up a quite widespread belief that teaching in 'mixed-ability' classes brought social benefits and little educational disadvantage. In the last twenty years the debate has intensified, as a perception has gained ground that the most able pupils are not fully stretched in mixed-ability classes and that the overall educational achievement of the school population in the UK gives cause for concern. For many schools there is now a live issue about the balance of 'streaming', 'banding' or 'setting' as alternatives to mixed-ability grouping – and a judgement to be made over whether maximum educational achievement should be given priority over social or wider educational objectives.

The third strand of this debate leads us back to Mr Gradgrind, what *methods and approaches* is it best to use? And, are these the same for every subject, or should we expect there to be more rote-learning in, say, modern languages and maths, than in history or English? A radical (and highly readable) critique of traditional methods was advanced in an influential book by *Neil Postman* and *Charles Weingartner* first published in 1969, and it related to a perceived change in the necessary philosophy and objectives of schooling. If, they argued, we now need schools to prepare students for the future in a highly dynamic and changing world, students will need flexibility of mind and the development of an independent capability, not merely the capacity to 'guess what the teacher is thinking when a question is asked'. The move which they advocated towards more enquiry methods, the use of experiential learning (games, role-play, etc.), group discussion, problem-solving and project work, gained credibility in many subject areas. It was underpinned by an optimistic belief that the 'basics' would continue to be picked up by an osmotic process as pupils worked on genuinely interesting and involving exercises. This turned out to be unjustified in many cases.

The pendulum has swung again in the last two decades, and the current educational concerns of all main political parties in the UK (and of Ofsted, the inspectional arm of government) as we enter the twenty-first century seem to be focused on the acquisition of basic skills and on an encouragement to return to more 'tried and tested' traditional teaching methods. Thus there is now renewed advocacy of the teaching of reading by phonics, and the learning of number tables in primary schools; and also of whole-class interactional teaching and expositional methods in both secondary and primary schools. It might be argued that, in the 1970s and early 1980s, process and experience became more important in schools than product, and that the transmission of knowledge was undesirably downplayed almost to the point of extinction by some teachers. The currently dominant view suggests that there must be a balance for pupils between acquiring basic information on the one hand and developing skills and desirable attitudes and values through which it is put to good use on the other.

WHAT CHANGES MAY THERE BE IN THE FUTURE?

The use of information and communications technology has yet to be fully integrated into classroom teaching and learning – despite the 'honeymoon' period of the late 1990s. ICT enthusiasts optimistically predict radical shifts in learning patterns, but these are unlikely to materialize until there are computers in every classroom and not merely in specialist rooms on which there are necessarily limitations on use. More radical prophecies suggest that the school itself may one day become redundant as an institution, as the Internet increases the power of home learning, but it seems more likely that the social attraction of schools, the quest for community life and the desire for personal interaction as part of learning will remain powerful and conserving factors. Unless a new era of Gradgrindery emerges, classrooms, schools and teachers are likely to remain enduring parts of the educational landscape for the foreseeable future.

Chapter 6

Use of Language in the School and Classroom

GABRIELLE CLIFF HODGES

LANGUAGE VARIETY IN SCHOOL

In school, students encounter and use a wide range of language:

- vocabulary peculiar to school, e.g. 'Principal', 'Head of Year', 'assembly', 'break', 'tutor time', 'PSHE', 'homework planner', 'detention'
- vocabulary in specialist subjects with sometimes the same word having different meanings in different lessons, e.g. 'space' used in Maths, Science, Art
- vocabulary associated with different technologies e.g. 'pen', 'book', 'mouse', 'cursor', 'screen'
- a range of language types, e.g. 'instruction', 'coercion', 'sympathy', 'discipline'
- a range of languages, dialects and accents

This diversity of language use is often taken for granted by teachers and students alike.

However, close observation of language in the classroom shows just how complex students' achievements are as they move between different languages, or between the spoken and written word, or formal and informal language in different contexts, for example: with peers in the playground; in tutor time or assembly; in lessons; in the dining hall, the library, the computer room; in the school council or the drama club. Much of this language appears to be assimilated by students simply through using it on a daily basis. But this is not always the case. A student may not have understood subject-specific terminology or usage, may not speak or write very much at all, and therefore misses opportunities to experiment with language, to learn or understand. There is much that teachers can do to help develop students' language, for example by planning work which involves wide-ranging language use and teaching students explicitly about it.

In the past there has been a tendency in secondary schools for language study to be seen as the domain of the English department despite long-standing calls for people to realize that 'every teacher is a teacher of English because every teacher is a teacher in English' (Sampson 1925). *English for ages 5–16* (DES 1989), commonly referred to as the Cox Report, which formed the basis for English in the National Curriculum, contained a paragraph which summed up well what language is, what it does and why *every* teacher should pay attention to it:

> Language is a system of sounds, meanings and structures with which we make sense of the world around us. It functions as a tool of thought; as a means of social organisation; as a repository and means of transmission of knowledge; as the raw material of literature; and as the creator and sustainer or destroyer of human relationships. It changes inevitably over time and, as change is not uniform, from place to place. Because language is a fundamental part of being human, it is an important aspect of a person's sense of self; because it is a fundamental feature of any community, it is an important aspect of a person's sense of social identity. (DES 1989, para. 6.18)

If language is a fundamental part of being human, then it is the proper concern of *all* teachers. The National Curriculum goes some way towards recognizing this in its statement on *Use of language across the curriculum*:

1. Pupils should be taught in all subjects to express themselves correctly and appropriately and to read accurately and with understanding. Since Standard English, spoken and written, is the predominant language in which knowledge and skills are taught and learned, pupils should be taught to recognize and use Standard English.
2. *Writing*
   In writing pupils should be taught to use correct spelling and punctuation and follow grammatical conventions. They should also be taught to organize their writing in logical and coherent forms.
3. *Speaking*
   In speaking, pupils should be taught to use language precisely and cogently.
4. *Listening*
   Pupils should be taught to listen to others, and respond and build on their ideas and views constructively.
5. *Reading*
   In reading, pupils should be taught strategies to help them read with understanding, locate and use information, to follow a process or argument and summarize, synthesize and adapt what they learn from their reading.

6. Pupils should be taught the technical and specialist vocabulary of subjects and how to use and spell these words. They should be taught to use the patterns of language vital to understanding and expression in different subjects. These include the construction of sentences, paragraphs and texts which are often used in a subject, e.g. *language to express causality, chronology, exploration, hypothesis, comparison, and how to ask questions and develop argument.* (DfEE/QCA 1999a, p. 40)

The National Strategy for Key Stage 3 (2001) also pays due attention to the role of language in learning, and literacy across the curriculum, albeit for slightly different reasons. David Blunkett's Foreword to the Strategy boldly states that 'language lies at the heart of the drive to raise standards in secondary school', before acknowledging that language is 'the key to developing in young people the capacity to express themselves with confidence, to think logically, creatively and imaginatively' (*ibid.*, p. 5). Like the National Curriculum, the Strategy emphasizes the contribution to be made by all teachers, not just English specialists, to students' development in this respect. However, the language in which it is written, suggests slightly different values from those of the Cox report (quoted earlier). Here we find notions of language as a 'tool' for learning and teachers having a 'stake' in strong language skills:

> Language is the principal medium of learning in school, and every teacher needs to cultivate it as the tool for learning in their subject. Other subjects do more than simply police English across the curriculum, or nurse pupils with poor skills. Teachers have a genuine stake in strong language skills because language enables thought. Language goes beyond just 'writing up' what is learnt and 'looking up' information in a text; it is in acts of reading and writing that meanings are forged. Finding the right words, giving shape to an idea, articulating what is meant: this is where language is synonymous with learning. (*ibid.*, p. 15)

The Strategy also has ambitious aims for transforming teaching about language, building on some of the features of the National Literacy Strategy for Key Stages 1 and 2. The extent to which secondary schools adopt and adapt the Strategy for Key Stage 3, however, still remains to be seen.

Whatever rationale schools and teachers profess, it remains the case that language learning and development is an entitlement of all students. Teachers should, therefore, from the first, consider the different needs and language strengths of every student in all their classes. These will vary, depending for example on whether students are monolingual, bilingual or multilingual; whether they have recently arrived from abroad and are learning English as an additional language; whether they attend language classes out of school. Levels of specialist support for those learning English as an additional language will vary considerably from school to school, as will school policies on inclusion or withdrawal. It is highly likely, however, that most teachers, some or all of the time, will find themselves working in multilingual classrooms. As Josie Levine argues, they therefore need to ask themselves a fundamental question:

> What do we need to know about additional language learning/subject knowledge/English mother-tongue teaching that will help us to teach our subject/class better? Such a question suggests that the intentions of teachers and the needs of their pupils are about to overlap in more fruitful ways than before. More fruitful for the children's learning and language and their social development, and more fruitful in furthering the development of teaching styles that are about the language, social and learning needs of all children. (Levine in Meek 1996, p. 53)

A further, challenging question about multilingual classrooms, again posed by Josie Levine, is: 'What are the tools of hospitality?' (*ibid.*, p. 53). It is a question she proceeds to answer in ways which are of immediate practical relevance to the classroom. Classrooms which are 'hospitable to diversity' are those in which, for example, students are encouraged to work collaboratively, take risks and join in, learning about the language demands of specific classrooms and subject areas as teachers or peers model the language for them, hearing how different questions are framed so that they can learn to use them for their own particular ends. Students should hear, as often as possible, 'the tunes and rhythms of English' read aloud, whether from a class novel, a newspaper article, a passage from a geography text book, a report on a science experiment, instructions for a game in physical education. Students should be encouraged to draw on their knowledge about languages in which they *are* already fluent and experienced to help them develop their skills in English in ways which do not diminish the significance of the first language.

Working in any classroom involves the teacher thinking about differentiation in as many ways as possible. Quite apart from the students' diversity of language needs, they have other needs relating to their knowledge, their understanding of the concepts of a subject, their skills and aptitudes, their motivation and their preferred learning styles (Hall 1995). The use of a variety of teaching styles and resources is as important as ever, as is the careful consideration which must be given to the demands of any task set and the support required for students to be able to achieve an outcome, at an appropriate level.

Mindful of the importance of differentiation, the National Curriculum also contains a general statement about inclusion (DfEE/QCA 1999a, pp. 32–9) which highlights teachers' obligation to provide effective learning opportunities and challenges to meet the diversity of students' needs. Ways to assist all students to achieve the highest standards are suggested, including those who exceed the expected level of attainment within any subject, those for whom English is an additional language and students with special educational needs.

LANGUAGE AND LEARNING

Whoever, or wherever, they teach, teachers need to understand the integral relationship between language, thought and learning. The theories of Vygotsky (Vygotsky 1978, 1986) are helpful in this respect. Vygotsky argues that young children learn to think by talking with others, by engaging in social and cultural practices which enable them to 'grow into the intellectual life of those around them' (Vygotsky 1978, p. 88). Later, speech divides into two particular strands: 'communicative' speech which we use to communicate with other people and 'egocentric' speech which we use to communicate with ourselves. In the early stages, egocentric speech is audible; but it eventually becomes silent 'inner' speech with its own idiosyncrasies of grammar, for individual thinking. (Occasionally, however, especially when faced with a complex challenge, e.g. learning how to use a new piece of computer software, we may talk aloud to ourselves again as a way of coming to know and understand how the software works.) Inner speech has different patterns from communicative speech: with inner speech, speaker and listener are the same person, so there is much that can be taken for granted. When we use communicative speech, the aim is to be understood by another person, so we have to make our ideas more explicit. Inner speech, therefore, is fundamentally different from communicative speech because it serves a different purpose. However, although inner and communicative speech are different they are nevertheless related, and it is the dynamic between them which, according to Vygotsky, enables intellectual development. It is therefore very important for teachers to have some understanding of this two-way process and how that understanding can be harnessed to help children become more effective learners.

Over the last few decades, researchers and teachers have studied the use of language in the classroom ever more closely. They have focused on the process of students' learning and the part played by different kinds of language: community dialects, mother tongues, spoken standard English. They have looked at the language for task setting or asking questions. They have observed the impact of the context and environment on teachers' and students' use of language. They have noted what linguistic difference is made by the relative urgency of the problems being solved. New understandings have subsequently emerged about the influence of exploratory talk on cognitive development, and how students talk themselves into understanding as they speculate, question, hypothesize, argue and negotiate. Of crucial importance is the understanding that:

> language provides us with a means of *thinking together*, for jointly creating knowledge and understanding. The inherent, open-ended flexibility and ambiguity of language makes it qualitatively different from other animal communication systems; it is not simply a system for transmitting information, it is a system for thinking collectively. (Mercer 2000, p. 15)

In the late 1980s and early 1990s, the National Oracy Project (Norman 1992) helped to disseminate more widely ideas about the role of talk in learning and to influence classroom practice. For example, teachers began to plan specific small group activities which involved students talking to solve problems, analyse texts, debate controversial issues. Or they made use of activities such as role play as an alternative way of exploring subject knowledge, be it in science, history or personal and social education. Whether students were learning *through* talk or learning *about* talk, it was clear that there could be no justifiable return to classrooms which were predominantly silent.

Students were taught *about* talk, teachers making explicit what students already knew implicitly; for example, that spoken language is affected by the context and purpose of the communication and by the audience to whom it is addressed, and why people alternate between speaking in Standard English or in a community dialect, between one language and another.

Given the complexity and importance of language in the classroom, all ITT trainees need to ask themselves the question: 'What, as a teacher, do I need to know about language?'

KNOWLEDGE ABOUT LANGUAGE

Grammar

In order to teach effectively about language it is necessary to have a clear understanding about grammar. Grammar is the system by which, in any language, words are formed and linked together to make meaning. Grammar includes the stock of words from which we choose (vocabulary or lexis); the forms of words (morphology), e.g. 'run' or 'ran', 'stop' or 'stopped'; the order of words (syntax), e.g. 'I was walking through the woods when I saw a fox' or 'I saw a fox as I was walking through the woods'. Any variety of English, whether Standard English or one of its dialects, is distinguishable by specific features of its grammar and vocabulary. According to Ron Carter:

> Standard English may be defined as that variety of English which is usually used in print and which is normally taught in schools and to non-native speakers using the language. It is also the variety which is normally spoken by educated people and used in news broadcasts and other similar situations. It is especially characterised by a rich and extensive vocabulary developed over centuries for a range of functions. Though it has been extensively described and codified, Standard English is not a homogeneous entity; it is subject to historical change and variation across the world. (Carter 1995, p.145)

Dialects spoken in different parts of the UK have their own different but equally systematic grammars and vocabularies. Indeed, it is by distinctive features of grammar and vocabulary that different dialects are identifiable, as you will discover if you try to identify from which regional dialects the following sentences come:

- They've wrote me three letters.
- I just ignores people like that.
- You're going, isn't it?
- How are y'all feeling today?
- We didnae think o' that.
- We couldn't see nowt.
- Who is it you'll be wanting?
- Can I give youse a lift?
- Why they do that?
- We was walking down the road.

(taken from Crystal 1996, p. 25)

As teachers it is important for us to know the grammar and vocabulary of dialects in the areas where we teach in order to be able to distinguish between when students are using the grammar and vocabulary of a local dialect and when genuine grammatical mistakes are being made in spoken or written Standard English. Students need to learn the advantages of using Standard English in certain contexts and be in a position to choose when and why to do so. For example, a student doing work experience as a receptionist will need to use spoken Standard English to ensure that clients from anywhere in the country or the world can understand clearly; when at home with family or friends, the same student may well use a local dialect as a mark of greater informality, familiarity and intimacy.

Another crucial distinction which teachers need to be able to make is between the grammar of spoken and written language. As Katherine Perera points out:

There are two important points to be made that concern the nature of speech on the one hand, and the nature of writing on the other. First, there is a fairly widely held but mistaken view that speech is some kind of careless or sloppy version of writing. This view leads people to make judgements of speech that are inappropriate because they derive from the written standard. Secondly, it is necessary to realise that written language is not merely a transcription of speech; so learning to read and write means not just learning to make and decode letter shapes but also acquiring new forms of language. Some difficulties in reading spring from the language itself rather than from the written code, because there are some grammatical constructions which are common in writing but which occur very rarely in speech. (Perera 1987, pp. 17–19)

Spoken-language grammar is strongly influenced by the fact that the speaker is almost always in the presence of the listener (telephone and radio being two of the rare exceptions). The presence of the listener and the spontaneity of most spoken language changes the grammatical ways in which meaning is conveyed. For example, speakers:

- make use of stress patterns, pitch, speed and volume so listeners can hear what is meant
- use gestures and body language to supplement what they say
- repeat themselves, make false starts, hesitate, trail off without the listener necessarily losing the thread
- interrupt each other or take turns
- link infinite numbers of clauses together (a pattern sometimes known as 'chaining') rather than speaking in sentences with clearly defined beginnings and endings

However fluent and careful spoken language may sound, its grammar is often very different from the grammar of written language. Look, for example, at the following transcript of a section of a Radio 5 commentary on the final game of a tennis match at Wimbledon in 1995:

Sanchez Vicario onto the Graf backhand and that is just inside the baseline the return and a forehand from Graf and a forehand reply higher from Sanchez Vicario now Sanchez Vicario pulled onto her backhand she goes across court with it but is beaten by the reply.

A tape recording of this extract reveals the commentator speaking at great speed in order to keep up with the pace of the point being played. His excited intonation conveys the spirit of the match to his listeners. His elliptical, telegraphic style is entirely appropriate for the context and purpose. If he used lengthier phrases and clauses he would quickly fall behind each shot. Notice, also, the unusual word order in the first two lines – 'that is just inside the baseline the return', where one might expect 'the return is just inside the baseline'. In tennis, winning the point depends upon whether the ball lands inside or outside the baseline. Here, then, the commentator gives his listeners the crucial information first ('inside the baseline') and then the additional information ('the return').

This is an example of spoken-language grammar which it would be misleading to describe as wrong. It is, however, different from what one might expect to read in a newspaper report on the match next day. Such a report might include the following sentences:

Sanchez Vicario played the return to Graf's backhand and it landed just inside the baseline. A forehand from Graf led to an even higher forehand reply from Sanchez Vicario. Sanchez Vicario was pulled onto her backhand, going across court with it, but was beaten by the reply.

Teachers can draw students' attention to such differences and thus assist them in making distinctions, in their own writing, between spoken and written grammatical structures.

Much of the writing students undertake in school is expected to be in Standard English. Students whose local dialect is similar to Standard English are at an advantage here. Nevertheless, even if a student's writing contains a number of errors, it is unusual for many of those errors to be grammatical. Instead they may involve the following:

- difficulty in making the transition from spoken to written, e.g. 'Well, when Queen Elizabeth came to the throne'
- oddities of style, e.g. 'I hope you will look on my application gladly'
- incorrect use of a correctly spelt word, e.g. 'I put the book over their'
- misconceptions about punctuation, e.g. 'I went home, I had my tea'

If they are grammatical then it may simply be a case of using local dialect grammar when Standard English was appropriate, for example 'we was' rather than 'we were'.

It is therefore helpful if, when correcting students' work, teachers consider any errors carefully, deciding whether they are to do with grammar, style, spelling or punctuation, and offer precise guidance for learning how to put them right, rather than loosely condemning the work as 'ungrammatical'.

Oracy

ITT trainees are often anxious about talk in classrooms, especially if they remember working in virtually silent classrooms when they were at school. They may have a tendency to equate silence with good discipline. It can, therefore, be very illuminating to observe closely how spoken language is used in order to understand its potential. If classroom activities are well planned you can observe the extent to which they provide opportunities for cognitive development through communicative speech, motivating students to hypothesize or predict, compare and contrast, express and justify feelings or viewpoints, consider the opinions of others, organize, interpret and represent ideas and information, ask questions and think aloud. You can also analyse how such planned activities support the language development of all students, including those who are not fluent in English.

You can observe the extent to which the teacher's own use of language makes a difference to students' learning, for example through careful questioning. There are two main kinds of questions: closed questions which attempt to elicit one single correct answer ('In what year did Queen Victoria die?') and open questions which attempt to elicit a range of responses, ideas or hypotheses ('Is 16 the best age to end compulsory schooling?'). A teacher's choice of questions depends upon the planned learning objectives: do they wish to discover what students already know or do they want them to talk themselves into understanding?

Reading

Reading forms a very considerable part of the secondary school curriculum and it is important for teachers to find ways to develop their students' reading skills. It is necessary to find out and build on what students already know and can do. Students for whom English is an additional language may be very fluent readers in other languages. We need to know as much as possible about how and what they read in other languages to ensure that they are offered reading material and levels of support which are appropriate.

Finding out what the students know and can do may best be done by asking them directly and taking a genuine interest in what they choose to read for themselves in their own time. Their answers may be very illuminating (Hall and Coles 1999). But there are other ways to find out, too: observing students informally in the classroom, library or resources centre and noting what kinds of reading sustain their concentration for the longest periods of time; analysing their ability to annotate or make notes from reading material; recording their preferences for different kinds of texts, for example electronic or print, visual or diagrammatic; reading their records from previous schools; looking at their results from statutory tests or other published reading tests. Listening carefully and systematically to them reading aloud may be revealing. However, any one of these approaches alone is unlikely to be sufficient. Reading is a multi-faceted process and it therefore cannot be adequately assessed by one method alone.

Many secondary schools use different schemes for what is known as 'reading intervention'. For example Paired Reading, where a less experienced reader is paired with a more experienced (often older) reader to read together on a regular basis, is one of a number of intensive, systematic schemes designed to help students whose reading is below the level deemed necessary to cope with the demands of the secondary school curriculum. The National Strategy for Key Stage 3 has produced materials such as the Literacy Progress Units for use with students in Year 7 who are still working at National Curriculum Level 3.

ITT trainees need to find out what literacy strategies are being used in their placement schools but they also need to ask relevant questions about how far such strategies substantially influence students' learning and what research evidence exists to support any claims being made. What is meant by the term 'literacy'? Upon what model of literacy is the school's policy for raising standards based? How far are students encouraged to become literate citizens who can demonstrate understanding of 'how the public gets information and how opinion is formed and expressed, including through the media' (DfEE/QCA 1999b)? Are students people whose literacy offers them (in the words of Gunther Kress) the potential to play a critical, innovative, productive part in society, locally and globally? Are they being prepared by the teaching of literacy across the curriculum 'not just to cope, but to control their circumstances' (Kress 1995, p.18)?

Writing

Students undertake a great deal of writing in schools. It is interesting to analyse when and how writing contributes to students' learning. The National Writing Project which was set up in the 1980s yielded extremely valuable insights into the nature of the writing process and the implications of this knowledge for teachers and students. Many different factors affect the writing process, so when students are asked to write, it is important to consider things like audience, purpose, genre and whole text structure and to assess students' achievements accordingly. Consider, for example, a task involving writing a letter of complaint to a local councillor about refuse collection and recycling arrangements. Will students be sufficiently familiar with the vocabulary of waste disposal? Will all the students in the class be fully aware of the discourse structure of such a letter, that is, how the shape and language of the letter is affected, even determined, by the power relationship between a councillor and an ordinary member of the public? Students' writing will need to acknowledge that the letter is:

- addressed to a councillor rather than a close friend
- in the form of a complaint rather than congratulatory
- a personal letter rather than a letter intended for publication
- a letter rather than a newspaper article, etc.

Their choice of vocabulary and syntax will also affect the way the letter is received. How the letter is finally judged by the teacher will depend on whether it is a draft version which is being formatively assessed or the final version being summatively assessed. Another consideration will be whether it is handwritten or word-processed and the different effects intended and achieved by one format rather than another. What appears, on the surface, to be a relatively straightforward task, is revealed to be a complex affair. Careful planning, teaching and assessment are therefore of the essence.

It is always important to consider the learning objectives for any piece of writing a student is asked to undertake, however apparently simple. For example, if notes are to be made, how is students' learning affected by whether the notes are copied, dictated or constructed by the students themselves? Have the students been taught how to make effective notes? Can they see a clear purpose for doing so? What techniques have they learnt to enhance the structure and layout of notes? In short, as teachers we should avoid taking the writing process for granted.

We need to consider what problems or misunderstandings may arise from setting a piece of written work and offer appropriate structured support and guidance. In particular, given the very different stages of writing development achieved within most classes of secondary students, even if they are setted rather than mixed ability, we need to differentiate the work to meet as precisely as possible the needs of individual students. Some students may welcome the support of writing frames, 'written structures to prompt writing [which seem] to mirror, but develop, the oral promptings that teachers have always instinctively offered to children' (Wray and Lewis 1997, p.122). The writing frames are skeleton outlines which offer students elements of the finished text, such as sentence openers ('When we lit the Bunsen burner we noticed'), or connectives ('however', 'meanwhile', 'therefore') which help to signal a change of direction in the argument or the start of an alternative viewpoint (*ibid.*). On the other hand, more fluent and experienced writers may welcome the teacher setting them very challenging but achievable targets, for example a tight word limit which forces them to communicate their ideas as succinctly as possible, or a requirement to explore an idea from a number of differing viewpoints, not just their own. Either way, the teacher must think through carefully the implications of the task set and the learning objectives against which it will be assessed.

CONCLUSION

Teachers need to be aware of the potential for students' use of language in the classroom to influence their cognitive development as well as their acquisition and communication of concepts and knowledge. To that end they need to plan for students to talk and listen, read and write for a range of purposes in a variety of contexts to give them the opportunity to develop. Teachers need to ensure that knowledge about language is made explicit, whenever appropriate, so that students understand how language works, are aware of the choices available to them and are confident in whatever uses they make of it.

Part II

Care, Opportunity, Community and Environment

Chapter 7

Pastoral Care and the Work of the Pastoral Tutor

MARY EARL

INTRODUCTION

This chapter can only very briefly introduce you to the vast range of material concerned with understanding adolescence and the relevance of this to the work of the pastoral tutor. What the chapter sets out to do is to ensure that, as pastoral tutors, you are aware of three important things:

- the fact that adolescence is one of several critical psychological and biological developmental stages in the growth of young people, and that successful negotiation of it is also affected by social and cultural factors
- the fact that this complex transition partly defines the pastoral problems with which we, as tutors, have to deal in secondary education
- the fact that the nature and the manner in which some of these pastoral problems are presented can lead tutors into difficult 'boundary issues' about which it is best to be forewarned and hence forearmed

BIOLOGICAL FACTORS

For some, talking about the pastoral issues related to dealing with pupils in the 11–18 age range, mainly means talking about the physical and biological effects of the onset of puberty. Puberty produces the biggest single set of changes to the individual's appearance and, indeed nature, that has happened since they learned to walk, talk and use a potty. At puberty, height and weight rapidly accelerate; secondary sexual characteristics manifest themselves; mature reproductive capacity develops; and there is further growth and differentiation of cognitive ability. Figures given for the onset of puberty state that the mean age of the menarche (the start of menstruation for girls) is thirteen (Year 8), though 15 per cent of girls in the UK now reach puberty before they leave primary school (Year 6). For boys, the average age of puberty is fifteen (Year 9/10). It is important to note, though, that the age for the onset of puberty for both boys and girls varies considerably.

Biological change affects every aspect of the adolescent's life. Many of the interactions, psychological, sociocultural and biological, which occur between young people themselves and between them and us as teachers, during puberty, are influenced by these biological changes. When you take a Year 9 PE lesson such as boys' football, the height, weight and hence strength, of the boys in front of you may vary astonishingly. When you take a Year 9 GCSE English or Drama class, you may find there are three to four years of 'maturity difference' in the ways boys and girls choose to engage with the emotional demands of studying a text about love or sexuality. Sometimes this can be irritating. The temptation to say 'Grow up!' to tutees is one that very few of us avoid completely. But we do have to keep in mind the idea that the fact that such anxieties keep re-appearing in our tutees' lives, often seeming completely overwhelming to them, is not entirely their *fault!*

Adolescents are young people waking up to the realization that they will soon be or are already becoming fully adult, fully capable, biologically, of not only living and breathing and dying, but also of reproducing, of fathering or of mothering. Puberty is not a minor life event and we should not trivialize the developmental problems arising from it.

For adolescents puberty often (not always) means the proliferation of worries often centring on whether all their new 'body bits' will ever grow, or change, or work, in the appropriate order/at the appropriate time. Dealing with all this anxiety, as a tutor, is not easy. Associated with all this anxiety there often comes a new set of secrecies and embarrassments, around the body and body image. Suddenly the girl in your tutor group who could win a House swimming match for you any day last year won't compete at all and has a period every time there is a match. Everyone seems to be keeping a (very private) diary. Your previously well-adapted, hard-working male tutees' faces break out into acne; their voices break; and their desire to work sinks through the floor. GCSEs are just around the corner. What do you do?

Adolescence and living with anxieties related to puberty is a 'phase' we all know we had to go through ourselves. But tutors need to remember, as the adults they now are, how much adolescents need and expect you to be *role models* of adulthood for them. This does not mean you have to be perfect but that you need to be able to tolerate tutees' anxieties, quiet them and show them how to manage them if necessary, and be able to help to pilot them through to calmer waters beyond adolescence.

Bullying, teasing and the miseries of being included or excluded from certain girl and boy 'groupings' due to peer group pressures, are other problems which stem partly from the both the variability and the inevitability of the biological onset of puberty. They may however also stem partly from psychological factors affecting adolescence.

PSYCHOLOGICAL FACTORS

When we come to consider what adolescence as such is, beyond the merely biological, consensus views are surprisingly hard to find.

Psychologists differ widely in their attitude to adolescence. Some have seen it as a near sickness, a difficult but inevitable period of *Sturm und Drang* (storm and stress). Teachers must, therefore, on this view, expect adolescents to be erratic and 'over the top' emotionally, to be scatty and uncertain about themselves and others – it's all part of adolescence.[1] Others, however, argue that there is no biological law which says the phase of physiological development we call puberty is inevitably accompanied by 'storm and stress'. Some have even said that as a definable life stage, adolescence does not, in any other than the merely biological sense, really exist. It is merely the sociocultural creation of increasingly leisured, technocratic, liberal Western pluralistic societies.

Developmental psychology, however, from Freud to Piaget, Erikson to Kohlberg, suggests that teaching adolescents involves guiding them not through a merely biological phase but through a distinctive psychological or perhaps more properly a bio-psychological stage of development. In other words, what is at stake, with the onset of puberty, is not only a change of physical appearance and the onset of the ability to reproduce, but a vast challenge to, and opening of possibilities for, wide-ranging *identity formation*. Erikson, in fact, characterized adolescence as one of eight life stages, each with recognizable tasks to accomplish and each with recognizable problems which could result from not negotiating the transitions adequately (Erikson 1984).

At Erikson's Stage Five (i.e. 12–18 years) the key task is given as *identity versus role confusion*, i.e. it is the task of setting out to make *oneself* and of making oneself in a role (or roles), without confusion with the roles of others. Significant influences, unsurprisingly, are peer groups and role models for leadership (including those in neighbourhood and school). It is fairly clear from this what the role of a tutor to pupils in this age group is going to involve. It is also fairly clear what the consequences, for both personal and social development, would be of failing to negotiate the stage effectively.

The fact that Erikson sees adolescence as a time for debating, very intensely, what it means 'to be or not to be' is also unsurprising. The anxiety arising from this debate is one reason why you can have such wonderfully existentialist conversations with adolescents, but it is also why they write so much poetry about death and disaster and sex and love. It is also why incidences of the onset of anorexia and abusive steroid use, along with other risky behaviours from very fast car and bike driving to unsafe sex, abound at this age. This identity formation, as we have already said, is inextricably intertwined with the biological changes of puberty. The high rate of suicide among 16–19 year old young men, for instance has been associated strongly with unresolved fears concerning gender identity.

Tutors have a responsibility to help tutees negotiate their way through this stage effectively, but we cannot solve everybody's problems, nor make the negotiation of the developmental phase successful for all pupils, all of the time!

This is because, as Erikson suggests, an adolescent is not a *tabula rasa* (blank surface). He or she brings to adolescence certain psychological assets and also certain liabilities arising from their previous negotiations of Life Stages 1–3 (see Table 7.1) Perhaps one way to look at the tutor's role then, psychologically, is to see it in terms of encouraging and strengthening the former, and counteracting and diminishing the effects of the latter no more, but certainly no less.

The psychological *assets* a child may bring to adolescence include:

- a sense of knowing what it means to be 'listened to', to feel one's views are being taken seriously (in little things, not only in big ones) and
- a sense of not being pressurized to 'perform'. One writer puts it like this: 'A child needs to know that there is no such thing as failure only unreal expectations'

The psychological *liabilities* a child may bring to adolescence include:

- fear of being 'nobody' with no experience of love, no sense of one's own substance, and no sense of one's own value

Table 7.1: Erikson's eight life stages

	Task	Meaning	Significant figure
Stage 1 (0–1)	Basic trust versus mistrust	Can I get and give in return?	Mother or mother figure/primary carer
Stage 2 (1–3)	Autonomy versus shame and doubt	Can I hold on and let go?	Parents
Stage 3 (3–6)	Initiative versus guilt	Can I make (going (after)? Can I make like (playing)?	Basic family
Stage 4 (7–12)	Industry versus inferiority	Can I make things (completing) and make things together?	Neighbourhood and school
Stage 5 (12–18)	Identity versus role confusion	To be or not to be?/ To share being oneself	Peer group, leadership models
Stage 6 (20s)	Intimacy versus isolation	To lose and find oneself in another	Partnerships in friendship, sex, competition and co-operation
Stage 7 (late 20s–50s)	Generativity versus stagnation	To make exist, to take care of	Divided labour and shared household
Stage 8 (50s and beyond)	Ego integrity versus despair	To be through having been; to face not being	Humankind, my kind

- feelings of neurotic rather than 'true' guilt, which can develop through an individual receiving bad training (or no training) in values
- fear of not being in the mainstream, for example being an introvert in a very extroverted society. Failure to handle this sort of fear can lead to an individual finding it hard to make friends and sometimes, to being bullied
- fear of being unable to cope with the world: the world of 'them', of sex, of stress, of fighting for a job

Failure to cope with any or all of these negative liabilities can lead an individual either to turn in on themselves or to become over-aggressive.

SOCIOCULTURAL FACTORS

How far a pastoral tutor is, or should be expected to be, a role model, counsellor, PSHE teacher, or even provider of a substitute 'family' structure, is viewed differently by different schools and in different cultures. What is crucial, however, is that you learn for yourself where to set the boundaries between these roles. Teachers are not trained counsellors, priests or social workers, but their work may at times contain elements of all three. The culture in which the school is situated also offers its own constraints for tutors.

Schools have to be aware of the sociocultural demands of the local and national context in which they operate as much as they are aware of the biological and psychological factors affecting their pupils. These, too, can and will affect your work as a tutor working with adolescents for, as some have said, 'adolescence begins in biology but it ends in culture'. For instance, in Britain today:

- 25 per cent of children under 16 have experienced a divorce in the family
- 1 in 3 marriages end in divorce
- there are changes in family structures overall
- working patterns have been, and still are, radically shifting
- lifestyle patterns (e.g. living near or far away from family of origin) have been and still are, radically shifting
- the onset of puberty is now earlier than before
- sexual experiences are also generally beginning earlier
- the availability of money to the young is very different from in previous generations. This may lead to being valued not by what you are but by what you have
- there are changing trends in use and abuse of drugs and substances
- the power of the media, availability of videos (including pornographic ones) and the strong influence of popular music heavily affects young people's views of themselves
- the role of religion is shifting continuously
- the way young people are seen in relation to crime and punishment is shifting

- the views of adults about how 'young people' should be are shifting
- some would say young people in liberal Western democracies have more choice and more freedom than ever before in any society. They differ as to whether this is a good thing[2]

Young people in the secondary stage of schooling need you to know about these constraints because they need: '*the ethical soundness, credibility and rational consistency of the society and the world around them in order to establish a stable identity and find meaning in life*' (Erikson 1984, p. 21). The pastoral system in many schools aims to provide that as one element in the experience of their pupils. You, as a tutor, are asked to contribute to the successful accomplishment of that task.

DEALING WITH BOUNDARY ISSUES

Even supposing there was all the time in the world to do the job of a pastoral tutor, we have all, at one time or another, found ourselves severely pressurized by pastoral work and unsure that we have the skills to deal with it. Teachers are not, after all, given much initial teacher training for this part of their role. Basically though, good tutors, like all other teachers, need relevant kinds of knowledge, understanding and skills to do their job well. The trouble is that it is never very clear how, when or from whom we are going to be able to get these. Take, for instance the problems of knowing that a young man on his first work experience has encountered racial abuse at work and doesn't know how to handle it other than by physically lashing out at his employer. Or the problems of knowing that a young woman is in deep distress (which she won't tell you about for fear of peer group recriminations), which turns out to be the result of having been pressurized by an older boy into a sexual relationship she does not know how to handle. In each case, an elementary knowledge of the law as it affects young people's employment, or sexuality, or race relations, is fairly essential. But what one also needs is skill in handling *boundary issues* – i.e. determining whether this problem is one you can or should be dealing with, and then determining either how to deal with it yourself or who to refer it on to.

Tutors often acquire what amounts to a pastoral 'caseload' and can then be stuck with enormous problems of time management and prioritization. Their skills lie in not ducking but in dealing effectively with this load, while still knowing that their prime role is that of a classroom teacher.

The prime skills for managing this load involve good basic administration skills, but also, sometimes, good basic *counselling skills*. Good counsellors set boundaries on when, where and for how long they will listen, but they also undertake to listen, within those boundaries, attentively and genuinely to that person as a person (not just as pupil X who is 'always in trouble' or pupil Y who is 'good at maths', etc.).

One such strategy involves saying to a young person, when they come to you for help (and particularly if you are very rushed): 'On a scale of 0–10 how serious is the problem now?' It may sound facile, but usually that person will immediately say: '4, or 7 or, oh, its only a 1 at the moment'. This really helps you to decide whether or not you need to put other issues 'on hold' while you deal with this particular pastoral problem. It also enables you, as things develop, to say casually at the start of each tutor period to that person: 'What point of the scale are we on today then, Donna/Ben?' Apart from anything else, this keeps you in touch with both the problem and the young person's abilities to solve it for themselves. We have to bear in mind that adolescents need (with apologies to Bruner) *emotional* 'scaffolding' to learn how to manage their own affective development. They also need you to know, for their own sake, when to remove some or all of that 'scaffolding' in order for them to become adult. Creating a collusive co-dependence that suggests you will solve all their problems is not the way to do this. Refusing to help them at all or not acknowledging that dealing with emotional 'stuff' is hard, is also counter-productive. Adolescents need to learn, as all of us have to, to take responsibility for their own actions. They have to learn to find solutions to emotional and other difficulties through their own reason, their own friendship groups and their own developing relationships with adult teachers who up until this stage in their development have largely been seen simply as 'authority'. They need to start to make the transition between teacher as out there 'parent figure' and teacher as potentially equal-status adult. This one transition provides, probably, at least half the work of the pastoral tutor working with this age group. We may act as better role models, for young people, of this adult attitude to life if we gently but firmly indicate the paths available to them to sort out their own issues rather than always solving their problems for them.

It is tempting, perhaps, to argue that dealing with an individual's psychological, social and emotional developmental problems is irrelevant to our primary teaching task, which, on the surface, is merely to do with their cognitive development. However, as the psychologist Arthur Maslow pointed out, it may be, on the contrary, that until those primary needs are met, significant cognitive development is impossible. Many schools implicitly recognize this by providing pre-school breakfasts for children, or just by recognizing that in times of deep emotional distress, some of the important things a young person needs to encounter are, as Maslow suggested when he produced his 'pyramid of needs', routine, trust and acceptance, the esteem and respect of others, being part of a group, and protection from potentially dangerous objects or situations (Maslow 1987). An adolescent bereaved, for instance, will certainly need these aspects of schooling to be there as s/he comes to terms with grief and loss.

Tutors have, legally, to adhere to rules in many aspects of their practice. These govern their ability to promise confidentiality to a pupil and their responsibility for knowing where, in relationships between pupil, tutor, school hierarchy, family and the local community, they are qualified and therefore allowed, to intervene. This takes time to learn, but is at the basic competence level of tutoring. What is far more difficult is learning how and when it is important to down 'teacher-as-educator' tools and pick up 'teacher-as-pastoral carer' ones.

In summary, however, the golden rules for tutoring seem to be:

- administrate efficiently and deal with problems as promptly as you can
- listen carefully – and genuinely. Take time to do so
- set clear boundaries to help the tutee know what they have responsibility for and what you have responsibility for in each situation
- know who to refer particular problems to
- never attempt to take a pupil's 'side' in a dispute without first checking:
  (a) that their side of the story fits with that of others involved in it (particularly important when there are disciplinary conflicts between staff and pupils)
  (b) which other staff should, or already do know about the problem (sometimes pupils start to tell several staff the same problem and end up getting everyone running round after them!)
  (c) what viable possibilities there are for pupils to solve the problem themselves, with or without emotional 'scaffolding'

CONCLUSION

As other chapters in this book point out, what we are doing, in all aspects of schooling, including tutoring, involves providing a good deal of implicit and explicit values education alongside the delivery of the formal curriculum. When we undertake, in maintained schools, the management of pastoral problems, we need to be very clear about what this means for us, both as individual teachers and as individuals collectively responsible to parents for the safekeeping of their children. Some schools see the tutoring role as merely instrumental, i.e. picking up problems as they arise and responding pragmatically to them. The dangers of this approach are, of course, that a lot of problems go unnoticed. There may also be, on this reading of the role of the tutor, little or no attempt by the school to deliver consistent values education within the tutor group. Given our responsibilities under the 1988 Education Reform Act and subsequent legislation for the pupils' spiritual, moral, cultural and social development, it is becoming less and less usual for tutor groups to function in this way. Many schools now see the tutor group as a space for encouraging not only cognitive and affective development but also, spiritual and moral development. This may be done in a variety of ways, from explicit collective worship to 'thought for the day' type explorations of current events and issues of general human concern. Either way, it is a clear attempt to influence pupils' values. This is new territory for many teachers and many feel reluctant, and certainly ill-equipped, to engage in such activity. It is worth noting, however, that while both the definitions and the practical outworking of a moral and spiritual, or indeed a citizenship education in maintained schools has yet to be fully formalized, discussion about it is very much alive and important within the educational community. Trainee teachers would be wise to engage with the debate in their initial teacher training since there may be less time to do so once they are full-time teachers.

Perhaps we can best regard different forms of pastoral tutoring as the attempt to find a 'best fit' solution to the need for schools, located in and representing very diverse cultures, to support their pupils through a crucial, if sometimes difficult phase of their psychological, emotional and cognitive development. This, done well, is part of the whole complex process by which schooling should enable young people to enter the increasingly complex world of adult community with as many cognitive and affective strengths, and as few liabilities as possible.

NOTES

1. Adolescence in the twenty-first century is subject to some pretty difficult and possibly unique pressures, but that doesn't mean it might not also be much the same thing as it always was. If you read this quote and try to date it you may get a glimpse of what I mean.

    > The young are in character prone to desire and ready to carry any desire they may form into action. Of bodily desires it is the sexual to which they are most disposed to give way, and in regard to sexual desire they exercise no self-restraint. They are changeful too and fickle in their desires, which are as transitory as they are vehement; for their wishes are keen without being permanent, like a sick man is prone to fits of hunger and thirst.

    > ... if the young commit a fault, it is always on the side of excess and exaggeration for they carry everything too far, whether it be love or hatred or anything else. They regard themselves as omniscient and are positive in their assertion; this is, in fact, the reason for their carrying everything too far.

    The date? Well you might be able to tell it's not recent from the language, but would you have guessed it was in fact written by Aristotle, 2300 years ago?

2. In her fascinating, though now rather dated and sometimes criticized study of adolescence in Samoa, *Coming of Age in Samoa*, the anthropologist Margaret Mead claimed to find little evidence of the existence of huge emotional disturbances which are sometimes regarded in our own culture as an inevitable (and incurably awful!) side effect of adolescence. But she did still see sociocultural factors as important. Mead put the apparent absence of emotional stress in adolescence in Samoan culture at that time down to the general casualness of Samoan society and its unhurried pace, to the looseness of its family and other interpersonal bonds, to the absence of economic, social or other crises; and, to a considerable extent, to the absence of a necessity for individual choice, vocationally, socially or morally.

    Such studies highlight the importance for us, as teachers, of being aware of the pressures our own society is making on its young people today. For instance, is adolescence becoming more stressful because of the increasing diversity and complexity of society today? To take one small example. Sitting down to help a Year 12 pupil look through the UCAS handbook, recently brought home to me the vast proliferation of courses (and universities!) to which she could go at 18, or at 21, or, indeed, at 41 or 81! Making career choices against such a background is very different from making them twenty, let alone forty or fifty years ago! The choice is affected by everything from economics, through gender to politics and family structures. To ignore all these factors would not make us good secondary school teachers, let alone good pastoral tutors.

Chapter 8

Special Educational Needs: Current Concerns, Future Opportunities

MARTYN ROUSE

SPECIAL EDUCATIONAL NEEDS: A BRIEF OVERVIEW

This chapter will consider some of the issues that teachers and schools face as they attempt to educate all students, in particular those who are thought to have special educational needs (SEN). The chapter will provide a brief overview of key developments in the field of SEN and will examine some of the assumptions that underpin recent thinking in this area. It will conclude by considering the responsibilities and opportunities that all teachers share in maximizing the learning of all children and young people in the light of these recent developments.

The history of special education in the United Kingdom can be traced back more than two hundred years to a time when the first special schools were founded for the deaf and the blind. Much of the impetus for these early developments in the education of disabled children was rooted in charity. In 1870, the introduction of compulsory schooling brought many children into schools who previously did not receive an education because it was believed they would not benefit from such an investment of time and money. Furthermore, the industrial revolution saw the mass relocation of populations from rural to urban communities and an associated decline in natural support systems for disabled people such as extended families and traditional crafts. In response to the concerns that this raised, separate special schools and institutions were created to cater for those children who were considered unsuitable for normal schooling and who were seen as so demanding of their families that they might undermine economic efficiency.

Associated with the growth of special education was the belief that disabled people, particularly those with learning difficulties or mental health problems, needed to be cared for, and that this could best be done by segregating them into asylums located away from populous areas. The reasons why this solution was adopted are complex. They result from a combination of factors including a humanitarian concern for those less fortunate than the majority and the growing need for social control. The influence of eugenic thinking was also apparent. This thinking suggested that such people should be segregated, controlled and not allowed to have children of their own for fear of contaminating the gene pool. Thus, the institutionalization of disabled people has its origins in *protection*; the protection of the community of 'normal' people from the disabled through segregated forms of provision and the protection of disabled people from themselves through 'humanitarian' care. Segregated special schools were often founded upon these same principles of protection and care.

During the twentieth century, special education developed as a separate but parallel system with its own career structures and teaching approaches. Over time, new eligible categories of handicap were established and at the time of the 1944 Education Act, ten categories of handicap were recognized. In spite of this growth in special provision, still not all children were entitled to education. Those with severe learning difficulties were the responsibility of health authorities and were placed in long-stay hospitals or junior training centres, rather than schools.

In England and Wales the 1970 Education Act made local education authorities (LEAs) responsible for the education of *all* children, regardless of the severity of their disability. This legislation recognized the right of all children to education and required LEAs to provide such schooling. What this meant in practice was that the existing junior training centres became ESN(S) schools serving what were then called educationally subnormal (severe) pupils. New teaching approaches developed in many of these schools and gradually it became accepted that no child was ineducable. Following this development, the seventies saw a rapid growth in the field of special education.

Much of this progress came about as a result of parental pressure. Parents and carers have played a major role in the struggle to establish and maintain the hard-won rights for their children to receive an appropriate education. Often this struggle was organized through the numerous voluntary societies, charities and pressure groups that have been instrumental in many positive developments in special education. Unfortunately, the field has been vulnerable to two negative aspects of this pressure. The first concerns the pressure to create new groups of children eligible for the additional funding that is associated with special education, and secondly the promise of 'miracle cures'; the history of special education is littered with initiatives that promised much but delivered little.

The Warnock Report (DES 1978), which was the basis of the 1981 Education Act, reflected a non-categorical, altruistic and benevolent view of special education. The Report introduced the concept of 'special educational need'. It broadened and loosened definitions suggesting that as many as 20 per cent of children could have a learning difficulty at some stage of their school careers. Parents were seen as playing a central role in the identification, assessment and education of their children alongside professionals. During the seventies and eighties, such thinking was the basis of developments in policy and practice in many schools and LEAs. Wedell (1990) suggests that it led to a reconceptualization of the special needs task based upon the following principles most of which are still influential today:

- *Interactive nature of difficulty*: special educational needs result from a complex interaction of factors, only some of which exist within the child. Other factors are found in the learning environment in which the child is educated. Acknowledging the importance of the context in which learning occurs has led to what is sometimes called an 'ecological perspective' which rejects the so-called 'medical model'. Interactive explanations recognize that a child might have a learning difficulty in one classroom but not in another. At their heart is the belief that teachers make a difference to how well, or badly, children learn.
- *Non-categorical nature of disability*: special needs are relative and context-specific. It is therefore impossible to draw a clear line between the so-called handicapped and non-handicapped. Furthermore the use of categorical labels, which might be useful in securing resources, often led to unhelpful stereotyping and lower expectations. Much of the provision that currently exists, together with many people's attitudes, remains based upon categorical assumptions of disability. The field has found it difficult to leave 'labels' behind and the recently revised *Special Educational Needs Code of Practice* (DfES 2001a) refers to four types of difficulty.
- *Common aims*: the aims of education are the same for all children, although the means may be different, as might the extent to which the aims are achieved.
- *Inclusion*: children have the right to be educated alongside their peers as long as their needs can be met. Additional support and different approaches to school structures and teaching may be required if this is to be achieved. Inclusive schools set out to educate all children, regardless of disability and diversity. They see diversity as a resource for learning rather than as inevitably leading to problems. Since 1997 the current government has backed a policy of inclusion through the introduction of a series of new policy initiatives, including the publication of *Inclusive Schooling: Children with Special Educational Needs* (DfES 2001b).
- *Positive discrimination*: some children might need additional help and support if they are to learn successfully in school. The current law aims to protect their rights by issuing a 'Statement of special educational need', a legal document detailing the form of provision and additional support required. However, it must not be assumed that additional help is always required, nor that such help necessarily leads to positive benefits for the child. Indeed there are many examples of inappropriate help harming children's learning, particularly when unskilled adult intervention separates the child from the curriculum and from other children, a major resource for their learning.

Evidence suggests that progress was made in implementing new policies and practice based upon these principles (Wedell 1990). Spending on special education increased during the eighties; LEAs appointed new advisory teams and there was a series of new teacher and school development initiatives designed to promote whole-school policies for meeting special needs.

In spite of these developments, problems in the field of special educational needs remain. It is possible to be critical of the consequences of the enabling and permissive special education policies that were so influential during the past twenty years. The lack of a clear framework and the absence of agreed definitions of what constitutes a special educational need, led to wide variation in practice both between and within LEAs. The special needs debate became dominated by questions about resources. Which children are entitled to receive additional help? At a time when funding was limited, there was pressure to relocate resources from certain existing groups to new or redefined kinds of special need.

As previously mentioned Warnock suggested that as many as 20 per cent of children might have special difficulty of some kind at some stage of their school lives. Of these children, the majority (18 per cent) would not require additional support. Under the current arrangements, schools are urged to follow a standard procedure for the assessment of a pupil's special educational needs prior to asking for a formal statutory assessment leading to a 'Statement'; this process is explained in the *Special Educational Needs Code of Practice* (DfES 2001a). Statements of special educational need are legally binding documents specifying the additional resources required to meet a child's need. They have been required for nearly twenty years, since the implementation of the 1981 Education Act.

An unintended consequence of the statementing process, however, has been that schools use it as the means through which they can secure additional resources from the local education authority. The resulting bureaucracy has not served children or schools well, because it is costly and consumes too much time and professional effort that could be focused on improving teaching and learning (Audit Commission 2002).

It has been suggested that the strengthened rights enshrined in the *Special Educational Needs and Disability Act 2001* (SENDA) that came into force in September 2002 may make the need for Statements obsolete. But some parents feel they 'have to fight' for a Statement as it provides important protection for them and for their child. For this reason, Florian (2002) suggests that they are still a necessary tool in the struggle for rights and access to education for all.

> It is worth remembering that Statements were introduced only one decade after children with severe learning difficulties became eligible for education. Judgements about the appropriateness of Statements should be made on the basis of whether they serve their intended purpose rather than only the cost of producing them. (Florian 2002, p. 165)

It was thought back in the early eighties that around 2 per cent of children would require the protection of a Statement of special educational need. Coincidentally, this was, overall, the same percentage that were being educated in special schools. However, by 2000, in some LEAs this figure (for special schools) was as low as 0.35 per cent (in Newham), but in others it was as high as 2.64 per cent (Manchester). In other words a child with a disability was more than seven times more likely to be educated in a special school in Manchester than they were in the London Borough of Newham (Norwich 2002). These differences cannot be explained by the relative incidence of disability in various regions; rather they are a result of the historic patterns of provision or of differences in interpretation of the government's guidelines by the LEAs. Newham for example has been pursuing a policy of inclusion for nearly eighteen years. In spite of the move towards inclusion in many LEAs, there continues to be confusion about the rights of the remaining 18 of Warnock's '20 per cent', the majority of whom are, and always had been, in mainstream schools.

The special needs task in many schools has been complicated in recent years by a number of changes that have challenged traditional thinking about the nature of disability and learning difficulty. These difficulties have been exacerbated by a shift away from legislation and policies based upon the principles of equity, social progress, altruism and towards legislation underpinned by the principles of academic excellence, choice, competition and parental self-interest. The new mantra is 'standards'. A spirit of 'educational Darwinism' has become apparent in which only the fittest students, teachers and schools survive. In a climate based upon the principles of the market, students with special educational needs have become particularly vulnerable because much recent educational legislation and policy development was formulated without reference to, or concern for them.

Recent reforms have had a radical impact upon the education of children with special needs. In particular, the National Curriculum, the Numeracy and Literacy Strategies and the associated systems of assessment would change the educational landscape and challenge the thinking of many parents and professionals about whether the educational aims for all children were, or could be, the same. Although the National Curriculum has been a challenge for all teachers of children with special educational needs, it is the impact of the curriculum and national assessment on the statemented group in particular (recently estimated as 3 per cent and rising) which has been most difficult (McLaughlin and Tilstone 1999). An encouraging recent development is the introduction of the so-called 'p levels' for children who are working at levels pre-national curriculum and the guidance that has been produced to help teachers with this group of pupils (QCA 2001).

The rapid changes have caused turmoil in the field of special educational needs. In spite of, or maybe because of, these changes there have been many innovative developments that might provide the impetus for improvements in future practice. There are a series of issues such as assessment, the relationship between teaching and learning, inclusion and the future of segregated special forms of provision, that face schools as they attempt to make sense of the special needs task in the context of recent reforms. Each of these will be considered below.

ASSESSMENT

Assessment has played a pivotal role in the development of policies and practice in special education. Traditionally, this task was directed towards categorizing and segregating children with disabilities and learning difficulties in order to find those children who would not benefit from mainstream schooling. Various screening and identification procedures were developed for this purpose so that problems could be named and diagnosed in order for appropriate placement and provision to be made. In addition, professionals have employed a variety of methods for the assessment of children in order to plan appropriate interventions for them. It could be argued that many of these approaches to assessment saw children's abilities as fixed, leading to negative consequences for children, because they were labelled inappropriately and teachers' expectations were lowered.

In recent years assessment in the area of special needs has focused on statutory assessment leaving little time or professional energy for teachers to undertake assessment designed to improve teaching and learning. Nevertheless, the power of formative (i.e. *informative*) assessment to improve learning in the classroom is increasingly accepted (Black 1996). The *Special Educational Needs Code of Practice* (DfES 2001a) attempts to address this dilemma of assessment but reinforces the status quo. Though the *Code* stipulates that ongoing observation and assessment should be undertaken, formative assessment is not required but left for 'schools to decide the procedures they should adopt for meeting the needs of all children, for observing and assessing their progress' (para. 5:38). It is when children begin to experience difficulties in learning, when there is sufficient concern about a child's progress to draw up an Individual Education Plan, that relevant assessments need to be undertaken, so that evidence can inform the development of interventions.

Although difficulties remain in developing a national system of assessment that will meaningfully include all children and enable them to demonstrate their learning, there is little doubt that the current preoccupation with raising standards has raised awareness in the profession. It has also has introduced a sense of urgency into the task of raising the levels of achievement of those children who find learning difficult.

CLASSROOM FACTORS: TEACHING APPROACHES

In a recent research project investigating the practice of nearly 300 secondary teachers working in inclusive schools, Florian and Rouse (2001a) found that many mainstream subject specialist teachers were able to identify, describe and use particular teaching strategies and approaches that successfully include all learners. These strategies include, peer tutoring, co-teaching, role-playing, co-operative learning and 'jigsawing'. The schools that took part in this investigation provide opportunities for teachers to learn about the use of such strategies in their own classrooms and encourage teachers to extend their range of teaching approaches.

In addition to the strategies mentioned above, there are other features that seem to characterize classrooms where children's learning needs are most effectively met. A good example concerns the use of praise. When appropriately used, perhaps in private, as part of the feedback process, praise can be a powerful means of improving self-esteem which is an essential component of successful learning.

Teachers who are effective in meeting children's special needs have high, but realistic, academic and behaviour expectations of the children they teach. They accept that all pupils can learn, but that some children may need alternative explanations and examples. In particular, it seems important for teachers to make connections between what is being learned, with what is already known and has been experienced. One way of doing this is to begin each session by explaining the aims of the lesson to the pupils and linking it to previous learning. Active learning plays an important part in successful classrooms. The experiences that are organized for the children should be as authentic as possible. Many children who find abstract classroom learning difficult have few problems learning out of school.

Grouping and organizational strategies should be appropriate for the activity that is taking place. For example, if it is necessary to give instructions, it is better to address the whole class and to ensure that they can all see and hear the teacher. Similarly children should only work in groups when they are working on a collaborative task. Properly structured collaborative group work has been demonstrated to be one of the most effective ways of meeting a wide range of learning needs within the classroom because it utilizes other children, one of the major resources for learning in the classroom.

Many schools are employing greater numbers of teaching assistants to support children who have special needs. While this additional help can be positive, it requires clear guidelines and should not lead to dependency on the part of the child. In some secondary schools, assistants are being attached to subject departments in order to allow the assistants to be more familiar with curriculum content and to provide greater continuity of learning experiences. Assistants should be seen as a resource to help the teacher to meet the needs of children, rather than only for direct intervention with the child. Why should those who find learning most difficult be taught by the least well qualified adults in the school? Helpful guidance has been produced by the DfEE (2000) to enable teachers and schools to review the role and deployment of teaching assistants.

INCLUSION

Inclusive education refers to a philosophy and practice of education based on the following principles:

- All children have the right to learn and play together.
- Children should not be devalued or discriminated against by being excluded or sent away because of their disability or learning difficulty.
- There are no legitimate academic reasons to separate children for the duration of their schooling.
- They belong together rather than need to be protected from one another.

Despite the difficulties associated with the implementation of inclusive education policies, there is a great deal of philosophical agreement about the rights of children with special educational needs to equal educational opportunity. The concept of inclusion is a central theme in the government's education policies. The extent to which the legislative process currently underway will help to ensure that pupils with special educational needs are justly included in the new education reform proposals is unclear. However, the acknowledgement that children with special educational needs are to be included in the drive for higher standards is a challenging and an exciting development though there are many problems to overcome.

Current government policy as outlined in the *Guidelines for Inclusion* (DfES 2001b) adopts a policy of increased inclusion but within a framework of special education. It clearly advocates a continuation of highly individualized approaches for children with complex needs. However, other policy revisions aim to develop an education system in which specialist provision is seen as an integral part of overall provision. Whether the actual policies which evolve from this process will help facilitate better educational opportunity for *all* remains to be seen. What is certain is that over a period of thirty years innovative teachers have been able to demonstrate that all pupils can learn, despite policies which excluded certain children from mainstream schools. Their contribution to the development of educational methods with applicability to *all learners* represented a significant advance in extending the right to education for all. Today, the human rights agenda which demands the adoption of inclusive education policies requires the same level of innovation from all professionals to demonstrate that all children can learn together.

Much of the research on inclusive classrooms has focused on primary schools and the difficulties associated with teacher resistance to inclusion or lack of knowledge about appropriate teaching approaches. It is therefore interesting to note that those schools that have made the commitment to support teachers in the development of their skills report fewer difficulties in implementation of inclusive practices which work to the benefit of all children (Ainscow 1999; Tilstone *et al.* 1998).

FUTURE OF SPECIAL SCHOOLS

Developments in inclusion have implications for the future role of special schools. One current view is that special schools could become regional resource centres to support developments in mainstream schools. This suggestion is, however, problematic. Many of the approaches developed in special schools, such as one-to-one teaching and daily monitoring of progress, are not mainstream-friendly and do not easily relocate from special to mainstream settings. In addition, many teachers who work in special schools have little experience of mainstream settings or of working with and through other adults as curriculum consultants. One area of expertise that special schools have developed is multi-professional collaboration. There is much that mainstream schools could learn in this regard.

Special schools are increasingly being judged against many of the same criteria that apply to mainstream schools. Questions about value for time and money are relevant here because of the significantly greater costs in educating a child in a special rather than a mainstream school.

CONCLUSION

The core debate in the area of special educational needs has been dominated in recent years by two main concerns. The first relates to *resources*: who should receive them and how should the distribution of any additional resources be monitored. The second has been about *location*: *special or mainstream*. These debates are likely to continue, but hopefully the future will see more professional energy being concentrated on the more fundamental issue of how children learn best. The task is not to identify more children with special educational needs, but to create classrooms and schools which do not produce learning difficulties as a consequence of the teaching approaches used. Associated with this aspect of the debate, there has been increasing interest recently in whether inclusion is compatible with raising standards for all children. In a series of studies, Lani Florian and I have looked at the features of schools that have been able to raise standards and become more inclusive (Florian and Rouse 2001a, 2001b). As mentioned earlier the London Borough of Newham adopted a policy of inclusion many years ago; in 1999 it was also the LEA with the best improvements in GCSE results. One thing is clear, teachers make a difference, and good teaching is the key to improving children's learning and to reducing the number of children who have special educational needs. This is the challenge for all teachers, not only those who have chosen to make their careers in special needs work.

Chapter 9

Equal Opportunities and Educational Performance: Class, Gender and Race

MADELEINE ARNOT

INTRODUCTION

It is one of the paradoxes of the 1988 Education Reform Act that, even though it was assumed that 'the pursuit of egalitarianism is now over' (Kenneth Baker, then Secretary of State for Education), the effect of the legislation has been to promote greater public concern about the unequal performance of different groups of children in the school system and onwards. Social inequalities now receive considerable public exposure from the publication of school performance tables, the breakdown of National Test results (SATs) into gender categories and, for example, the publication of Ofsted reviews such as that by Gillborn and Gipps (1996) on the achievement of ethnic minority pupils, Arnot, Gray, James and Rudduck (1998) on recent research on gender and educational performance, and Gillborn and Mirza (2000) on mapping race, class and gender educational inequalities.

Although the level of support offered to schools from LEA advisers and specialist teachers on equal opportunities, financial assistance, and networking between schools, declined in many areas of the country in the mid-1990s , there were signs in 1995 of a 'third wave' of interest in gender equality issues, particularly in the rural shires (Arnot, David and Weiner 1996). The increased attention given to differences in academic performance in the standardized tests and in the GCSE results especially by Ofsted inspectors highlighted for schools the importance of monitoring and reducing gender inequalities in outcomes (Arnot *et al.* 1996). The debate about girls' and boys' schooling was directly related therefore to issues of standards and performance rather than to the more general concerns of social equality (Arnot *et al.* 1999).

The 'principle of the market as a method for co-ordinating education'

(Robertson and Lauder 2001, p. 223) which framed the governance of schools under successive Conservative governments has, since 1997, continued to be promoted by Labour in government. However, the more that social class and racial inequalities were found to block progress in meeting national performance targets (the first through evidence of poverty and the second through concern about the high rate of school suspension and exclusion of black pupils), the greater the need for the government to re-address the issue of social inequality. A new ethos emphasizing 'real opportunity', 'civic responsibility' and 'social inclusion' (*ibid.*, p. 224) was promoted to complement rather than replace the market ethos. These new agendas aimed to reduce the forms of social exclusion associated with such competitive performance cultures. In this context, the Labour government attempted to break the 'cycle of welfare dependency and poverty through its Welfare to Work and New Deal Strategies' (Hodgson 1999) and to encourage inclusion through diverse educational initiatives such as the *Sure Start* and *National Childcare Strategies*, the *Excellence in Cities* initiative and the *National Literacy and Numeracy Strategies*. During this period of intensive reform, it appears that there has been a substantial rise in terms of the average number of qualifications achieved by students. Each of the main *ethnic* groups has participated in this improvement in GCSE attainments (with the improvements of some minority ethnic groups even greater than that of white students). It is not clear, though, that the same could be said for members of all social *classes* (Gillborn and Mirza 2000).

SOCIAL CLASS AND ACHIEVEMENT

Social class inequalities are notoriously difficult to measure – historically these inequalities have been traced by social scientists rather than by government. As a result recent available data is not always reliable. Free school meals, for example, are often used as rough indicators of social class, when in fact they measure family poverty (Gillborn and Mirza *op. cit.*, p.18). Nevertheless, using currently available indicators, it *is* possible to see the connections between higher social class and higher educational attainment. In 1997 the Youth Cohort Study (YCS) found that:

> children from the most advantaged backgrounds (classified as 'managerial/professional' in the YCS) were more than three times as likely to attain five or more higher grade GCSEs than their peers at the other end of the class spectrum (in the 'unskilled manual' group). This is one of the longest established trends in British education but the association is not static. There is evidence that the inequality of attainment between social classes has *grown* since the late 1980s. For example, in relation to the five higher grade benchmark, between 1988 and 1997, the gap between 'managerial/professional' backgrounds, and 'unskilled manual groups' grew from 40 to 49 percentage points. (Gillborn and Mirza 2000, p. 18)

Contemporary educational debates are now focused mainly on the issue of creating 'real opportunities' for all young people to reach *higher* education. Earlier, the National Commission on Education (1993) reminded us that:

Children from social classes I and II do better, on average, in examinations at 16, are more likely to stay on longer in full-time education and are more likely to go to university than those in social classes III to V. There has been little change over the years in the proportion of entrants to higher education who come from working-class families (p. 8).

The gap between the working classes and the upper middle (and especially professional) classes reaching higher education is still very substantial. Plummer (2000, p. 38) quotes UCCA figures for 1992 which showed that students from the middle classes (classes I, II, IIIa) represented 71 per cent of applications and 75 per cent of university places. In contrast students from manual working-class backgrounds (Classes IIIb, IV, V) represented approximately 29 per cent of applicants and 25 per cent of places. Only 1 per cent of applicants were from students from Class V (unskilled manual) and they were allocated 1 per cent of places. Despite the doubling of student numbers in higher education and the increase in qualifications at 16 and 18, it is still the case that some 80 per cent of children from low income groups do *not* go to higher education, while 80 per cent of higher income children do. Arguably this class gap has been aggravated in the UK by the removal of grants to cover university fees and maintenance (Reay *et al.* 2001).

Behind the annual educational statistics, therefore, lie 'the myriad ways in which social class differences contribute to social inequalities' (Reay 2000). A series of sociological studies (e.g. David, West and Ribbens 1994; Gerwitz, Ball and Bowe 1995; Reay and Ball 1997; and Reay *et al.* 2001) provide evidence that an educational system based on concepts of 'choice' differentiates between social classes while hiding the fact that it does so. Thus, middle-class families have been found to use their managerial and symbolic advantages (often referred to as cultural capital) to increase their privileges through market strategies and the choice of high-status subjects, courses, and institutions. In contrast, working-class families appear to choose schools, courses and higher education routes according to different principles which rationally reflect their much reduced material circumstances.

Gillborn and Mirza conclude that an ironic consequence of the last twenty years of educational reforms is that the educational attainment gap between the highest and lowest social classes substantially dwarfs both the race and gender gaps, although the effects of race and gender aggravate the effects of social class. The complex connections between class, race and gender inequalities within the educational system and within society have therefore made it difficult for teachers and schools to know how to respond to such social and educational disadvantage.

Of considerable concern are the interconnections for example between class and ethnicity (see Chapter 10). Class differences exist within all ethnic groups but, even more disturbingly, factors linked to race can aggravate class inequalities. Gillborn and Mirza's data revealed, for example, that African-Caribbean pupils from non-manual homes were the lowest attaining of the middle-class groups: 'In some cases they are barely matching the attainments of working-class pupils in other ethnic groups' (p. 21). In contrast, while there *are* gender differences in the educational attainments of different social classes and ethnic groups, these are not always substantial. There are in fact rather small gender gaps in performance among the upper middle-class high-performing students as well as among those pupils who fail to obtain any formal qualifications at 16 (Arnot *et al.* 1999).

Evidence from a major Australian study (Teese *et al.* 1995) *Who Wins at School?* found not only that working class girls had higher rates of failure in some subjects than other girls (for example, in English) but that working-class boys were more likely to depress the overall scores for boys in literacy and in language more generally. The lower the social status of girls, the less likely they were to take mathematics and the more likely they were to fail when they did. Working-class boys, in contrast, over-enrolled in mathematics and physics, and were more likely to play truant in classes in literature, history or modern languages. Unfortunately there is no comparable study of such class and gender patterns in the UK (although the gender gap in subject take-up and performance is mapped in Arnot *et al.* 1996).

Gillborn and Mirza reminds us that the association between class and attainment does not necessarily lead to the conclusion that the *explanation* for such 'failure' lies with working-class pupils themselves, or with their families and communities. They point out that 'the ways in which social class affects educational opportunities are multiple and complex: some factors lie outside the school, others operate through institutional process that disadvantage particular groups of pupils' (p. 19). The organization of the school, family circumstances and the nature of the locality can all be critical influences on pupils' achievement. Inside the school, differential teacher expectations can lead to working-class, male or black pupils being assumed to have behavioural difficulties and to receive a greater number of exclusions and suspensions. Setting in different subjects can also involve forms of social selection and lead to different levels of access to higher status subjects, top grades and top tier examination papers etc. (Gillborn and Mirza 2000). The demands for more individualized learning processes may also lead to subtle forms of social differentiation. Gillborn and Youdell (2000) found in their study of two secondary schools that, under the pressures of educational performance in what they call 'the A*–C economy', the machineries which construct educational failure may become more rather than less sophisticated in their sifting of each new cohort. Teachers employ a widening range of diagnostic techniques which, under competitive marketized regimes, identify those children who have the potential to improve to the critical grade C benchmark and are therefore 'suitable cases for treatment' (a decision not unlike medical concepts of *triage*). Working-class boys who rebel or show signs of disengagement are the most likely victims of such processes.

The considerable increase in the proportion of all pupils achieving higher grades in GCSE masks the serious effects of unemployment and poverty in certain parts of the UK and in particular communities where a high proportion of single-parent families live close to the poverty line and there are few local employment opportunities for young people. Such circumstances can lead to low pupil aspirations and motivation, and to high levels of conflict, disaffection and disengagement. The loss of traditional transitions from school to work challenges secondary schools in particular to find new ways of motivating pupils to 'stay on' and to become more flexible in their life choices. In such areas, teachers attempt a range of strategies: for example, working more closely with the community, encouraging parents to express their values and needs in relation to their children's schooling, signing up parents to contracts over homework, and becoming involved in pupil mentoring and setting homework targets. Concern about social inequality also encourages schools to engage more actively with their local communities. The introduction also of citizenship education with its emphasis upon community involvement can provide a spur to breaking down school–community barriers.

THE GENDER ACHIEVEMENT DEBATE IN SCHOOLS

Concerns about gender, class and race issues often come together in discussions about boys' educational experiences. The relatively low academic performance of male pupils, especially of black and white working-class boys, has become a matter of great concern, especially for schools attempting to improve their literacy levels and overall performance. The media have labelled the relative underachievement of boys a 'crisis in masculinity'. Various chapters in the Epstein *et al.* collection *Failing Boys?* (1998) suggest how and why this debate developed in the 1990s in the UK (in much the same way as it developed in Australia, see Gilbert and Gillbert 1998). Two key gender gaps in performance were identified by a recent Ofsted review (Arnot, Gray, James and Rudduck, 1998). Firstly the literacy gap and secondly the different patterns of male and female success in achieving 5 or more higher grade GCSEs. The gap between boys and girls in terms of literacy is already established by the age of 7. By the time pupils reach secondary school, girls are ahead of boys. DfES statistics for 2000 suggests that at the end of Key Stage 2, 'around 10 per cent more girls than boys achieved level 4 in English, and far more girls than boys reached level 5'. The gender gap was larger in writing than in reading. In Maths and Science, however, there was much greater parity: similar numbers of boys and girls reached level 4 in KS2 in both subjects, although curiously more boys reached level 5 in Maths and more girls reached level 5 in Science (see DfES website: *The Standards Site*).

As pupils progress through secondary schooling the gender gap in language-related subjects remains sizeable, affecting not just English but also modern foreign languages. This difference in male and female performance is especially significant because not only have girls kept their advantage in such conventionally 'female' subjects but they have, with the support of teachers and schools, substantially reduced boys' traditional advantage in terms of entry into, and performance in, 'male' subjects such as mathematics, chemistry, and physics (Arnot *et al.* 1996 and 1998)

In terms of overall differences at sixteen plus, by the mid-1990s, only 80 boys compared to every 100 girls achieved five higher grade GCSEs, compared with over 90 boys in the mid-1970s. This pattern has since remained relatively stable. To some extent, girls' progress in improving their qualifications over and above that of boys' levels of progress is associated with the introduction of GCSE, the National Curriculum and the changed patterns of subject entry which followed. Boys and girls are now expected to succeed in subjects which traditionally they avoided. Many theories have been put forward to explain why boys have failed to match the substantial improvement in girls' performance (see Francis 2000). Cultural and economic factors, for example, are seen to play their part in that those boys who traditionally used to 'pick up' in terms of academic achievement in secondary schools, may now no longer have the motivation to work especially by Years 8 and 9. Many working-class boys, particularly the most *macho*, now appear to celebrate football, fighting and sex (Mac an Ghail 1994) rather than celebrating hard physical manual labour. Such cultures, rather than being seen by schools as a response to economic restructuring and a new competitive educational ethos, may be read more simplistically as 'opposition' to schooling.

Attention has also been focused on the spread of boys' 'laddish' culture (which had previously been associated mainly with unskilled white working-class boys – Willis 1977), to middle-class boys (Mac an Ghaill 1994, Martino and Meyenn 2001). 'Laddishness' leads to boys seeing schooling and especially 'feminized' subjects such as English and literacy, as 'not cool'. The increase in anxiety associated with high performance and less time for teacher–pupil sociability is thought to aggravate boys' worries in a context where masculinity is associated with success or superiority. Research on masculinity and teachers' projects focus on rethinking teachers' assumptions about male pathology as learners and the various concepts of masculinity now to be found in schools (Skelton 2001, Sewell 1997, Wright *et al.* 1998).

Considerable attention has been paid to boys' learning preferences and the reasons why boys report lower levels of enjoyment at school. There is interest in whether boys and girls prefer different subjects, and whether they respond differently to, for example, coursework and project work, extended writing, factual teaching, also whether they are motivated differently in relation to the same subject. Research has also encouraged an interest in whether boys and girls are equally comfortable with different styles of assessment: for example, is their performance affected by the choice of items for assessment, terminal examinations, multiple choice versus coursework, etc? The Ofsted review on gender research (Arnot *et al.* 1998) offered the following summary of research findings:

- Girls are more attentive in class and more willing to learn. They do better on sustained tasks that are open-ended, process-based, relate to realistic situations and require thinking for oneself. Girls may overrate the difficulty of particular subjects. Girls find timed end-of-course examinations less congenial. Teachers believe that coursework favours girls but other factors (including syllabus selection) may be more important.
- Boys show greater adaptability to traditional approaches which require memorising abstract, unambiguous facts which have to be acquired quickly. They are more willing to sacrifice deep understanding for correct answers achieved at speed. Boys do better on multiple choice papers, whatever the subject.

Research on learning differences between girls and boys has been identified as an important area for raising teacher awareness, encouraging the view that gender blindness (treating all pupils alike) may no longer be helpful (Arnot and Gubb 2001). Investigating the similarities and differences in learning styles of boys and girls is likely to be more fruitful for identifying appropriate strategies. Similarly, the current interest in developing more effective models of pupil consultation suggests that teachers have a lot to learn about learning from pupils themselves.

A number of other gender issues in schooling are being brought into focus by such concerns about boys' education. Of central importance are teachers' gender values, especially in relation to their pupils' concepts of masculinity and femininity – and the effect such values might have on pupils' learning experiences. Gender values can affect how teachers deal with, for example, male and female pupils' anxieties, their motivation to learn, their choices of subjects to study, their work experience placements and the careers advice they receive at school. In certain contexts, teachers can encourage rather than discourage male disaffection. Increasingly, researchers (cf. Arnot *et al.* 1998 for references) are highlighting the following:

- Images of masculinity being legitimated by the school (through the hidden curriculum) and by teachers' interactions with boys. There is evidence from research of conflict between male and female teachers and boys, especially over overtly 'masculine' behaviour (Abraham 1995, Sewell 1997, Mac an Ghaill 1994, Skelton 2001).
- Teacher expectations about boys' abilities insofar as they affect, for example, the diagnosis of special needs (especially behavioural and emotional difficulties), learning support provision and disciplining strategies (expulsions, suspensions). Boys are considerably over-represented in all these categories. Each year over 10,000 pupils, mainly black and white working-class boys, are excluded from schools (Gillborn and Mirza 2000).

• The levels of bullying reported by pupils in the UK raise concern about teachers' responses to such incidents, especially when they involve boys. If teachers' responses are considered unfair or not sufficiently protective by pupils, then they may contribute to the lower levels of male enjoyment and engagement with schooling (Chaplain 1996). There has been increasing interest in the incidence of violence and bullying among female students which has been associated in some research with the alleged increase in the number of 'laddettes'.

LIFE CYCLES OF INEQUALITY

There is a concern that the strong level of interest in boys' underachievement will ignore not just their successes (boys outperform girls in several subjects), but will fail to engage with the continuing problem of both girls' lesser involvement in science and also with the 'underachievement' of working-class girls. At A level, a cross-over in patterns of performance is apparent compared with results at GCSE since more men than women achieve the highest grades (Equal Opportunities Commission 2001). The statistics of male and female achievement reveal not only that boys do better at A level, even in female subjects such as English but that they are far more likely to study the sciences, technology and computing at this level than girls. The Equal Opportunities Commission found that: 'All the Sciences are dominated by men except for Biological Sciences, whereas all the Arts are dominated by women (website). Despite girls' success in performing comparably in the sciences and mathematics in primary and secondary schools, boys gain a slight advantage as they progress through school and many more boys than girls sit single science GCSEs in Physics and Chemistry (Arnot *et al.* 1998). At A level these subjects are getting more rather than less 'masculinized', with the statistics of further and higher education also demonstrating the low proportions of girls going on after school to study science or science-related courses/degrees.

There are also marked gender differences in the proportion of women and men studying vocational subjects at 18 and beyond. Vocational courses remain strongly sex stereotyped, with young women opting for traditional female training courses for work in the service sectors (e.g. hairdressing, beauty care, caring courses and social studies). In this respect, they continue to make 'poor choices' in terms of post-16 training and careers, since such courses typically have low economic benefits. It also remains the case that women experience what is called a 'glass ceiling' in relation to advancement in top jobs. Gender stereotyping by pupils (and possibly teachers) therefore remains an ongoing issue for schools.

The EOC's 1999 Report (Rolfe 1999) argues that the careers service and school-based careers education programmes should take responsibility for promoting equal opportunities, but that this should not be interpreted solely as 'promoting entry into non-traditional areas, but focus on equal access and achievement at all levels, including in management and the professions' (p. xi).

The DfES has intervened into vocational preparation in secondary schools. The White Paper, *Schools Achieving Success* (DfES 2001) encourages greater diversity of curriculum provision and pathways in secondary schools. The proposals suggest that

> Supported by effective use of ICT, young people's learning from the age of 14 will increasingly take place across a range of institutions and in the workplace, complemented by extra-curricular activities such as sport, the arts and voluntary work. There will also be more opportunities for vocational study and we look forward to a time when many more young people gain some experience of vocational education. And for the first time there will also be the opportunity of a predominantly vocational programme for those with the aptitude, beginning at 14 and going right through to degree level. Such a programme might include a significant element of work-related learning from 14, followed by a Modern Apprenticeship or full-time vocational study at college and then a Foundation Degree for those who have the potential. (DfES 2001, para. 4.4)

The EOC is especially concerned about the impact of sex-stereotyping that might emerge as a result of these new vocational educational initiatives, as a consequence of the uncontrolled use of ICT and because of the procedures which allow pupils to disapply from key National Curriculum subjects (a procedure that has already led to stereotyped choices). No strategies have been identified which would assist these choice processes in such a way as to prevent greater gender differentiation in subject and career choices. The EOC argues that the high rates of achievement at GCSE already 'masks choices which close career doorways' leading to a 'lifetime of inequality'. For women, school curricular choices can lead to poorly paid female work and adult poverty. The government's White Paper appears to have ignored the 'limiting effects on gender stereotyping of their proposals' (EOC 2001). The EOC recommends that legislation should provide each child with an entitlement to additional time with an advisor; additional information should be provided on choices, and opportunities should be given for non-traditional taster work placements. Heads should also be trained in the requirements of equality legislation.

Every year a number of boys and girls leave school at the age of 16 without any qualifications. Statistical data on achievement also suggests that the success of girls in raising their achievement of 5 higher grade GCSEs mainly applies to white middle-class girls rather than girls from other ethnic groups or working-class girls. Data presented by Gillborn and Gipps (1996) also suggest that the interconnections between gender, ethnicity and class patterns of achievement can differ substantially in different localities. Some groups of Asian boys, for example, may perform better than equivalent groups of Asian girls; while working-class African-Caribbean girls might be affected by the same difficulties in school as working-class African-Caribbean boys.

Research has shown that gender never works in isolation: it affects and is affected by ethnic and class cultures. Many schools recognize the need to break down gender performance data into social class and ethnic subgroups, and some Local Education Authorities provide excellent databases which allow schools to target particular groups of underachieving pupils.

SCHOOL EQUALITY STRATEGIES

Various agencies (e.g. the Qualifications, Curriculum and Assessment Authority, the Equal Opportunities Commission, the Secondary Heads Association, and Ofsted) have entered the fray, with suggestions about how teachers might improve pupils' academic performance. The gender gap became a matter of national concern when it was seen that improved overall school performance was dependent upon the efforts of schools to tackle those boys who were most disaffected. The then Schools Standards minister Stephen Byers pointed to the fact that 83 per cent of permanent exclusions were of boys and that 7,000 more boys than girls left school at 16 with no qualifications. He argued that the 'laddish anti-learning culture' should be challenged and that schools should not simply 'accept with a shrug of our shoulders that boys will be boys'. He commented:

> Failure to raise the educational achievement of boys will mean that thousands of young men will face a bleak future in which a lack of qualifications and basic skills will mean unemployment and little hope of finding work.

At the same time, he argued, it was vital that 'policies aimed at disaffected boys are not introduced at the expense of girls whose improvement over recent years has been a real success story'. Despite such professed concerns about girls, many recent projects have in fact focused on how to raise boys' academic achievement (for example, the Raising Boys' Achievement, project 2001-3, funded by the DfES and directed by Michael Younger and Molly Warrington) – but with noticeably less attention being devoted to the achievement of girls.

The Ofsted review's conclusion that 'there are no simple explanations for gender differences in performances; in any one context several factors are likely to have an influence' (Arnot *et al*. 1998) is reflected in the range of school approaches to gender equality developed in the UK. The West Sussex County Council project (Arnot and Gubb 2001) and the new DfES project on gender and achievement, have identified a range of different approaches which schools have adopted to promote gender equality (raising boys' achievement while not damaging girls'). Arnot and Gubb, for example, distinguished three school approaches: *targeting boys*; *promoting equal opportunities for all*; and, *the pastoral approach*. These three perspectives led a range of often overlapping initiatives to encourage both sexes to perform well at schools. Preliminary findings of the DfES project on gender and achievement identifies the following four strategic approaches among their sample of secondary schools:

- *Organisational Strategies* identify the importance of a positive school culture through, for example, a carefully designed prefects' system, a high quality physical environment, celebrating boys' achievements, support clubs, success days, merit systems and single-sex groups.
- *Individual Strategies* which involve the active development of use of performance data and formative target settings, and such supports as tutor interviews, mentoring, etc.
- *Pedagogic Strategies* focus for example on classroom management, teaching and learning strategies, literacy across the curriculum, identifying texts that are appealing to boys.
- *Sociocultural Strategies* which involve, for example, targeting students as key leaders and image makers, challenging conventional images of masculinity, formal and informal behaviour management schemes.

MacDonald *et al.*'s (1999) report on boys' achievement advises schools to take a whole-school approach to gender issues, putting into place a range of departmental strategies and management techniques, one of which is the annual monitoring of gender performance (SATS, GCSE and measures of value-added performance), or the targeting of particular pupils – particularly in Years 8 or 9. Short-term single-sex learning groups have been tried in mixed secondary schools in order to explore gender stereotypes about learning and to offer 'safe' contexts to review pupils' preferences and attitudes (e.g. in English). More opportunities have been provided in different subjects for boys and girls to explore their interests. Some schools have given more recognition to the need to work directly with boys and to build their confidence in themselves and their abilities. Teachers are also now called upon to research for themselves how gender works within the culture and structure of the school, in relation, for example, to male and female responses to different teaching styles and learning demands, to different modes of assessment and to various types of classroom organization (see also Chaplain 1996; Bray *et al.* 1997; Bleach, 1998).

Christine Skelton (2001, p. 175) argues that a relevant gender equity programme would need to encourage students to question taken for granted assumptions. She argues that primary schools should address four key questions to challenge gender identities and characterizations. These questions, which are equally relevant to secondary schools, are:

- What images of masculinity and femininity are children bringing with them into school and what types are they acting out in the classroom and playground?
- What are the dominant images of masculinity and femininity that the school itself reflects to the children?
- What kinds of role model does the school want and expect of its teachers?

- What kinds of initiatives/strategies/projects should teachers be under-taking with children to question gender categories?' (*ibid.*, p. 175)

Such models of masculinity and femininity are closely associated to, indeed are often the expression of, ethnic and class identities (Reay *et al.* 2001). The challenge for teachers and schools is to find ways of engaging constructively, critically and dynamically with pupils' identities and the choices which follow from them. Care must be taken not to assume that masculinities and femininities are in opposition to the school, rather they are expressions of social survival and change.

CONCLUSION

There is a need therefore not just to close the gender gaps in performance but to ensure that opportunities are offered for the lowest-achieving pupil to succeed and for racial prejudices to be eliminated from the school system. Schools are aware of the controversies over social class inequalities and how best to organize themselves in ways that do not reinforce such inequalities. There is much debate over how to establish compatibility between the need to encourage a learning culture in which all can excel and the ways pupils are grouped (setting, streaming, banding and mixed ability teaching). Class stratification and indeed class values in relation to subject content, language and modes of communication between teachers and pupils can be built into the school in ways that are often masked. At the same time, there is still considerable concern over the reasons why African-Caribbean pupils appear to start schooling well but to conclude their school days as one of the lowest-achieving groups. There are, therefore, still many more debates to be engaged with over the most appropriate organization, and the culture and ethos of schools, so as to ensure genuinely 'inclusive education' that is able to cope with and indeed celebrate diversity. New pro-active ways of encouraging all pupils to excel are being sought therefore by teachers keen to think creatively about the challenges schools are faced with today. Improving the effectiveness of schools in relation to all their pupils is a task engaging teachers in a range of 'egalitarian' initiatives which involve thinking critically and constructively about social class, gender, and ethnic patterns as part of the professional ethos and practice of teaching.

Chapter 10

Race and Schooling

JACQUI STANFORD

INTRODUCTION

Sir Herman Ouseley, in the foreword to his 2001 report on social and community relations in Bradford, highlighted that his investigation

> focused on the very worrying drift towards self-segregation, the necessity of arresting and reversing this process and the role of education in tackling ignorance and bigotry as well as identifying excellent exemplary projects and initiatives that point the way forward for future developments in the District. (Ouseley 2001, p. ii)

Bradford is an urban area which is multicultural by virtue of its overall demographic composition, but one whose population by the summer of 2001 had nevertheless become increasingly *divided* along lines of race, ethnicity, religion and social class. These divisions, Ouseley maintained, were rooted in ignorance and fear, and compounded by the economic decline of a once prosperous locality.

When *subsequently* 'the necessity of arresting and reversing' the drift towards self-segregation seemed to be underscored by the events that came to national attention in what the media labelled the 'Race Riots' of Oldham, Burnley and Bradford (in May and July 2001), Ouseley's Bradford Report proved a timely document. It was timely, however, not just for Oldham, Burnley or Bradford; the questions highlighted by these disturbances served as a means by which Britain would revisit, once again, the issues of race and multiculturalism and the possible role of education in engendering a cohesive and inclusive society.

RACE AND SCHOOLING IN BRITAIN: A BRIEF HISTORICAL OVERVIEW

Although the historical juncture at which Britain became 'multicultural' could be endlessly debated, the *concept* gained currency in the second half of the twentieth century. The subsequent multicultural debates that have occupied the public imagination since then would suggest that Britain only started down its multicultural trajectory with the docking of SS *Windrush* in 1948. Britain's history of empire would, of course, challenge such an assertion. Britain has clearly had centuries of a multiracial, if not a multicultural, past, even if the arrival of people from the Caribbean in 1948 has undeniably become something of a landmark (Ramdin 1999; Runnymede Trust 2000).

Britain actively encouraged immigration after the Second World War as it sought to rebuild its economic and social life. The *Windrush* passengers, for example, were literally taken from their Caribbean shores to Britain's in a bid to supply urgently needed cheap labour. They were not the only migrants at the time; vast numbers of Europeans, for example, also emigrated to participate in and benefit from Britain's recovery. Nevertheless, as by the late 1950s Britain's relative economic decline proved intractable, changed immigration policies initiated and focused new patterns of engagement with the issue of race.

'Immigration' became synonymous with black and, in time, Asian people entering Britain. Further, 'immigration' became associated with, and a euphemism for, social problems attributed to these particular newcomers; their presence became implicated in the perceived economic and social decline they had initially been recruited to help stem. As they settled, invariably at first into working-class (and often 'inner-city') areas, they and the established residents within these communities had to negotiate both the populist (often racist) notions of the day as well as the reality of increased competition for resources (Cohen 1988). Immigration, political discourses and the collective public imagination became racialized in particular ways as race became a primary lens through which many in Britain understood or explained their lived reality (Solomos 1992; Hall 1978).

Hall (1978) argues that a 'convenient amnesia' resulted in which Britain's long history of ties with the peoples of the Caribbean, Asia and Africa was forgotten, being displaced by ignorance and fear of those people settling in Britain. This sat alongside attempts by the New Right to delineate a British and/or English identity that was premised on 'kin', 'stock' or 'breeding' and which, consequently, would not include people who were not white (Parekh 1986; Gilroy 1987). Further, effective rights as full citizens were denied to black and Asian people as they faced continual racial harassment and often found their access to social services and employment obstructed (Ramdin 1999). So, it was not long before there was tension and resentment on all sides. These would from time to time erupt into civil disturbances, while more insidiously laying the foundations for the development of entrenched boundaries separating both ethnic identities and communities.

In the early phases of non-white immigration it had been assumed that the newcomers would adopt 'British' norms and practices. This assumption was reflected, for example, in the absence of any educational policy designed to meet the distinctive needs of the immigrants' children entering the educational system. Despite the evidence of racial tension between the settled and immigrant groups, and white hostility in and outside schools, it was thought that these problems would eventually disappear. The immigrants would be absorbed into a tolerant society and the immigrant children would mix with and learn from the British.

By the mid-1960s, however, this *laissez-faire* approach gave way to a strong push at the government level for assimilation (Fuller 1984). Ramdin (1999) points out that in 1958 racial tensions and hostility erupted into riots which emphasized that racial disharmony and racism had become part of daily life within British society. Faced with civil disturbance, political leaders sought to generate racial harmony by discouraging cultural diversity, that is, the immigrants would be actively encouraged to replace their own cultural norms and practices with British ones.

Education was seen as having a primary role to play in achieving this end. Fuller (1984) reveals that, officially, some in the teaching profession sought to abstain from this lead by the government, resisting responsibility for either fostering or discouraging assimilation into British culture among immigrant children. Nevertheless, there *was* significantly increased 'English as a second language' tuition targeted mainly at Asian pupils. And in some LEAs, Asian, along with black children, were dispersed or 'bussed' away from their homes to schools in surrounding areas, in a bid to further their assimilation as well as to protect the education of British children.

Black children, in particular, were also at greater risk of being removed from mainstream schooling and placed into centres for the educationally subnormal. An influential paper by Bernard Coard (1971) voiced the concern among black parents and teachers regarding their children's over-representation in such centres. His publication initiated the wider documentation of the ways in which the educational system was failing to meet the needs of black children. The next three decades would continue to generate more evidence of black children's disproportionate exclusion from mainstream schooling and their low levels of academic achievement within it (Gillborn and Gipps 1996; Blair 2001).

For a long time there seemed to be an official consensus that black children were removed or performed poorly because of cultural differences and/or within-group deficiencies of various kinds (Nehaul 1996). Black parents, however, continued to resist these views and eventually found a degree of acknowledgement in the 1985 *Swann Report* of their contention that racism was implicated in their children's poor experiences of school (DES 1985). While Swann maintained that black children did fair badly in examination results, it also drew attention to the *intra-group* performances of all groups of children, and in this way challenged the stereotypical notion that all black children performed worse than all white children or that all Asian children were doing well. Swann demonstrated that the response to the complex issues of race within schools and in society at large impacted negatively on the school careers of black and Asian children, and called for an approach that met the needs of all pupils and prepared them for life in a society which was both multiracial and culturally diverse.

The Swann Report's official support for multiculturalism became embroiled in intense debates, within and outside education, between those contending for a multicultural approach and those in favour of an *antiracist* approach to the problem of racism in British schools and the wider society. Nevertheless, while there were fundamental disagreements, the debates did mark an important moment in the trajectory of recent race relations. Along with the race riots of the early 1980s, the debates served to highlight the fact that neither the assimilationist project of the 1960s nor the subsequent strategy of integration growing into cultural pluralism, had generated a cohesive and inclusive society at peace with its diversity. The wider public consciousness was also being challenged as Britain faced decisions about the correct response needed in coming to terms with the permanent presence of black and Asian people within the society.

Antiracists, in general, favoured policies that clearly exposed existing patterns of inequality and the reproduction of racial inequality over a multicultural approach viewed primarily as the teaching and learning of the cultures of different groups in the society (Troyna 1992). However, both sets of arguments were in some respects marginalized by the 1988 Education Reform Act, which conspicuously charted a different agenda for education. Neither the insights generated in the race debates nor Swann's vision for an 'education for all' was developed at the government policy level. Instead, the introduction of the National Curriculum, the cornerstone of the ERA's reforms, effected a return to the stance taken in the 1950s: there was a marked *absence* of policy that addressed the problems of racism within or beyond schools, alongside an approach that treated all children in British schools as one and the same.

It would be a full decade before the Macphearson Report (1999) would ignite renewed widespread public debate on race. The Labour government which came to office in 1997, initiated a renewed investigation into the murder of the black teenager, Stephen Lawrence and the Macphearson Report documented the enquiry. Like Swann, though more strongly, the report highlighted racism as a force that impacts negatively on the life chances of black people. Macphearson went further than Swann in providing a definition of *institutional racism* and identifying it within the Metropolitan Police Force as that which prevented a proper investigation of the murder initially. The report also made three direct recommendations for education:

- It called for the amendment of the National Curriculum such that it better reflected the needs of a diverse society by endorsing cultural diversity and preventing racism.
- It suggested that schools should actively implement strategies that prevented and addressed racism.
- It proposed that Ofsted inspections should scrutinize the implementation of these strategies.

The government 'accept[ed] in part' (Home Office 1999, pp. 33–8) these recommendations. It contended that the National Curriculum (as revised in 1995) already endorsed cultural diversity and would enhance this recognition with the introduction of citizenship education in all schools early in the next century. The Home Secretary accordingly revealed that the citizenship programme would include a focus on learning about each other and learning to live peacefully together. There was some resistance, however, to taking on the harder-edged Macphearson recommendations with respect to racism and particularly institutional racism.

There was acceptance of Ofsted's role in monitoring the implementation of strategies against racism; however, the government only accepted in part the second recommendation that schools should implement strategies that addressed and prevented racism. This effectively undermined, even nullified, any response specifically addressed to racism (Stanford 2001a). Osler and Morrison's (2000) research into Ofsted's role subsequent to Macphearson, would maintain that those given the lead role to monitor strategies aimed at addressing and preventing racism in schools often failed to do so. This was partly because schools commonly addressed race issues by employing the notion of 'educational inclusion', an umbrella term intended for a range of inequality issues including race equality, but which, nonetheless, operated to silence open discussions about race equality. The researchers demonstrated that:

> School inspection reports often fail to report on those aspects of race equality that the Ofsted framework itself requires them to inspect. When they do report on them they do so with little consistency and often without rigour. Whether or not race equality outcomes are inspected or reported on appears often to depend on the interest and understanding of the particular reporting inspector. Inspectors themselves seem to feel unprepared and untrained to meet the race equality requirements of their own inspection framework. Headteachers appear to be largely unaware that inspectors will inspect race equality outcomes, and the inspection of these issues, when it occurs, rarely provides them with Key Action points. (Osler and Morrison 2000, p. xii)

In effect then, the response to the Macphearson Report was a revisiting of the debate between multicultural and antiracist approaches, and the less contentious multicultural approach was, arguably, the one most often officially adopted. This is noteworthy given that institutional racism was arguably Macphearson's major finding.

LOOKING TO THE FUTURE

In September 2002 the National Curriculum was amended to include citizenship education as a Foundation Subject (see Chapter 15). This new subject has been designed, *inter alia*, to promote understanding of today's multicultural society. Accordingly, for example, the government proposes that 'for the first time, 11–14 year olds will be taught about "the diversity of national, regional, religious and ethnic identities in the UK and the need for mutual respect and understanding"; 14–16 year olds will be taught about "the origins and implications" of such diversity and again the need for mutual respect and understanding'. Pupils in primary schools will be taught to 'identify and respect the differences and similarities between people' and 'to realise the consequences of anti-social and aggressive behaviours, such as bullying and racism, on individuals and communities' (DfEE 1999, p. 1).

The various reports published around the time of the Oldham, Burnley and Bradford race riots of the spring and summer of 2001, would appear to endorse the government's present approach to race and schooling. With some consistency there is a call for greater knowledge, contact and respect across cultural boundaries to promote community cohesion and tolerance (Ouseley 2001; Rashid 2002; Home Office 2002). It is possibly something of a coincidence that there is such agreement between government policy and these independent reports. One factor may be that unlike past civil disturbances, *Asians* constituted the dominant minority group involved in the 2001 disturbances. Their particular religious and cultural practices generate specific interfaces with the wider society.

Like Macphearson, the Ouseley and Cantle reports had a specific focus, which limited their ability to address the entire project of race relations in Britain. Even so, it is noteworthy that while both the Ouseley and Cantle reports acknowledged the value of the citizenship component in the revised National Curriculum, they also called for its development and expansion. Both want to see fundamental changes to how citizenship is perceived in the society. They want to see local communities responding to their own unique mix of cultural resources in the wider society alongside the official call for 'a greater sense of citizenship based on [a few] common principles which are shared and observed by all sections of the community' (Home Office 2002, p. 10).

Both reports were also agreed, and were most emphatic about the need to remove the fears around the difficult issues of race. These fears, it was argued, inhibited the possibility of open and honest discussions and ultimately undermined the possibility of truly embracing cultural diversity. Perhaps, these findings provide some explanation for the long-term reluctance to embrace explicit antiracist approaches within education, and why it has taken so long for even the citizenship component to constitute part of the educational terrain.

Ouseley spoke of the fear of 'challenging wrong-doing because of being called "racist" – and that applied across all ethnic groups' and the fear of confronting all white and/or all Muslim schools about their contribution, or rather lack of contribution, to social and racial integration' (p. 1). Stanford (2001b) has shown that fear of being called racist, separate from and in addition to an actual accusation, has significant personal and professional impact on teachers. The impact can be disabling.

However, teachers who felt that they could discuss their concerns to do with race, and had some protection from unfair accusation, actively took on their full professional responsibilities to black and Asian children. Blair and Bourne's (1998) study also revealed evidence that would support this view. The creation of a safe space to talk about race without fear, therefore, suggests itself as a major site for development within education as in the wider society. Perhaps an honest and open discussion, would recover, re-centre and explore racism as part of educational discourse and facilitate the realization of a truly inclusive and cohesive multicultural society.

Chapter 11

Schools, Parents and the Community

TERENCE H. MCLAUGHLIN

INTRODUCTION

Schools do not, and cannot, conduct their work in a vacuum, isolated from 'external' influences, forces and claims. It is not only practically impossible for schools to do this, but also wrong for them to try to do so. The 'external' factors with which schools are confronted involve not only influences and forces, but also *claims*. Some of these claims assert *rights* to (for example) information, consultation, shared decision-making or control. For reasons of principle as well as practical reasons a school must therefore attend to, and, where necessary, respond to, 'external' realities and demands.

The 'external' realities and demands which surround the school are varied and wide ranging, and they give rise to many complicated questions of a social, moral, political and economic kind. This chapter will focus attention upon two prominent sources of 'external' demand with respect to the school: parents and the community. Although there is much to be said about practical aspects of the relationship between schools, parents and the community, the emphasis here will be on some central matters of principle which arise.

It is useful to conduct our discussion in relation to a series of models of relationship between schools, parents and the community.

MODELS OF RELATIONSHIP BETWEEN SCHOOLS, PARENTS AND THE COMMUNITY

It is important to stress that the models presented here are 'ideal types' intended to act as a framework within which issues can be mapped. There is no suggestion that these models capture in any precise way the complex realities of existing relationships, either past or present.

1. Distance and separation

As its name implies, this model involves the school attempting to conduct its work, as far as possible, in a significantly isolated way from parents and the community. A model of this sort is discernible in relation to schools of all kinds in Britain, from the nineteenth century until relatively recently. Salient in this model is the notion of schools seeking to protect and even 'rescue' their students from the potentially negative influences of parents and communities. Victorian Elementary schools often saw themselves as 'citadels of civilization' in the midst of wastelands of ignorance, poverty and squalor, a self-perception which was reflected in the architectural design of the school buildings. Grammar schools were often suspicious of the anti-educational influences of some parents and communities, and were particularly concerned to wean working-class students away from the potentially limiting and constraining effects of their home background. The elite Public schools, particularly boarding schools, were keen to protect their students from possibly indulgent and decadent families who were seen as failing to instil in their children appropriate virtues of mind, character and leadership.

This model of 'distance and separation', particularly weaker forms of it, does not imply that schools were, or could be, completely isolated from parents and the community. The relationships involved were, however, often limited and restricted. Reports on pupil progress were often perfunctory, and parent involvement with the school was often restricted to invitations to be present at sports events, dramatic performances and the like.

It is possible to discern three broadly philosophical claims embedded in this model of relationship between schools, parents and the community:

- that education is a kind of activity which is best conceived and pursued independently of the immediate surroundings, concerns and lives of the students. Education should be seen (in some sense) as 'academic'
- that educators (and, in particular, teachers) are in the best position to determine what is and what is not in the educational interests of students
- that it is appropriate to be suspicious of the educative influence of parents and the community

All three of these claims are significantly controversial, and have been extensively challenged in recent years.

The view that education should be confined to 'academic' matters unrelated to the immediate surroundings, concerns and lives of students has been countered by the claim that education has an important part to play in the personal and social education of students, and that these aspects of education must necessarily make reference in various ways to the families of students and to the society in which they live. More generally, it has been argued that a fully rounded education requires ingredients which go beyond the merely academic. On motivational grounds alone, it has been claimed, education should relate to the existing interests, experience and interests of students and be (in some sense) 'relevant'. Education, therefore, cannot and should not be seen as 'distant' and 'separate' from life outside the school.

The view that educators (and, in particular, teachers) are in the best position to determine what is and what is not in the educational interests of students has been countered by the claim that, while teachers have some professional expertise (particularly in relation to methods of teaching), this expertise does not encompass all that is required in order to determine the aims and 'content' of what is to be taught. The expertise required to determine these matters requires, among other things, the ability to answer such questions as: 'What knowledge is of most worth?' and 'In what ways should we shape the next generation?'. These questions, like the question 'What kind of life is worth living?', are not ones which can be answered definitively by easily identified experts. In part this is because the questions are complex and in part because the questions involve judgements of value which are significantly controversial (for further discussion of matters of this kind see Chapter 13). In a liberal democratic society, it has been argued, questions of this kind must be settled by wide-ranging discussion which includes parents and the community as a whole. Parents and the community therefore have rights to participate in educational decision-making, and teachers lack a mandate to settle all educational questions by themselves.

The view that it is appropriate to be suspicious of the educative influence of parents and the community has been countered by an acknowledgement of the potential educational benefits of this influence. In part this is seen in the beneficial effect on achievement which has been shown to follow from the well-conceived involvement of parents and the community in various aspects of teaching undertaken by the school. A prominent example of this kind of beneficial influence can be seen in the improvement in reading performance of pupils whose parents play a role in structured teaching programmes that have been developed in this area. The general point here is that parents and the community can offer to the school educational insights and resources of various kinds which it is unwise to ignore.

2. Mutual involvement

This model articulates the closer relationship between schools, parents and the community which is now common in contemporary educational practice and in educational legislation.

Five broadly philosophical claims can be discerned in this model:

- that parents and the community be seen as having rights to appropriate forms of *information* about various aspects of the work of the school. The sorts of information involved here include details about the courses of study offered, the performance and progress of individuals, school policies and procedures of various kinds, school inspection reports and examination results
- that parents and the community be seen as having rights to engage in

consultation with the school on a range of matters of policy and principle
such as (for example) the approach that the school should take to the
handling of sensitive and significantly controversial issues such as sex
education
- that parents and the community be invited to engage in *co-operation* with
  the school in relation to such matters as pupil learning (as in the example
  of parent assistance with reading improvement mentioned above), the
  educational programme offered by the school (as in a situation where local
  employers participate in various aspects of the school curriculum), and the
  provision of practical resources (as in fund-raising of various kinds and the
  sharing of facilities such as swimming pools and playing fields between the
  school and the community)
- that parents and the community be seen as having rights to engage in
  shared decision-making with the school on various matters of policy and
  practice through (for example) representation on governing bodies and on
  committees of Local Education Authorities
- that schools be seen as having *a wider focus of educational concern* than the
  merely 'academic'. Thus, for example, personal, social and health
  education and the provision of appropriate forms of pastoral care are
  seen as part of the educative task of the school, and parents and the
  community are seen as important educational resources

This model of the relationship between schools, parents and the community is
supported by arguments of both a practical and a principled kind. On the
practical side, it is clear that these forms of mutual involvement between
schools, parents and the community are associated with greater educational
effectiveness and efficiency. The beneficial effects of partnerships between
schools and parents with respect to the promotion of aspects of student
learning have already been mentioned. The financial and other efficiencies
associated with facilities such as swimming pools jointly provided for schools
and for communities are also noteworthy. However, the arguments
supporting this model also have a principled character in that it is claimed
that the model does justice to the *rights* which parents and the community
have to the various forms of involvement which have been indicated.

While each of the broadly philosophical claims associated with this model
seem relatively unproblematic, questions and difficulties arise in relation to
each of them. With regard to the claim about rights to the provision of
information, for example, questions arise about the most appropriate way in
which certain kinds of information should be provided. The publication of
school 'league tables' based on examination results may give a misleading
impression about the real educational performance of a school because the
'value added' element of the school's contribution (the extent to which the
school has extended the achievements of its pupils since entry relative to their
ability) may be invisible. Difficulties such as these generate a challenge to
schools about how they can present information in a full and fair way to
interested parties. Another specific issue which arises in relation to the

provision of information concerns the possible controversiality of some information. Who, for example, should have access to the school records of individual pupils, and should all information held by the school be made available?

With regard to the claim about rights to engage in consultation, questions arise about how, where and on what grounds the line can be drawn between consultation and shared decision-making. The same questions arise in relation to the claim that parents and the community be invited to engage in co-operation with the school.

With regard to the claim about rights to shared decision-making, questions arise about which party should have the final say on matters which are disputed, and about the grounds on which the allocation of the final say should be determined in relation to the differing kinds of matter at stake.

With regard to the claim that schools should be seen as having a wider focus of educational concern than the 'academic', questions arise about the proper emphasis and priority to be given to various aspects of the educative task. These questions surface regularly in familiar and long-running educational disputes, some of which are expressed in terms of 'traditional' versus 'progressive' or 'academic' versus 'pastoral' conceptions of the educative role of schools.

3. Dominance of parents

This model embodies a conception of 'parents as determiner' with respect to their children's education. On this conception, parental rights in education are seen (within minimal limits) as fundamental, overriding and extensive. There is a suspicion of the priority of 'professional' or 'political' judgement in educational matters and there may also be suspicion of a common form of educational provision offered by the state. The child's educational experience is seen as properly determined to the greatest possible extent by the child's own parents and family.

The model involves one major claim of a broadly philosophical kind:

- that parents have the capacity and right to determine exclusively what is in the educational interests of their children

However, this claim has been subjected to a number of significant criticisms. A prominent line of criticism is that the most fundamental right which requires acknowledgement here is the child's 'right to an open future': a right of children to reach maturity 'with as many options, opportunities and advantages as possible' (Feinberg 1980, p.130). This, it is argued, is the fundamental educational interest of the child which the parent has a duty to facilitate and which acts as an important limitation on parental rights. It involves (for example) parents avoiding the foreclosure of options for children through the making of certain 'crucial' or 'irrevocable' decisions determining the course of lives at too early a stage (*ibid.*, p. 143) and a requirement that children be provided with a broad education aimed at the development of their autonomy which acquaints them with 'a great variety of facts and diversified accounts and evaluations of the myriad human arrangements in the world and in history' (*ibid.*, p. 139). Another source of limitation on the 'parents as determiner' model of parents' educational rights is the rights and needs of other parents and of society. Among other things, this limitation generates the need to take account of imperatives of fairness and justice in the distribution of educational goods, and the need to expand the educational entitlement of all pupils to include education for citizenship. (On education for citizenship see Chapter 15.)

Arguments of this kind do not, of course, result in undermining all parental rights with respect to education. A more modest conception of the parent as 'trustee' of the child's educational rights can be readily defended. On this view, the parent has the right to determine the child's 'primary culture', including certain forms of separate schooling, and has the right to co-ordinate and review the educational experiences and development of the child. However, these educational rights are seen not as fundamental moral rights possessed by parents but rather as rights derived from parental duties to secure their children's autonomy and citizenship rights, which are merely 'held in trust' by parents until the child is capable of exercising them for him or her self. Parents are not seen, therefore, as having fundamental moral rights which infringe the right of their children to achieve autonomy and formation as democratic citizens; nor do they have the right to infringe the rights and needs of other parents and of society. On this view, parents have important educational rights and are important agents in the various aspects of the 'mutual involvement' model which has been discussed. However, they are not seen as dominant in relationships between schools, parents and the community and they do not enjoy the role of an exclusive or wide-ranging 'determiner' with respect to their children's education (for further discussion of these matters see McLaughlin 1994a).

Acceptance of the general notion of 'parent as trustee' leaves room, however, for much detailed discussion about what precise parental rights can be derived from it.

4. Dominance of the educational marketplace

This model is often associated with the preceding one. Although it can take many forms, the essential feature of this model is the view that education is best provided through a 'marketplace' of different kinds of school, each competing for 'customers' (parents) who are in the possession of information and of resources (e.g. through possession of a 'voucher') to choose schools in line with their own educational desires. Included among the arguments in support of this model are those relating to the need to counteract complacency and inefficiency on the part of schools, and to provide an antidote to undue state power and monopoly in education.

Apart from the claim about the justifiability of the 'parents as determiner' conception of parental rights which has been discussed in the last section, this model involves at least one further broadly philosophical claim:

- that an educational market can best secure an adequate education for all

Central to the evaluation of this claim is the question of how we should understand the notion of an 'adequate education'. Often, proponents of this model do not specify what is meant by 'adequate' here and suggest that this question should itself be determined by choices exercised within the marketplace. However, as we saw in relation to claims about parental rights, there are compelling reasons to think that there is an educational entitlement related to the development of personal autonomy and democratic citizenship which should be secured for all pupils. It is widely acknowledged that in the same way that the demands of the development of personal autonomy and democratic citizenship act as a brake upon parental rights, so they act as 'moral limits of the market'. The central issue between advocates and critics of markets in education then becomes: Which system can best ensure the provision not of some unspecified 'adequate' education whose definition is itself determined by the market, but the provision of this entitlement?

Given the relationship of this entitlement to fundamental matters of personal dignity and democratic agency, the duty of extending it to all children becomes clear. The question then takes on a more precise form: Which system can best secure the provision of this entitlement for *all* children?

One difficulty which arises in relation to the claim that markets can secure this educational entitlement for all relates to doubts about whether all parents are in a position seriously to evaluate such an entitlement for purposes of choice. There is a danger that, in the situation of a significantly free educational market, parents will make unwise and limiting educational choices on behalf of their children. In the light of this, there seems to be a strong case for exempting this entitlement, if not other aspects of educational provision, from market forces, and securing its achievement for all pupils through forms of democratic state control and regulation (for further discussion of these matters see McLaughlin 1994b).

5. Dominance of the community

This model can take at least three forms, depending on how the notion of 'the community' is understood. The notion of 'the community' is capable of interpretation in a number of different senses. Three senses will be considered here, each related to variants of this model: the 'local' community, the 'culturally specific' community and the 'general' community.

The 'Dominance of the Local Community' model is apparent (for example) in the vision of 'Village Colleges' developed by Henry Morris in Cambridgeshire in the 1930s (on this see, for example, Ree 1973) and also in urban variants of this model developed in the 1960s and 1970s in comprehensive schools such as Sidney Stringer in Coventry, Stantonbury Campus in Milton Keynes and the Abraham Moss Centre in Manchester (on urban variants see, for example, Midwinter 1975). Common to all these models is a view of the need to link education closely with the local community, and to break down in a radical way the barriers between the local community and the school. One broadly philosophical claim which is associated with this model is as follows:

- that the local community should provide the focus for what is learnt in the school and be particularly salient in educational decision-making

This claim is open to question on grounds of the potential narrowness and restrictiveness of what might result. In the light of the sort of educational entitlement for all, which has been sketched earlier, why should attention be focused particularly upon local matters and why should educational decisions be made particularly at local level? The educational entitlement mentioned earlier seems to call in part for a national, international or even global perspective on certain matters, and the need for the entitlement to be secured for all seems to require consistency across potential variabilities between local differences. Relevant to these questions is the widely held view that a properly liberating education should lead pupils beyond 'the present and the particular' (on this notion see Bailey 1984). These arguments do not undermine the claim that local considerations should have a part to play in educational arrangements, as distinct from the more wide-ranging claim that these local considerations should be dominant.

'Culturally specific communities' include communities which exhibit (say) ethnic or religious distinctiveness, as in, for example, the Afro-Caribbean or the Muslim community within the UK. The 'Dominance of the Culturally Specific Community' model involves the following broadly philosophical claim, which is often expressed in relation to arguments for certain kinds of separate educational provision (for example, Muslim schools):

- that 'culturally specific communities' should have decisive educational decision-making rights in relation to the sort of educational experience which is appropriate for its children and young people

This claim is open to question on a number of grounds. There are potential tensions between the claim and both the educational and other rights and needs of individuals who may be members of 'culturally specific communities', and the educational and other rights and needs of the broader community. A prominent line of argument is that whilst these 'culturally specific communities' can constitute 'primary cultures' in which children can be brought up, they should not completely prevent the sort of development of autonomy and democratic citizenship in individuals which has been alluded to, nor undermine the development of the sorts of general understandings and loyalties which society as a whole requires. Thus, it is claimed, while 'culturally specific communities' have an important role to play in educational decision-making (for example in illuminating what is required in a fair treatment of cultural diversity), it should not necessarily be a dominant role. The demands of the sort of educational entitlement which has been referred to, and which is closely related to the development of personal autonomy and democratic citizenship, must be borne in mind. While these demands do not rule out the justifiability of certain sorts of separate school (on this matter see McLaughlin 1992), the demands do need to be taken into account in the overall judgements about educational policy and practice which need to be made.

The 'general' community can be regarded as the overall community in which individuals and citizens live. A 'liberal democratic' variant of 'The Dominance of the General Community' model involves the following broadly philosophical claim:

- that a liberal democratic society has the right and duty to ensure for all young people the sort of educational entitlement which is necessary for the achievement of personal autonomy and democratic citizenship

Such a society may secure this entitlement through various strategies, including state control and regulation of education through (for example) a national curriculum. It is important to note that this variant of the model does not seek justification of state control over education of *any* kind. What is envisaged is control limited by the values and demands of the sort of educational entitlement which has been indicated, and subject to democratic discussion and mandate. There is no suggestion that the education envisaged on this model will be totalitarian or nationalistic in any objectionable sense. This may allay fears of state manipulation of, and indoctrination through, the educational system. Nor is the control envisaged seen as extending to all the details of the educational process, as distinct from its broad aims and framework. The model can accommodate, it is claimed, a proper role for teachers, parents, local communities and 'culturally specific' communities to contribute to educational decision-making. The role of the state, it is argued by supporters of this model, is simply to ensure that education satisfies its fundamental purposes.

An assessment of the adequacy of this model in principle needs to be separated from the particular features associated with the increased state control of education in England and Wales since 1988, which are not seen as necessarily corresponding to the principles which the model embodies. The philosophical claim which is made by the model is open to a number of lines of criticism. One of the most prominent of these is how the nature and limits of state control can be fleshed out in some detail, and how this control can be insulated from the potentially destabilizing effects of involvement in party political debates and processes (on this model see White 1990, chapters 1 and 9).

CONCLUSION

As indicated at the outset, the relationships between schools on the one hand and parents and the community on the other, give rise to many varied and complex questions of principle. Getting clearer about these matters of principle does not, and cannot, in itself settle all the equally varied and complex matters of practice which arise. Clarity may not be a sufficient, but it is nevertheless a necessary, requirement for an adequate approach to these important practical questions.

Given its centrality to much of our discussion, one of the central tasks in articulating a justifiable account of the principled relationship between schools, parents and the community is an articulation and defence of the notion of an educational entitlement related to the development of personal autonomy and democratic citizenship.

Chapter 12

Environmental Education: Education for Sustainable Development

MICHAEL YOUNGER AND ANGELA WEBSTER

ENVIRONMENTAL EDUCATION: EVOLUTION AND AIMS

Debates about the role and importance of environmental education within the secondary school curriculum have been around for a long time, and various attempts have been made to get environmental education more formally established on the curriculum. At different times, such attempts have been supported by pressure groups as diverse as the National Farmers' Union and Friends of the Earth, the Royal Institute of British Architects and the Women's Environmental Network. Environmental and rural studies, outdoor education, education for conservation and urban studies have each, in their own way, attempted to give a higher profile to environmental education, but progress has been slow, and there developed through the 1970s and 1980s curiously ambivalent relationships between the environmental education movement and established school subjects, such as geography, history and the sciences, which saw aspects of the environment as their own specialized, protected domain.

It is paradoxical in some respects that environmental education received more attention following the establishment of the National Curriculum in the years after the Education (No. 2 Act) of 1986 and the Education Reform Act of 1988. It was almost as if policy-makers felt the need to balance a prescriptive, subject-oriented, content-laden curriculum with more open, cross-curricular perspectives. Whatever the rationale, the publication of *Curriculum Guidance 7* (NCC 1990) raised the profile of environmental education nationally and brought the issue more centrally on to school curriculum planning agendas, as one of five cross-curricular themes. As such, environmental education was explicitly cross-referenced with the original National Curriculum documents in history, geography, technology, the sciences, and seen as having the potential for exploring links with drama, the arts and English. Such cross-curricular themes were intended to pervade and infuse the whole curriculum, encouraging schools to develop links between different aspects of their curriculum, and to develop a view of the curriculum as a whole. Many of the topics and themes with which they were concerned were core issues within the National Curriculum; the struggle for the tropical rainforests provided a cross-curricular theme for study in geography, in science, in art, in dance, in drama, in English and in PSE; the water cycle, and issues of drought and pollution, was studied in science and in geography, in technology and as a focus for modern language work; urban redevelopment and industrial regeneration featured in maths, technology, history, geography and religious studies. Other aspects of environmental education focused upon skills and enquiry; thus town trails and streetwork exercises, for example, were designed to reveal the intrinsic interest and fine grain of a relatively ordinary part of an urban environment, and to focus upon the potential of unexceptional environments and typical environments for environmental education. There were explicit references, too, to the gender angle, with studies of the urban built environment which focused on issues such as urban safety and mobility, and access to urban services.

Many schools responded by auditing their current practice, and there were expectations in some schools that each subject-based curriculum unit would include reference to cross-curricular themes; other approaches involved cross-curricular events, such as environmental theatre projects and 'theme weeks', often with the support and involvement of organizations such as World Wildlife Fund for Nature and the Body Shop. Thus there appeared to be an emerging consensus on the scope and role of environmental education, such that Duncan Graham, then the chair of the NCC, could claim that: 'Environmental education is an essential part of every pupil's curriculum. It helps to encourage awareness of the environment, leading to informed concern for and active participation in resolving environmental problems.'

The curriculum overload which characterized the early years of the National Curriculum at key stages 3 and 4, and the fact that the National Curriculum Council's guidance on cross-curricular themes was at no time translated into statutory prescription, ensured that much of the rhetoric about environmental education was not translated into effective action in the school context. The revisions to the National Curriculum implemented in September 2000, however, led to suggestions that environmental education 'will receive a major boost in primary and secondary schools in England and Wales [because of] the substantially increased emphasis on environmental education evident not only in the science and geography curricula, but also [because] it is a prominent feature in a revised introduction to the whole curriculum' (Summers *et al.* 2000). Just as *Curriculum Guidance 7* talked of the need to raise student awareness, stimulate interest and understanding, and establish the foundation for active participation in environmental issues, so one of the requirements within Curriculum 2000 is for schools to develop (pupils') awareness and understanding of, and respect for, the environments in which they live, and secure their commitment to sustainable development at a personal, local, national and global level. (The National Curriculum Handbook for Secondary Teachers 2000, p. 11)

EDUCATION ABOUT, IN AND FOR THE ENVIRONMENT

Within the context of the secondary schooling system in England and Wales, environmental education is perceived as having three closely integrated aspects. Education *about* the environment aims to develop a basic knowledge and understanding through the study of the environment, focusing on topics such as climate, soils and rocks, materials and resources, plants and animals, people and their communities. Such a perspective is concerned with the factual and conceptual understanding of environments at a variety of scales, seeking an understanding of the interactions which take place within environments, and examining the environment from a variety of viewpoints. As such, this perspective on environmental education puts the emphasis on increasing people's understanding of the multiplicity of factors which influence the environment, but at a level which acknowledges and accepts the existing social order and social relations. Growing out of a concern for environmental management, conservation and control, it adopts a techno-centric perspective to environmental education, presenting environmental issues as 'asocial or universal problems, which are rarely examined in terms of their structural causes' (Huckle 1990, p. 154).

Education *in and through* the environment stresses the use of the environment as a resource for learning experiences and the development of a broad range of enquiry, communication and participation skills. The environment is thus seen as a resource to give reality, relevance and practical experience to learning, with emphasis upon active enquiry and investigation in the field, developing skills and aesthetic responses. The emphasis is upon student-centred learning, fieldwork and enquiry which helps to develop an appreciation of the environment, 'education for environmental awareness and interpretation' (Huckle 1993a). This approach has a long-established pedigree, in terms of giving a focus for discovery approaches to learning about the environment, and it has the potential to contribute to a raising of awareness and consciousness about the environment, without necessarily informing about the real causal processes which affect and govern the environment.

Education *for* the environment is envisaged as presenting pupils with opportunity to explore their personal response to environmental issues. Such an approach is concerned with considering ways of ensuring caring use of the environment now and in the future, considering solutions to environmental problems (taking into account that there are conflicting interests and differing cultural perspectives), and informing the choices which have to be made. It recognizes that there is no clear consensus about many environmental issues and that people hold different, equally legitimate points of view. This approach was initially developed at the small scale, focusing on local issues related to housing, environmental quality and congestion. Some of the early work was described in admirable issues of the *Bulletin of Environmental Education*, and in texts such as *Streetwork: The Exploding School* (Ward and Fyson 1973). Implicit within this work is a concern with values education, helping students to become active decision-makers and develop a critical eye for environmental issues, within a coherent and consistent set of values. Taken to its logic conclusion, of course, this approach to environmental education inevitably focuses upon controversial issues, and issues about which there may be more societal conflict than consensus. At face value, the emphasis is not simply on heightening pupils' awareness of environmental issues and developing their aesthetic appreciation of environments, but on encouraging active participation in resolving environmental problems, of integrating all aspects to engender critical thinking, responsibility and action, in enabling students to 'think globally, act locally'.

SUSTAINABLE DEVELOPMENT AND EDUCATION

The concept of sustainable development came into the public domain following the UN Conference on the Human Environment in Stockholm in 1972. Global environmental crises began to make headline news throughout the western world. The loss of tropical forests, the intensification of the nuclear debate following Chernobyl, atmospheric contamination on a vast scale in the form of increased acidity and greenhouse gas warming, growing alarm over the distribution of toxic chemicals in consumer goods all emphasized clear messages of global environmental deterioration. Into the 1980s further concerns developed about population growth and the depletion of resources, and the incompatibility of economic growth with the preservation of environmental systems. The World Commission on Environment and Development (the Brundtland Commission), identified a series of overlapping crises which stemmed from a mismatch between the capacities of natural systems and human activities: a crisis of development, linked to poverty, nutrition and debt, particularly impacting upon countries of the South, and especially on women and children in those countries; a crisis of the environment, with insufficient resources to feed growing populations, a loss of biodiversity and forest resources, and resource degradation through misuse and pollution; more recently still, a crisis of global insecurity, resulting in wars, global terrorism and refugee trails.

The notion of sustainability is thus defined as the capacity to meet the needs of the present without compromising the ability of future generations to meet their own needs. Within the concept, there is the recognition that economic growth is both desirable and possible, to meet the basic needs of humankind, but must be sustainable at a global level. Sustainable development emphasizes the need to reconcile economic development and conservation of the environment, to place a consideration of environmental issues within a social, economic and political context. This concern with sustainability links with education *for* the environment, and gave a new impetus globally to environmental education. The Brundtland Report had itself emphasized the crucial role which the world's teachers had to play 'in helping to bring about the extensive social changes needed for sustainable development' (p. xiv), and Agenda 21, the programme for action following the UN Conference on Environment and Development (UNCED), in Rio in 1992, devoted similar attention to education for sustainability: 'Education is critical for promoting sustainable development, and improving the capacity of the people to address environmental and development issues' (UNCED 1992, chapter 36, p. 2).

Such perspectives on environmental education for sustainability linked naturally with the rising concern for development education, with its integrative approach to global issues and its commitment to experiential styles of learning and to developing the culture of co-operation in the classroom (see, for example, the seminal work of the Centre for Global Education [Pike and Selby 1988]). Focusing initially on 'Third World' poverty, development education evolved in such a way as to enable development and under-development to be explored as one and the same process, impacted upon by global economic and political systems. As inequalities between North and South, and within and between countries of the South, became increasingly evident, so the development education focus on distributive justice, with meeting the basic human needs of all the population, became more emphatic. Linked to this was the notion of equity and social justice, highlighting the distribution of a country's income and services among its peoples, and stressing equality of access for all, regardless of age, status, gender or ethnicity. The focus upon development education also emphasized, if further emphasis were needed, the link between poverty and environmental issues, and the need to consider such issues within economic and cultural perspectives.

In this overall context, then, sustainable education can be seen as a process which, as well as stressing the interdependence of peoples and environments through the globe, 'develops people's awareness, attitudes and values, enabling them to be effectively involved in sustainable development at local, national and international level, and helping them to work towards a more equitable and sustainable future' (Sterling *et al.* 1992).

ENVIRONMENTAL EDUCATION FOR SUSTAINABILITY

Such approaches to environmental education for sustainability embody a number of challenges to teachers and to teacher educators. At a basic level, while there can be no doubt that there has been a seismic shift in public attitudes to the environment in the past decade, there is still an enormous ignorance about environmental issues. An NFER review (Rickinson 2001) reported on the generally low levels of young people's factual knowledge relating to environmental issues, and on their misunderstandings of the scientific basis of specific environmental issues. Most, for example, did not know the main sources of carbon dioxide, and few respondents were aware of the link between pollution, consumption and lifestyles. Studies of trainee teachers' knowledge of the greenhouse effect, the ozone layer and acid rain revealed significant gaps in understanding, and showed that student' awareness and knowledge of environmental concepts was frequently super-ficial and lacked an understanding of causal chains (Dove 1996). Many experienced teachers, responding to such issues from a subject-specific perspective, feel underprepared to tackle issues which are so complex, multi-faceted and subjective.

It is in defining the essential nature of environmental education for sustainability (EEFS), however, that we expose the extent of the challenge to teachers. EEFS is not only concerned with generating an understanding of the concept of global interdependence, of a global ecosystem in which the future of all species, humans included, is inextricably linked, but with embracing a commitment to action on that understanding – a commitment to change. There *is* a concern within society, a belief held by many, and particularly by children, that the preservation of environmental quality is important, but few extend this to a consideration of how their own consumption patterns and ways of living might need to change if environmental sustainability is to be achieved (Rickinson 2001). The challenge for EEFS is to translate a concern for the environment into an understanding that it involves personal costs and constraints, and this means developing understanding and commitment. A key part of the role of environmental education is thus 'to empower present and future citizens to act responsibly on issues of importance, both to them individually and to society' (Stoltman and Lidstone 2001). This point is well developed by Tilbury:

> In order to contribute to EEFS, environmental work will need to be relevant to the student, through increasing their understanding of themselves and the world around them. It must encourage pupils to explore links between their personal lives and wider environmental and development concerns, by dealing with issues such as consumerism, and how the practices of banking and industry affect their lives. (Tilbury 1995, p. 199)

Similarly, Fien, in outlining an environmental and development education project for teacher educators in Australia, identifies the fundamental questions which have to be faced:

> Issues of environment, social justice and sustainable development pose important questions for the future of human society. Those involved in environmental and development education, at whatever level, need to activate the socially critical or reconstructionist tradition in education and promote approaches to curriculum planning and pedagogy that can help integrate social justice and ecological sustainability into a vision and a mission of personal and social change. (Fien 1995, p. 25)

In this context, it is clear that EEFS raises a number of uncomfortable challenges for schools and politicians. Young teachers have a number of explicit issues to consider when learning to teach about environmental issues; they 'have to select appropriate subject matter and teaching strategies, decide on their aims for students' values education and decide on their own role as teachers in handling controversial issues with their students' (Corney 1998, p. 90). It is Corney's emphasis on teaching strategies and controversial issues that is of central concern. EEFS gives legitimacy to concerns with affective, value-based responses, as well as with cognitive understanding. Such teaching acknowledges that children are to be given opportunities to develop their own value-based responses, and recognizes that we are concerned with teaching about issues which may engender conflict and controversy. Handled skilfully by experienced teachers, this might not be too problematic, but at another level, such a focus for environmental education, with the central concern on values and attitudes, is complex and challenging, and many teachers feel ill-equipped, in terms of their own teaching strategies, to cope with such issues. Even for experienced teachers, a major concern is the lack of extensive teacher support materials with activities to boost confidence in handling controversial issues in the classroom.

But there is a still further issue of concern. Central to the concept of sustainability is a holistic approach to the study of the environment and development issues, an approach which stresses global interdependence, and interactions between people and their whole environment: 'Many definitions of environmental education lay emphasis on interconnectedness, interdisciplinarity and viewing the environment in its entirety, consistent with a holistic perspective' (Sterling 1993, p. 74). In many countries, however, the approach to teaching about environmental issues is fragmentary, unco-ordinated, usually discipline-based (Huckle 1993b). Ironically, in the United Kingdom context, such moves as there were towards an integrated approach to environmental education were hindered and in some instances overthrown by the implementation of the subject-specific National Curriculum after 1988. Similarly, the content-heavy nature of such curricula meant that there was less time and space for innovative teaching strategies which had the capacity to be adapted for EEFS teaching. The work associated with the Humanities Curriculum Project, and teaching methodologies central to the ethos of Schools Council projects such as Geography for the Young School-Leaver and the Schools Council History Project, with their emphasis on discussion, open-ended enquiry, simulations and values exploration, became less pivotal and influential, at the very time when they had the capacity to transform environmental education teaching. Where environmental education was given recognition, the emphasis was upon didactic teaching methods and fact gathering, receptive learning approaches (Gayford 1991), upon transmission modes of teaching which gave low priority to open and controversial areas of knowledge, and downgraded crucial issues which cross disciplinary boundaries and could not be contained within a specific subject.

Hence in the United Kingdom there is the fundamental paradox: on the one hand, successive governments have subscribed to and advocated environmental sustainability at the international and national policy level, and promoted EEFS as an important component of this strategy; at the same time, a prescriptive, subject-based, content-oriented National Curriculum has been imposed upon schools which even now severely limits the scope and the methodologies available for teaching EEFS. Despite the publication of *Curriculum Guidance 7* and the revisions to the National Curriculum in 2000, environmental education has in reality lost ground in the United Kingdom's schools. As the education system shifted its focus to an emphasis on raising standards, defined in terms of knowledge and understanding, aspects of affective education, including beliefs, values and attitudes received less attention and prominence.

The extent of the challenge is clear; how have teachers and teacher educators responded to the challenge? From the time of the Humanities Curriculum Project, and its advocacy of the teacher as a neutral chair, environmental education has faced the challenge of devising strategies through which to teach about controversial environmental issues, while avoiding the promotion of the teacher's own values and opinions. Approaches have been sought which have allowed students to understand certain controversies, while appreciating the range of perspectives available, and gaining an expectation that there is not necessarily one right answer.

The emphasis upon values education is one such approach, for it is clear that central to environmental education is the difficult and politically sensitive task of helping children to develop a more sophisticated and critical understanding of the values that inform everyday life (Bonnett 1997). Here the emphasis on enquiry as a route to personal beliefs and actions (Naish *et al.* 1987) gives students opportunities to use discussion and logical analysis of evidence to analyse and investigate real issues with a values dimension (values analysis, as defined by Fien and Slater 1985). It enables students to focus on opinion, to explore the possibility of prejudice and bias, and to consider stages in decision-making about environmental issues. But it also allows students opportunities to come to a personal decision and judgement, to help students become aware of their own values in relation to their behaviour and that of others (values clarification), and offers the possibility of a personal response. In this context, it is analogous to active learning,

> encouraging students to see themselves as interacting members of social and environmental systems, through having them clarify and analyse values with the intention of enabling them to act in relation to social and environmental issues according to their value choices. (Fien and Slater 1985)

Other approaches have involved the production of workshop materials for teachers and teacher educators, which have aimed to develop critically reflective teachers who have a sound grasp of the debates linked to sustainability, and who are enabled to involve pupils in action-research learning, through teaching strategies such as simulations, role-plays, games and discussion. In Australia, this approach has been adopted by the environmental and development education project for teacher educators entitled *Teaching for a Sustainable World* (Fien 1995), and in the United Kingdom the Worldwide Fund for Nature spearheaded an in-service education initiative, *Reaching Out: Education for Sustainability* (Huckle *et al.* 1995), which provided a comprehensive course in the theory and practice of EEFS. Handled well, such strategies can give students some insights into the cultural-laden aspects of many environmental issues, allowing for discussion of these issues within economic contexts, and giving scope for appreciating the different values of other, non-European, non-white cultures. The emphasis on futures education (Hicks 1994; Hicks and Holden 1995) is a further aspect which needs consideration; at one level, the study of environmental issues and problems can lead to feelings of despair and helplessness, to indignation and compassion fatigue, whereas 'encouraging students to explore their preferred futures can lead to greater feelings of hope and empowerment' (Hicks and Holden 1995). In such a context, a responsibility to introduce young people through environmental education to 'the extensive traumas of the world' (Hicks and Bord 2001), must be balanced by teaching with optimism, building environmental success stories into the curriculum, developing awareness of sources of hope and inspiration, offering empowerment strategies to young people so that they are better equipped to cope with the forces of social and technological change (Huckle 1990).

CONCLUSION

There has been little opportunity here to consider the aesthetics of environments, but implicit within EEFS is the assumption that the world is worth sustaining! As our home, and essential to our survival, the point needs little development. But a consistently neglected aspect of environmental education has been the concern with the quality of *individual* places and localities, a consideration not only of the cognitive but of the aesthetic and the spiritual. Thus each of us has our own sense of place, a subjective, unique interpretation of place, which frequently defies rationality and logic. Images from literature, music and art, feelings and emotions linked to sights, sounds and smells of a place, intangibles linked with experiences and half-forgotten memories, all contribute to our subjective impression of place, to a perception of place which is both real and unreal, and which is an essential part of our being. Each of us has that special place, which quickens the heartbeat, which excites; a place to which perhaps we retreat, in mind if not always in body, which revives and sustains us. No environment exists in isolation from humankind; environments have different meanings for different people, in time and space; we respond to environments differently, we evaluate them differently. Given this, we need to be aware that one of the tasks of environmental education is to open up environments and places for students, to encourage them to explore their own feelings, emotions and understandings of environments and places, to allow them experiences, encounters and opportunities whereby they will develop a sense of place and an understanding of valued environments, and to appreciate and be deeply affected by 'the sheer otherness of non-human things' (Bonnett 2002). An environmental education without this dimension of environmental literacy, divorced from the context of valuing and caring for places, will be an environmental education devoid of spirit. In the words of Stables and Bishop, 'an environmental education which runs independently of an exploration of the cultural, aesthetic, personal and even irrational views of the environment will prove insufficient to our needs, as it will harness not 'hearts and minds' but merely part of the mind, in a limited range of contexts, and with a limited view of the world as essentially mechanical and liable to breakdown but not to improvement' (Stables and Bishop 2001).

The last decade has seen an increasing national and international prominence given to issues of sustainability. Educational policies within the United Kingdom have been at odds with these environmental policies, however, and, despite the efforts of a number of radical educationalists, teaching for environmental education still focuses heavily upon didactic and knowledge-oriented approaches. There remains the challenge of developing effective and flexible teaching resources and strategies which allows students to consider value- and issue-based environmental challenges in a critical way. Such approaches will have the potential to reduce the sense of powerlessness and frustration which are often generated by a study of environmental problems, and sustain a continuing interest and involvement in environmental issues.

It needs to be explicitly acknowledged, however, that the aims of environmental education for sustainability go beyond an exploration of students' value positions and their understanding of current debates about sustainability. Earlier work on values education, particularly in the context of geography and the humanities, placed the emphasis on the valuing process and on 'values probing', on students clarifying their own value positions and acting consistently within their own values framework. Such an approach enabled students 'to consider the implications of the environment and society of alternative courses of action, to make judgements about the respective merits of such actions, and to decide their own responses, behaviour and future courses of action in relation to sustainable living' (Corney and Middleton 1996, p. 329).

But the aims of EEFS go further than this, than simply providing students with a process whereby they come to an independent value position:

> EEFS does not merely hope that learning activities will lead to the development of an (environmental) ethic. Instead it sets out positively to develop environmental awareness and concern to a level which will result in the acquisition of a personal environmental ethic ... teachers

actively promote the consideration of values required for the development of sustainable lifestyles and do not hold a neutral stance. (Tilbury 1995, pp. 201–2)

From such a perspective, the analogy with education about issues of race, gender and disability is very clear.

Part III

**Values, Morality and Citizenship:
Issues in Personal, Social and
Health Education**

Chapter 13

Values in Education

TERENCE H. MCLAUGHLIN

INTRODUCTION

Education cannot be value-free. Every action (and every omission) of a teacher is value-laden and so is every aspect of the ethos and organization of the school. Education is inherently saturated with value. Since education cannot be value-free, we cannot therefore avoid fundamental questions such as: which values should education embody and transmit, why? and how?

What is meant by the term 'value'? Although much more needs to be said about this question, for the purposes of the present chapter values can be regarded in a rather broad way as criteria (standards or principles) for judging worth. There are, of course, many things which may be valued or judged worthy (including, for example, personal qualities, forms of understanding and states of affairs) and many respects and aspects in which they may be seen to be valuable or of worth. A significant range of values are of relevance and importance for education.

EDUCATION AND THE INESCAPABILITY OF VALUES

The inescapability of values in education is obvious. Let us reflect on the activity of the teacher in the classroom. In seeking to bring about learning, the teacher engages in a wide range of activities including describing, explaining, initiating discussion, prescribing study-related tasks, encouraging, admonishing and the like. All these complex and interrelated activities presuppose that the kind of learning which is being aimed at is thought valuable in some way. The teacher of history, for example, assumes that it is valuable for students to study history in general and valuable that the students study the specific periods and aspects of history which are being taught. Further, the teacher assumes the value of the particular kinds of learning within history which he or she wishes to promote (the achievement of an empathetic understanding of forces and motives, say, as well as a knowledge of facts). In addition, since teachers not only teach their own subject, but impart wider lessons about, say, learning in general and about matters relevant to the individual, social and moral development of students, the value of what is taught in these wider lessons is also assumed. As well as presupposing the value of *what* is taught, teaching also involves value presuppositions about *how* teaching should be conducted. Not any way of bringing about learning is educationally desirable or acceptable, and educational values must be appealed to in determining what educational desirability or acceptability amounts to here. It is necessary to acknowledge that in teaching it is not easy to separate 'what' is being taught from 'how' it is being taught; in many cases 'how' lessons are taught constitute 'lessons' in themselves. These remarks about the value-laden nature of teaching apply also to the life and work of the school. Its aims and processes are value-laden in similar ways.

It is important to note that attempts sometimes made by teachers and schools to be 'neutral' or 'non-judgemental' with respect to matters of value, involves not the absence of value judgements but the presence of complex ones. For example, teachers may feel for various reasons that they should not express their own views to students on certain controversial issues, or judge that they lack a mandate to teach or transmit a specific value stance to students on such matters. However, the forbearance of expression and influence on the part of teachers in cases like these is far from being value-free. A teacher who is reluctant to tell students whether God exists or whether a given political party has the correct approach to a particular matter is not seeking to abdicate all value responsibility. On the contrary, such a teacher is trying to transmit to students certain 'value messages'. These 'value messages' include the need for students to think and judge for themselves about significantly controversial matters, and for students to recognize the limits of the expertise and mandate of the teacher in relation to such questions.

The value-laden character of the activities of teaching and schooling (and more broadly of education) is not merely a matter of practical inescapability. It is also one of logic. A value-free education is not merely a practical impossibility but also a contradiction in terms. The very idea of education involves value.

THE PERVASIVENESS OF EDUCATIONAL VALUES

Values in education are pervasive. Education in values is taking place in everything that a teacher says and does (and in everything that a teacher does not say and do) and in all the aspects of the life and work of the school. It is far from the case, therefore, that education in values takes place only when 'value issues' are explicitly addressed with students, as in specifically designed and labelled lessons or course units, for example. Nor are 'value issues' uniquely and exclusively associated only with certain subjects and topics.

It is vital to realize that the value influence on students exerted by teachers and schools is not confined to influence which is deliberately intended. Unintended value influence can take place through the 'hidden curriculum' of teaching and schooling, and in some cases this influence can contradict and undermine what teachers and schools intend. Thus, for example, various forms of unacknowledged prejudice may infect a teacher's interactions with some pupils, and cast doubt on claims that all members of the student body are being treated with equal respect. Further, rigid policies of setting and streaming on the part of the school may give the lie to the claim that equality of opportunity is being provided for all. It is therefore necessary for the value influence exerted by teachers and schools to be kept under careful and sensitive review.

THE VARIETY AND COMPLEXITY OF EDUCATIONAL VALUES

We often tend to assume in speaking of educational values that we are referring to moral values. Educational values, however, are of many different kinds. Moral values and moral education are only a part, albeit an important part, of the 'value responsibility' of teachers and schools. (For a fuller discussion of moral values in education see Chapter 14.)

The values inherent in the aims, content, processes and achievements of education are wide-ranging. They include judgements about human good implicit in general educational ideals and aims (for example, the ideal of personal autonomy or of the 'active citizen'), particular judgements within subjects or areas of study (such as the criteria for a good poem or an adequate scientific explanation) and commitments of a social and political kind (seen, for example, in policies aimed at equality of opportunity in its various aspects). Even if these broader educational values have moral aspects or implications, they extend beyond the moral to include values which are intellectual, aesthetic, social and political in nature.

There are a number of complexities which arise in relation to educational values. Five complexities are worthy of mention here. First, the fact that educational values are so pervasive and varied makes it difficult for us to discuss them with any degree of clarity and coherence. A persistent temptation when discussing educational values is to fall into 'edu-babble' (a form of imprecise and platitudinous rhetoric similar to 'psycho-babble'). Yet it is important for teachers and schools to bring questions relating to educational values clearly into focus, not simply at the level of theory and principle but also at the level of practical implications for the classroom and school. A second complexity relates to the fact that not all educational values are mutually consistent or harmoniously realizable. They can conflict with each other and therefore call for judgements about priority and emphasis. Examples of such conflicts include the tensions between freedom and equality in education and between breadth and depth of study. A third complexity relates to the diversity and dispute which arises in relation to at least some educational values. This matter will be considered in more detail below. A fourth complexity concerns the question: who should properly determine educational values: teachers, schools, students, parents, the state, the local community, the democratic community as a whole, employers, or the mechanisms of an educational marketplace? Teachers and schools do not, and cannot, conduct their work in a vacuum, isolated from other influences, forces and claims. Fifth, and as a consequence of the preceding four complexities, it can be very difficult for teachers and schools to develop an approach to educational values which is unified and coherent.

VALUES, EDUCATION AND CONTROVERSIALITY

Teachers and schools exercise influence not only upon the thoughts and minds of students, but also on their wider development as persons. In an important sense, education shapes persons and their lives. It is therefore appropriate and necessary for the values inherent in education to be carefully assessed by teachers, parents and the community more generally. Many values with which education is concerned are relatively uncontroversial in that they enjoy widespread support from informed academic and professional opinion and from parents and the community as a whole. It is important not to over-emphasize controversiality in relation to educational values. A reasonable and well-grounded consensus exists on many issues. In the area of morality, for example, few doubt that teachers should urge their students to respect other people and their property, to be honest and responsible, to exercise self-control and to be fair and just. The immorality of bullying and child abuse, for example, is not in doubt. A reasonable and stable consensus also exists in relation to many other educational values. The general nature of a balanced curriculum and of appropriate teaching processes, for example, are the subject of wide agreement.

However, education is an area which does give rise to significant controversy. The notion of *significant* controversy is worthy of emphasis here. Not all disagreements and disputes are significantly controversial. Some disagreements and disputes arise from misunderstanding and ill-will. Significant controversy exists when contrasting views on an issue are based on well-grounded and non-trivial differences of judgement, and where these contrasting views are not contrary to reason. Significant controversy may exist for various reasons. Sufficient evidence to settle the matter at stake may not yet be available; the weighting or interpretation to be given to evidence or aspects of evidence may not be agreed; what counts as evidence may be in dispute and (in the most wide-ranging cases of disagreement) whole contrasting frameworks of understanding, belief and value may be at stake. A complexity here is that what actually constitutes a matter of significant controversy can itself be a matter of significant controversy.

Some matters of educational controversy do not appear to involve matters of value directly but seem to take the form: if we value the learning of X by students, what is the best way to bring that learning about? Caution is needed, however, in relation to educational disputes which appear to be merely 'technical' about means rather than ends. We noted earlier that it is not easy to separate 'what' is being taught from 'how' it is taught. 'Means' and 'ends' are often inseparable in an educational context. A dispute about the best way to teach a given subject matter may be partly evaluative in character. Disputes between 'traditionalists' and 'progressives' in education, for example, often involve competing evaluations of what is to count as learning of the appropriate kind.

Other educational disputes have a more directly evaluative character, as in the famous question of Herbert Spencer: 'Which knowledge is of most worth?' Disputes of this more directly evaluative kind are found at different levels. Spencer's question is at the most general level, where disputes about different conceptions (or 'philosophies') of education are to be found. Familiar disputes here concern the aims and 'content' of education (for example, about the relative importance of traditional academic disciplines, study 'relevant' to 'life' and to social and personal development, vocational preparation, and breadth versus depth in study); the processes of education (for example, about how the role of the teacher in its different aspects should be conceived); and about matters of institutionalisation and control (for example, about the extent to which diversity of schooling should be permitted or encouraged and about the extent of the rights of choice of parents). Often, particular evaluative assumptions are built into the language we are invited to use in relation to education (terms such as 'delivery', 'input/output' and 'learning outcomes' are clearly value-laden in this way). Evaluative disputes do not merely arise at the most general level of educational thinking, policy-making and practice; they are manifest in different ways at all levels.

Adequate attention to the full range of questions which arise in relation to educational values requires extensive discussion. Henceforth, this chapter will focus attention upon one specific question: the principles which should govern the teaching of controversial value issues in schools.

EDUCATION AND THE TEACHING OF CONTROVERSIAL VALUE ISSUES

In the light of our earlier discussion it is clear that the explicit handling of controversial value issues is only one aspect of the overall 'value influence' of schools. It is also clear that not all value issues explicitly dealt with in the curriculum give rise to significant controversy. Any education worthy of the name, however, cannot ignore significant value disagreement in its different aspects. It has recently been insisted, for example, that an examination of controversial issues is an inescapable part of Education for Citizenship (Advisory Group on Citizenship 1998, Section 10; Qualifications and Curriculum Authority 2000, Appendix 2). (For further discussion of Education for Citizenship see Chapter 15.) The need for the explicit handling of significantly controversial issues does, however, arise in relation to a number of aspects of the curriculum of the school. While personal, moral, social, political and religious issues notably give rise to well-grounded and non-trivial disagreement, such disagreement is not confined to these matters. In the approach of teachers and schools to significant value disagreement the following general considerations are relevant.

Liberal democracy, diversity and public/non-public values

We are confronted in modern liberal democratic societies by people holding many different, and often incompatible, values, including 'comprehensive' theories of the good, or overall views of life. Catholics, Jews and Muslims live alongside atheists and agnostics. These comprehensive views are significantly controversial because, it is claimed, there is no way of objectively and conclusively adjudicating between them to the satisfaction of all citizens. Nor are these disagreements likely to be conclusively resolved in the future. They are deep-seated and tenacious, the result of fundamental differences of belief and value. Yet many of these comprehensive theories of the good can be regarded as 'reasonable' or 'within the moral pale'. They do not conflict with, even if they go beyond, values acceptable to all. Liberal democratic societies, and the philosophical theory of liberalism in terms of which they are frequently articulated, approach questions of value diversity by invoking a distinction between 'public' and 'non-public' values and spheres. The nature of this distinction is illuminated by the observation by Jonathan Sacks in his 1990 Reith Lectures, that in modern democratic societies, people 'speak' two 'languages of evaluation': a 'first' language of public (or common) values and a 'second' language of their own substantial traditions reflected in familial, religious and cultural communities (Sacks 1991).

'Public' values can be regarded as those which, in virtue of their fundamentality or inescapability, are seen as binding on all persons. Frequently embodied in law and expressed in terms of rights, they include such matters as basic social morality and a range of democratic principles such as freedom of speech and justice. 'Public' values can be affirmed by persons whose wider frameworks of belief differ from each other. They do not presuppose some particular metaphysical theory of the self, or of the nature of human destiny. For example, atheists and Catholics differ profoundly on such matters, but they can share common ground in condemning cruelty and supporting a democratic way of life, even if their different overall frameworks of belief give them a distinctive perspective on such matters. It is the 'public' values which constitute the common or unifying values which are necessary for a democratic society and on which its characteristic notions of pluralism and multiculturalism depend. 'Public' values, in virtue of their fundamentality and inescapability, give wide-ranging relativism pause for thought.

In contrast to the 'public' values, 'non-public' values go beyond what can be affirmed by, and insisted upon for, all members of a society. They are part of a range of options from which, within a framework of justice, persons might construct their lives. Such values may involve wide-ranging views of life as a whole, such as a religious faith or a substantial political creed. Since such 'comprehensive' theories of the good are significantly controversial, they cannot be imposed or insisted upon for all members of society but are seen as matters for individual and family assessment and decision. It is in relation to these 'non-public' values that the notion of 'respected difference' associated with pluralism and multiculturalism arises, and the difficulties with evaluation to which relativism presents itself as a response.

The distinction between 'public' and 'non-public' values, and the precise determination of the 'content' of each of the categories, is not without difficulty. The distinction is, however, helpful in discerning principles for the handling of significantly controversial matters in schools (for further discussion see McLaughlin 1995a).

Pluralism and multiculturalism

Two other concepts which are often encountered in relation to the discussion of significantly controversial value issues are pluralism and multiculturalism. Both notions, however, need to be carefully understood. They point not only to the mere existence of diversities of various kinds within a liberal democratic society but also to need for these diversities to be (in some sense) positively valued.

In discussions of pluralism and multiculturalism, emphasis is often laid on the significance of diversity. It is important to note, however, that the very notions of pluralism and multiculturalism imply elements of commonality as well as diversity. Without common values, ideals and procedures, a pluralist multicultural society would not only disintegrate but would also lack, among other things, freedom, equality and tolerance: values essential to pluralism and multiculturalism themselves, as well as to democracy. The respects in which pluralism and multiculturalism involve a balance of unifying and diversifying elements is well brought out in the vision of a democratic pluralist multicultural society outlined in the report of the Swann Committee (Committee of Enquiry into the Education of Children from Ethnic Minority Groups 1985; and see also Commission on the Future of Multi-Ethnic Britain 2000).

One of the central questions raised by the notions of pluralism and multiculturalism is the nature and extent of the diversity which should be valued, and on what grounds. Clearly, there is nothing about diversity or difference *per se* which is valuable. Murder, theft and exploitation are aspects of diversity. Clearly only *certain sorts* of diversity are candidates for favourable evaluation. What, however, does 'favourable evaluation' mean here? Is the diversity at issue to be judged worthy merely of toleration, or of some more full-blooded acceptance?

Relativism

A general attitude or perspective which is often encountered in relation to the discussion of significantly controversial value issues is relativism. Relativism is the view that judgements of value (and, possibly, also of knowledge and truth) are relative to, and dependent upon, such variables as time, place, society, culture, moral codes, practices, forms of life, conceptual schemes or frameworks, and personal background, circumstances and perspective. In its most extreme forms, relativism holds that there are no general standards or criteria of evaluation and no neutral or objective ways of choosing between the different sets of standards or criteria associated with these relative variables. There are no objective values, but merely *my* or *your* or *their* values. Among the educational consequences of relativism is an undermining of the point of discussing alternative views with the aim of rationally evaluating these views and not merely becoming aware that they exist.

However, the extreme claim that all values are relative, and that it is impossible to appeal to any well-grounded basis on which we can claim that some values are better or more adequate than others, is both overstated and incoherent. The claim is overstated because it overlooks the extent of the reasonable consensus on many value questions which was alluded to earlier. It is incoherent, because in calling into question in a radical way the value of, say, general standards of argument, the claim does not provide any grounds on which it can itself make sense. The claim presents itself as stating something which is true (that there are no valid general standards of argument). But if there are no standards of truth or argument, how can the claim be coherently articulated, given that it involves an argument about what it true? A perspective of thorough-going relativism, apart from its inherent difficulties, makes the task of education both impossible and incoherent.

A rejection of an extreme form of relativism leaves us, however, with the question of how precisely we should approach matters of evaluation in relation to significantly controversial issues.

Differing schooling contexts and mandates for value influence

The general mandate for the exercise of value influence which is enjoyed by schools of all kinds can be roughly expressed in the following way. All schools, regardless of their character, are on firm ground in presupposing and transmitting the 'public' values which have been referred to. Schools do not regard the morality of bullying or racism as open questions and nor do they hesitate to promote democratic values such as respect and toleration (within principled limits) for the views and decisions of others. Day by day, schools of all kinds urge their students to respect other people and their property, to be honest and responsible, to exercise self-control, to think for themselves and to achieve appropriate forms of autonomy in relation to many matters. 'Public' values such as these can be regarded as fundamental or basic: they are constitutive of civilized life in any human community – and, more specifically, in a democratic one, and are therefore in a sense 'non-negotiable' for any school. These values are 'shared', not in the sense that every person shares them (murderers and despots do not) but that they are not matters for reasonable and civilized dispute.

What value influence should schools exert with respect to the more complex and controversial value issues which are characteristic of the 'non-public' domain? What, for example, should schools say about the truth or otherwise of a particular religion, the adequacy of a particular code of sexual ethics or the coherence of the policy of a political party on a matter of contemporary interest? Here it is important to note the differing mandates for value influence enjoyed by different kinds of school. 'Common' schools are intended for students of all backgrounds and are not based on a particular 'view of life'. Since the value influence exerted by such schools must be broadly acceptable to society as a whole, they lack a mandate to present values in the significantly controversial 'non-public' domain as if they were unequivocally true and good. Rather the mandate of the common school is seen as that of illuminating the nature of the controversies which arise and of helping students to explore, understand, discuss and make critically reflective judgements of their own about the matters at stake. In contrast, 'separate' schools, which are based on a particular 'view of life' (usually a religious one) enjoy a mandate to exercise more wide-ranging value influence in the 'non-public' domain than their 'common' counter-parts. Thus Anglican and Catholic schools, for example, enjoy a mandate to form their students in a particular religious faith, together with the ethical, social and political sensibility associated with it. Such schools, do not, of course, enjoy a mandate crudely to indoctrinate, and they face the challenge of offering their distinctive value influence to students in a way which respects the demands of criticism and personal autonomy (for more discussion of common and separate schools respectively see McLaughlin 1995b and 1992).

TEACHING APPROACHES AND STRATEGIES IN RELATION TO CONTROVERSIAL VALUE ISSUES

A number of approaches and strategies can be discerned in relation to the teaching of significantly controversial value issues. These include ignoring or evading the issues, seeking balance, adoption of a form of procedural neutrality, invoking the notions of reasonableness and impartiality and engaging in counter-advocacy. These approaches and strategies all require assessment in the light of the principles and considerations discussed in the previous section. (For a detailed discussion of particular approaches and strategies and related ideas see, for example, Bridges 1986, Advisory Group on Citizenship 1998, Section 10.)

CONCLUSION

This chapter has confined itself to a discussion of some of the key issues which arise in relation to values in education from a philosophical perspective. Philosophy alone, however, cannot deal with all the issues which arise in relation to educational values, much less determine the practical implications for teachers, schools and educational policy-makers which arise. Educational values require illumination from many academic perspectives (including sociological, psychological and historical ones) and from the practical insights and experience of those working in classrooms and schools. Philosophical considerations of the sort which have been outlined, however, have an indispensable role to play in our understanding of educational values and the practical implications and demands to which they give rise.

Chapter 14

Moral Education

CHRISTINE TUBB

INTRODUCTION

Few would deny that schools have a part to play in moral education, but exactly what that means can be elusive. There is an expectation that 'teachers should be contributing more directly to the promotion of moral values appropriate to the creation and maintenance of an orderly and law-abiding society' (Best and Lang 1997, p. vii).

Perhaps, in the wake of intense media attention focused on crimes of violence committed by children, it is felt that a significant number of young people somehow lack all sense of morality and that schools ought to teach children what is right and wrong. Certainly concern is often expressed about a perceived decline in moral standards and a rise in the level of offences committed, and this may be behind the calls for values to be taught in schools.

It is important to be aware of the dubious nature of some common assumptions underlying this demand before deciding what moral education in school ought and ought not to involve.

QUESTIONABLE ASSUMPTIONS

There appears to be an implicit conviction that there is a direct causal relationship between knowing what is right and refraining from crime, and thus between moral education and the achievement of a more law-abiding society. However, it is not obvious that people generally act in morally objectionable ways because they do not know what they ought to do. Even murderers rarely seem to be confused about the morality of murder. They do not argue that murder is good, but, in their own defence, are more likely to claim that they were not responsible, that there was no choice on this particular occasion or that a particular incident was not a case of murder, but accidental killing or manslaughter. Sometimes people can have clear conceptions of right and wrong and yet be weak, giving in to temptation and failing to live up to their moral principles. At other times they may be intentionally doing wrong as a protest or a means of rebellion. None of this is incompatible with *knowing* right from wrong.

There is little to suggest that our pupils have no conception that certain acts might be morally unacceptable. They certainly talk as if they believe some things are wrong and they complain eloquently when they think they are the victims of wrong-doing. The problem may be, not that children have no ideas about what is right and wrong, but that adults do not always agree with their ideas. After all, when there is talk of children having little or no sense of morality, 'morality' is often intended to signify that which is morally good (or rather what the complainant *deems* to be morally good). In other words, the assumption here is that children lack a proper understanding of morality in that their ideas of right and wrong, good and bad, are mistaken.

However, 'morality' might equally be taken to refer to the *sphere* of morality (to the whole area which concerns what is morally good or bad rather than, for example, what is aesthetically good or bad). The underlying presumption may be that young people's moral sensibility is undesirably diminished or limited, such that moral considerations are not always recognized or acted upon. The force of expediency, self-interest and instrumental arguments may be thought to take precedence over, or to obliterate, reflection on moral factors in some situations. While conceding that murder is readily identified as a moral matter, there may yet be anxiety that practices such as tax-dodging are not perceived as moral issues, but as socially acceptable – what everyone would do if they could get away with it. The worry may be that 'What ought I to do?' is being ignored in the face of 'What can I do?' Thus the young are perceived as less discriminating and less scrupulous than is desirable.

It is also possible that there is concern that the nature of morality is misunderstood in other ways, and the fear is that young people's commitment to moral values is eroded by unreflective adherence to a relativist or subjectivist position. Plainly one does not need to engage in sophisticated philosophical thought to gain the impression that moral values are primarily cultural, relative to time and place, or to conclude they are just a matter of taste. A lack of certainty, and a consequent attitude of 'anything goes', with respect to what is right or wrong may well be feared.

How far these implicit assumptions or the fears which ride on them are well-grounded is, of course, highly debatable, but even if they *were* justified, it is a further question whether or not teachers must simply teach children what is right and wrong. The issues raised already intimate that the answer is likely to depend a great deal on what precisely is meant by this.

MORAL EDUCATION

If education is under consideration, the aim cannot be merely to train pupils to act in certain ways, as if they were dogs or parrots. There can be little doubt that many people would very much like teachers to concentrate on producing young adults whose conduct conforms to that which is deemed to be desirable, law-abiding and morally acceptable. But education concerns more than trained behaviour: education concerns teaching with regard for children's capacity to understand, know and reason. Moral education, and any other education, must involve cognition and should not be reduced to training or conditioning behaviour. Similarly, with respect to beliefs, moral education is not reducible to indoctrination or to the inculcation of moral values such that children are brought to believe certain actions are morally right or wrong just because teachers say so:

> ... there are rational considerations. As a matter of rationality, there are moral claims which we have to recognise. But we have to recognise them, rather than blindly following answers given by others. If something like this is right, then the idea of imposing morality on others becomes a contradiction in terms. People will have to appreciate the force of moral thinking for themselves, and there will be a role for moral education, not in imposing anything, but rather in enabling people to see what in the end they will have to see for themselves. (Haydon 1997, p. 84)

Moral education is surely intended to help children to be able to think and act morally for themselves to develop as moral agents. Despite some doubts over what might be meant by 'moral development', moral education must at least be about developing those capacities needed to function in the moral sphere. Being moral is not a matter of blind obedience to others, or doing the right thing for fear of reprisals; it requires that people act autonomously, freely acting in the light of beliefs which in some significant sense they have made their own.

If teaching what is right and wrong amounts to coercing or manipulating pupils into unthinking conformity then it is clear that this is not the task of schools. If, on the other hand, it means enabling children to be full moral agents, building on what they already understand of moral concepts, right and wrong, good and bad, this is surely at the heart of moral education.

It must be absurd to imagine that secondary school students have no moral beliefs at all, but believing something to be morally wrong is not the same as understanding the moral sphere itself. One of the first concerns for moral education surely should be to address the nature of moral beliefs as such.

THE NATURE OF MORALITY

Moral beliefs are not the same in kind as beliefs about scientific or mathematical propositions. Morals are not facts or knowledge that can be arrived at simply by assessing empirical evidence or pursuing logical argument. Questions of morality are questions about what is right and wrong, about what people ought to do, not just about what is the case. Answering moral questions involves making judgements in the light of principles held and moral values. Facts and reasoning are not irrelevant, but, in the final analysis, morals are unverifiable and are the proper object of belief rather than knowledge. It cannot be proved beyond doubt that it is wrong to torture, in the way that the correct height of a tree can be established. Evidence and reason are important in showing that torturers inflict agony, but it is the belief that we should not unjustifiably inflict pain which is crucial in deciding whether or not torture is morally acceptable and not the fact that torture is still widely used in some prisons. We *believe* rather than know that some acts are wrong.

To say that morals are not reducible to facts is not, however, to say they are exclusively subjective or merely arbitrary, nor is it to suggest that all beliefs about morality are equally valid. Moral beliefs based on misapprehension of the relevant facts, on incoherent reasoning or chosen at random are evidently less defensible than judgements arrived at through coherent reasoning and taking into account relevant evidence. Yes, moral education aims to help children to hold moral values they have chosen for themselves, but this should not be thought of as some trivial 'pick 'n' mix' process, reflecting mere taste or whim.

Moral beliefs are *controversial* in their nature and open to question in the sense explained by Terry McLaughlin (Chapter 13). They are values. At the same time, moral values are distinct from other values such as aesthetic, political and intellectual values. That which is believed to be morally acceptable may coincide with or overlap the law, social mores, cultural traditions and religious beliefs, but is also distinguishable from these. We may derive the particular moral beliefs we hold from, for example, religious teaching or what society approves, but morals are also separable. What we believe to be morally right may at times contradict the law of the land or conflict with a particular religious tenet. In judging an action to be morally good or bad, relying on convention and conviction will be inadequate: 'That a principle is backed by tradition, intuition, power or revelation does not make it a moral principle. Only if it is rationally justifiable is it that' (Hirst 1973, p. 140). Moral considerations are generally held to be overriding; transcending social conventions, expediency and other values.

Morality is controversial in its logical status, but is also the subject of controversy in the ordinary sense. People vary in their specific moral beliefs and disagree over what is morally right or wrong. Understanding the moral sphere includes appreciation of the diversity of moral values, of different conceptions of right and wrong.

If moral values are so varied and uncertain, it may seem that we should not be attempting to teach right and wrong since cultural relativism may appear to be the only appropriate stance in a pluralist society. But diversity does not *have* to entail thorough-going cultural relativism or equal acceptance of irreconcilable views.

Nevertheless, given the evident diversity, it is clear that moral education is a sensitive matter. Our moral values are usually important to us. A significant value is something held in high esteem, something dear to us, and in addition our moral beliefs are part of who we are and a reflection of our ideals. Consequently arguments about what is morally right or wrong are not only likely to be intransigent, they may also often be heated.

CAN ANY MORAL VALUES LEGITIMATELY BE TAUGHT?

Whose moral values?

The potential for conflicting views on what is morally acceptable and what is not, between parents and schools or between teachers and children, is plain. Who is to decide which moral values should be promoted in schools? While there are no good grounds for accepting that teachers *qua* teachers are the only proper arbiters of what is right and good, by the same token parents and others do not always know better. Troublesome clashes are unlikely to be avoided by passing the decision-making over to parents who may disagree among themselves, or indeed to any other body of people.

There are no moral experts to whom we can apply for information about what is right and wrong or what the content of moral education ought to be. Some people may be better than others at making moral judgements; nevertheless, such people do not form a class comparable to other sets of experts, to whom we might apply to make certain judgements for us. Even a degree in moral philosophy would not necessarily signal the specific expertise required. Undoubtedly training in moral philosophy would be useful in clarifying and analysing the nature of particular ethical dilemmas, but more is needed. The expertise required includes practical wisdom and being a good person, and there is little reason to suppose that moral philosophers are morally better persons than others.

Far more importantly, even if there were an identifiable set of moral experts, the notion of leaving decisions about what is right or wrong to them would remain unacceptable – morally unacceptable. To rely on the moral understanding of others and to surrender one's choice of moral action in unreflectingly accepting their advice, would be to relinquish part of being a person. A person thinks and acts morally in virtue of doing so with some relevant *autonomy*. In simply conforming to the ideas of the expert, one has abdicated from making further moral choices with respect to their sphere of enquiry and cannot properly be said to think or act morally in any consequent conformity. (This is not to suggest that no expert judgement is ever relevant to making moral decisions, but to maintain that mere conformity to another's advice cannot be autonomous thought or action. It is of course distinct from applying to experts for their specialized knowledge of a particular area, and relying on their authority in their own fields, or taking their views into account in arriving at one's own decision.) We may not be all equally qualified for or good at making moral judgements, but to permit others to decide for us is to stop being moral at all. We need to achieve more expertise ourselves and to acquire the disposition to act in the light of it, not to leave it to others.

Should moral education be only *about* morality?

It might be thought therefore that schools should concentrate on teaching *about* morality and avoid any attempt to teach right and wrong in any more direct sense. But refraining from exerting any influence over pupils' moral beliefs does not seem to be an option that is in practice open to teachers. It is easy to recognize that the hidden curriculum, in the sense of all that is implicit in the way teachers present lessons and treat their pupils, is full of messages about what they value and believe with respect to morality. A school's ethos reflects and embodies values. Whether acknowledged or not, the hidden curriculum is unavoidable. Moreover, this implicit presentation of moral values can be highly influential. It may be that we arrive at many of our moral convictions from the example of others and from how we are treated, rather than from direct instruction or discussion.

If this is the case, it must be important to reflect on what, if any, moral values can be legitimately taught, and to confront the issue explicitly in moral education.

Fundamental values and specific moral beliefs

In The National Curriculum 2000 handbook for Key Stages 3 and 4, the guidelines for PSHE include the 'Statement of Values' produced by the National Forum for Values in Education and the Community. The remit of the Forum was to identify, if possible, those values which are 'commonly agreed upon across society' (DfEE and QCA 1999, p. 195) and could be promoted in schools in England and Wales. It was made explicit that the statements of value agreed upon were not intended to be 'a definitive and complete list of all the values people hold' (National Forum for Values in Education and the Community 1996, p. 1); moreover, it was emphasized that:

> the shared values will not necessarily be the values that all people believe to be the most important. By their nature, for example, 'shared values' do not include those distinctive of any particular religious or cultural group. (*ibid.*, 1996, p. 5)

Evidently the values sought are those on which agreement seems possible and indeed likely. There is no claim that such values are the objects of universal consensus, only that there may be agreement on values that 'schools should promote on society's behalf' (ibid. 1996, Introduction).

A MORI 'omnibus' poll of 1,500 adults apparently showed that 95 per cent of those consulted were agreed on the values put forward in the statement: 'This overwhelming consensus is empirical evidence for the claim that, despite the fact that we are a pluralist society, there is a robust set of values that are shared by all of us' (Talbot and Tate 1997, p. 3).

Nevertheless, the fact that there may be wide agreement or even consensus with regard to particular moral or any other values cannot alone justify their inclusion in the school curriculum. While broad agreement might well in practical terms facilitate the teacher's task, for example by helping to avoid conflicts with parents and others, it could not *justify* the intentional promotion of particular moral values in school. Other grounds too are needed.

However, it may be that there is wide agreement on certain moral values, not purely as a matter of coincidence, but because in some way they are fundamental. It may be the case that these are readily shared values, not because contingently there is agreement about them, but because without appreciating them it is difficult to see how one could understand what it is to be a moral agent.

Some values seem to be fundamental to understanding morality itself. The Statement of Values includes:

> We value truth, human rights, the law, justice and the collective endeavour for the common good of society (DfEE and QCA 1999, p.196)

> We value others for themselves, not only for what they have or what they can do for us (*ibid.*, p. 196)

Valuing others 'for themselves' appears to be fundamental to understanding what it is to be moral. In other words, it is difficult to imagine how one could begin to act and think as a moral agent without appreciating the value of respect for persons. In the same way, notions such as impartiality, justice and truth are also held to be basic to moral agency:

> treating other people with respect, not causing unnecessary hurt or pain, taking seriously other people's interests, telling the truth and keeping promises. It is difficult to conceive a morality that did not subscribe in some way to such principles. (Pring 1987, p. 65)

If such concepts are fundamental to functioning morally, it must be legitimate, and indeed necessary, to promote them in moral education.

A distinction can be drawn between such *fundamental values* and *specific moral beliefs*. Fundamental values do seem to be in a different category from specific beliefs. The principle that human life should be respected is fundamental, but a range of differing specific beliefs might follow from this. Whether or not respect for life demands a stand which is pacifist, anti-abortion or anti-euthanasia is contentious. Pacifism comprises a specific instance of respect for life, but is not the only defensible position to take on war. Accepting others for themselves could also be cashed out in a variety of ways. Believing in this as a fundamental value is significantly different from believing that it must be reflected specifically in, for instance, generous donations to charity or never arguing.

In pluralistic societies such as our own, consensus that specific moral beliefs are right must be unlikely, perhaps because beliefs in this category are inherently so contestable. But it is important to note that even fundamental values are not incontrovertible or uncontentious. In this respect they are no different from many specific moral beliefs. To value everyone as having intrinsic worth may be basic to moral thinking, but it is not morally neutral nor incontestable (cf. Cohen 1969, p. 160).

Promoting or teaching *specific* values will always be educationally dubious, but it may be entirely appropriate to foster a concern for *fundamental* values in moral education. This will involve nurturing and refining the understanding that certain concepts are central to morality.

Moral Development

Aim 2 of the National Curriculum handbook begins, 'The school curriculum should promote pupils' spiritual, moral, social and cultural development and, in particular, develop principles for distinguishing between right and wrong' (DfEE and QCA 1999, p. 11). Schools, then, are expected to educate for moral *development*.

Kohlberg's research (1966, 1969) led him to conclude that there is a pattern to moral development, and that there are consecutive levels and stages through which children and young adults pass. His work focused closely on children's moral reasoning. His developmental scheme can be briefly summarised as shown in Figure 14.1.

If a developmental view is adopted, presumably moral education should, in terms of this model, aim to help pupils to move towards Stage 6 (although Kohlberg himself believed that few adults actually achieve this level of sophistication in their moral reasoning). This would involve enabling and encouraging children to move from heteronomy and being led by self-interest, to recognition of the claims of others and, eventually, to being guided by concern for others and impartiality.

Kohlberg's influence on moral education has undoubtedly been significant, perhaps especially because his description of the stages of moral development has been taken to be a scientific theory, based on evidence and open to proof. Such a view must, however, be misconceived for the criteria against which children and adults can be categorized are surely value-laden, reflecting prior judgements about what counts as more or less developed, better or worse. The stages may be *prescriptive* rather than descriptive, listing desirable changes rather than describing the way things are.

Nonetheless, recognition of the prescriptive character of such theories of moral development need not lead to a complete rejection of cognition in moral education. In the context of schooling, focusing on the development of moral reasoning seems entirely appropriate and desirable.

It would, however, be foolish to suppose that an intellectual grasp of reasoning, however sophisticated will, of itself, preclude anti-social behaviour. Few instances of criminal behaviour can have been the consequence of misunderstanding the finer points of moral philosophy. As Wringe wryly

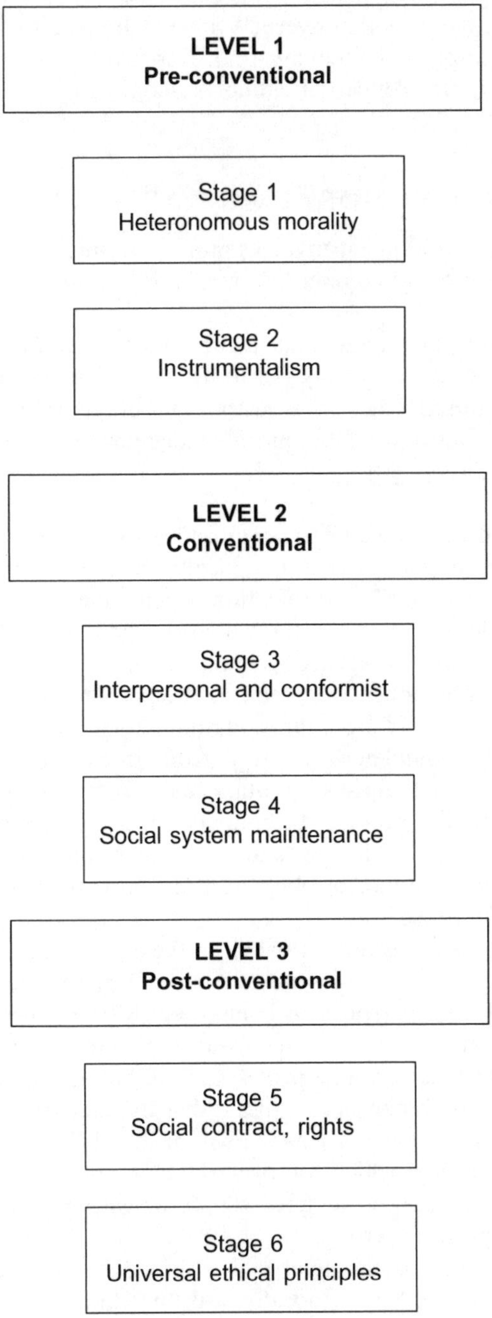

LEVEL 1
Pre-conventional

Stage 1
Heteronomous morality

Stage 2
Instrumentalism

LEVEL 2
Conventional

Stage 3
Interpersonal and conformist

Stage 4
Social system maintenance

LEVEL 3
Post-conventional

Stage 5
Social contract, rights

Stage 6
Universal ethical principles

Figure 14.1: Kohlberg's developmental scheme

notes, 'it is unlikely that the young mugger or joy-rider will have asked herself, "Can I will the maxim of this act to become a universal law?" and simply hit upon the wrong answer' (Wringe 1998, p. 226).

Developing moral judgement and improving moral reasoning are important, but moral education cannot be confined to this if it is to affect moral action.

EDUCATING FOR MORAL AGENCY

To develop as a moral agent involves more than intellectual comprehension of the moral sphere and coming to appreciate certain fundamental values:

> children may be taught a great deal about morality without being taught to be moral agents; they may fail to use the information and the skills they have acquired, when faced with a real-life moral decision, or they may fail to act upon the moral judgements they have formed. (Straughan 1982, p. 90)

Children do need to be able to *act* morally as well as to think, to be taught 'that right and wrong are real and applicable, not merely verbal distinctions' (Warnock 1996, p. 49). Moral education which aimed to have no bearing on behaviour would surely be extraordinary. There should in this regard, however, be no suggestion that schools ought to engage in behavioural conditioning or non-educative practices designed to regulate conduct, not only because this would be unduly manipulatory, but also because moral action cannot be completely divorced from intellectual processes. Acting morally is not to act always spontaneously, on whim or at random. A measure of rationality needs to be cultivated if people are to make decisions about what they ought to do and to act on them, but in addition moral agents are those who have a sense of obligation to follow their own principles and the disposition to do so.

Moral principles are beliefs or values in the light of which the moral agent makes judgements and decides how to act. They can be seen as rules or guidelines to which a person feels committed. Moral education involves the cultivation of dispositions: not necessarily the disposition to perform a specific action such as joining a protest march, but at least the disposition to act in accordance with one's principles rather than ignoring them. This is not to say that morally educated persons will always behave according to their moral beliefs or in ways which conform to their consciences, but moral agents will be aware when they have acted rightly or wrongly. In this sense moral agents know right from wrong.

Other dispositions of character which should be nurtured surely include those listed by White: 'to be morally and physically courageous, generous, friendly, confident, moderate in their appetites for food, drink and in due course sex, self-controlled in matters of anger' (White 1994, p. 374). To develop virtues such as these is to go well beyond the purely cognitive.

Spiecker would also want moral education to include attention to moral emotions and attitudes, pointing out that: 'Educators not only try to teach children to act according to moral rules, they also want them to do so with "heart and soul" and "in the right spirit" ' (Spiecker 1988, p. 53).

Whether they are best described as emotions and attitudes or in different terms, the affective aspects of morality cannot be ignored. It must be possible to lead a morally blameless life and even to perform good deeds out of a strong sense of duty without feeling empathy with other human beings, but, for many of us, understanding what we ought to do springs from feeling for others, and our sense of moral obligation is strong because we feel inclined to be altruistic, kindly, fair or whatever. Our feelings contribute to our motivation to act in certain ways. Moreover, a range of emotions are *appropriately* experienced by moral agents on occasion, so it is fitting to feel ashamed when we think we have done wrong and it is appropriate to be appalled and outraged when faced with an instance of dreadful cruelty. Feelings too need to be recognized, understood and encouraged in moral education.

Trying to conduct one's life in the light of one's moral principles may also require resolution or strength of will, so moral education may need to include empowerment – raising and maintaining pupils' self-esteem and developing their assertiveness, as well as providing knowledge and understanding – in order to help young people to adhere to their principles in the face of opposition and to stand up for what they feel to be morally right.

CONCLUSION

In this chapter the aim has been to draw attention to some of the problems inherent in the whole idea of moral education and to raise some issues relating to any demand that schools should be teaching children to be good. There are of course many ways of looking at moral education which have not been mentioned here. The emphasis on educating for moral action could, and some would argue should, be replaced by a concern for virtues and the nurturing of virtuous people. This might cause particularly intransigent problems for moral education in schools, but the 'ethics of care' propounded by Gilligan (1982) and Noddings (1984) offers for many a viable, alternative approach.

Chapter 15

Citizenship and Citizenship Education in England

JOHN BECK

THE DEVELOPMENT OF CITIZENSHIP EDUCATION IN ENGLAND AND WALES

In England and Wales, as compared with many other countries, official education for citizenship has been neglected until quite recently.[1] At certain moments of crisis, efforts have been made to promote it, a case in point being the formation of the Association for Education in World Citizenship, established in 1935 in response to the rise of Fascism and Communism. Similar concerns to educate for democracy as a safeguard against totalitarianism motivated a brief period of enthusiasm for citizenship education in Britain in the post-war years. But the Ministry of Education proved equivocal in its support and gave no national lead (Ministry of Education 1949). From the mid-1960s, the growth of comprehensive schooling provided an impetus for curriculum expansion in social studies, with new GCE and CSE syllabuses in subjects like Politics, Sociology, and Integrated Humanities, as well as the growth of General Studies in sixth forms. But even then, such subjects were typically offered only as options and there was little support for *universal* citizenship education.

The introduction of the National Curriculum from 1988 saw the first effort to include citizenship as a *required* element in the education of all young people in England and Wales. However, this took the form of introducing Education for Citizenship as one of no fewer than five 'cross-curricular themes' which schools were supposed to include in their curricula alongside the statutory subjects of the National Curriculum (see National Curriculum Council 1990). In the event, the sheer weight of the statutory elements meant that few schools had either the time or energy to pay much attention to citizenship education. Not only that, but many teachers felt that their efforts were in any case hampered by a lack of clarity about the meaning and content of this area of the curriculum. Several pieces of research conducted in the 1990s reinforced this picture of uncertainty, revealing that many teachers were uneasy and unconfident about citizenship education, that citizenship was not a particularly meaningful notion in their lives, and that insofar as they did have a concept of citizenship, it was often apolitical. Arnot, for example, reported that 'English and Welsh student teachers held impoverished notions of political discourse' (1997, p. 288) while Davis *et al.* state that 'among primary teachers there is little evidence of citizenship as directed to the political sphere' (1999, p. 44).

As far as official support for citizenship education was concerned, a decisive change occurred when David Blunkett became Secretary of State for Education in Tony Blair's first administration in 1997. One of Blunkett's first acts was to set up an Advisory Group on Citizenship, chaired by his former politics tutor at Sheffield University, Bernard Crick, a long-time advocate of political education in schools (see Crick and Porter 1978). The Group's remit was to provide 'advice on effective education for citizenship in schools, to include the nature and practices of participation in democracy; the duties, responsibilities and rights of individuals as citizens; and the value to individuals and society of community activity' (Advisory Group on Citizenship 1998, p. 4). Accepting this guidance, the group's Final Report highlighted three key elements of citizenship education: social and moral responsibility, community involvement, and 'political literacy'. The Report was favourably received by ministers and the upshot was that with effect from September 2002, Citizenship became a Foundation Subject of the National Curriculum at key stages 3 and 4, and part of the non-statutory 'framework for PSHE' at key stages 1 and 2. The KS3&4 Programmes of Study, though couched in rather different terms, broadly followed the Crick Report in highlighting the importance of pupils becoming informed and responsible citizens; participation in community activities is also strongly emphasised (QCA and DfEE 1999). Since then, schools have received significant further guidance to help them in the task of developing the new subject (e.g. QCA 2000, QCA 2001).

For all that this was a remarkable change of fortunes for citizenship education, there are good reasons to think that many schools and teachers continue to feel a sense of unease and uncertainty not only about *education* for citizenship but about the meaning and indeed the meaningfulness of citizenship itself. It is worth mentioning two significant reasons why this may be so. One is that, in Britain, there is no strong language of citizenship: a situation which contrasts strongly with the USA and many European countries, where a widespread sense of citizenship identity can be traced back historically to national independence movements and, in some cases, revolutions. Britons, it is sometimes said, have been 'subjects' rather than citizens though this is an oversimplification in that Britain actually has strongly entrenched *rights* of citizenship. But it remains true that people in this country do not, in most situations, think and talk about themselves in terms of a *language* of citizenship.[2] A second important reason why there is uncertainty and reticence about citizenship education among many teachers, is that citizenship is a *contested* concept (Beck 1998, Chapter 5). Different intellectual and political traditions are in fundamental disagreement about what the scope, content, rights and duties of citizenship should be. As a result, citizenship, at least in liberal democracies, is to a greater or lesser degree *controversial*. And this makes citizenship *education* a difficult and delicate task.

WHAT IS CITIZENSHIP?

Oddly enough, some people have seen relatively little problem here. For example, the authors of the House of Commons Commission on Citizenship which reported in 1990 and which gave strong support to the introduction of citizenship education, confidently suggested that it was possible to identify a broadly consensual 'British' approach to citizenship : 'the definition, framework and approach to be found in the work of T. H. Marshall seems to reflect the British approach to citizenship' (Commission on Citizenship 1990, p. 4). The reference here is to Marshall's *Citizenship and Social Class* which revived interest in citizenship, particularly among social scientists (Marshall 1950, see also Marshall and Bottomore 1992). Marshall's ideas were certainly influential, but as we shall see, his approach has proved far from uncontroversial.

T. H. Marshall's conception of citizenship

Marshall told a persuasive story about the nature of citizenship and its historical development. The book is a 'grand narrative' – a story of what Marshall himself regarded as moral and political progress, an account of a long march towards enlightenment. Marshall argued that, at least as it had developed in Britain, citizenship emerged over three successive centuries, each of which saw the growth of a different 'element' of citizenship. Each of these elements involved the extension of different kinds of *rights* to individuals: rights which provided important kinds of *protection* – protections against the exercise of arbitrary or unaccountable power, and against adverse economic and personal circumstances.

The 'civic' element/civic rights

These developed mainly in the eighteenth century. They included a range of legal rights and protections, some of the most important of which were:

- the establishment of the rule of law and the principle of equality before the law so that even the most powerful individuals and institutions (including the State and its rulers) were subject to the rule of law
- freedom of conscience and religious observance ('freedom of speech, thought and faith' as Marshall himself put it)

- freedom to own property, to transmit it to one's heirs, to enter into legally binding contracts

The 'political' element/ political rights

In Britain, political citizenship rights were achieved mainly in the nineteenth century though we do well to remember that many of these rights were not won by *women* until well into the twentieth century. Most important were those democratic rights that enable all adult citizens to have at least some influence over the laws by which they are governed. As Ralph Dahrendorf has put it:

> unless all citizens have an opportunity to feed their interests into the law, the rule of law leaves serious inequalities of entitlement. That is why political rights were necessary to supplement civil rights. (Dahrendorf 1996, p. 38)

The key political rights include:

- freedom of expression and freedom of association (e.g. press freedom, the right to belong to political parties, trade unions, pressure groups, etc.)
- the extension of the franchise (eventually to all adult men and women), i.e. the right to vote in national and local elections
- rights for eligible citizens to participate in the governance of smaller-scale institutions within 'civil society' – e.g. school governing bodies, National Health Service Trusts, as well as a whole range of voluntary associations

Of course, the desirable *extent* of such rights remains contested in many respects: relevant current examples include employees' claims to be represented in the boardroom, or student representation on governing bodies and management committees in higher education.

The 'social' element/social rights

The most novel and most controversial of Marshall's three elements of citizenship was the social element. Marshall wanted to extend the concept of citizenship to include a set of entitlements which would protect individuals from certain risks which are inseparable from the operation of market forces in capitalist economies. The key risk was that of being plunged into poverty as a result of unemployment, ill-health, old age, etc. – i.e. risks associated with being unable to support oneself by one's own labour in a 'free' economy. To put it differently, he was concerned with what he saw as the real 'unfreedoms' which the free play of market forces entailed for some people at key points in their lives. He therefore proposed that rights of citizenship should be extended to include a basic entitlement to *welfare*: 'the right to a modicum of economic welfare and security'. What was novel about Marshall's position was not, of course, the notion of welfare benefits as such, but the claim that access to a certain minimum of such benefits should be a *full right of citizenship*. As Marshall himself unambiguously put it, the social element of citizenship involved 'a universal right to a real income not proportionate to the market value of the claimant' (*ibid.* p. 39). Similarly, he proposed, citizens (or future citizens) should have rights to an appropriate level of 'free' education and health care.

Marshall advanced three key arguments in support of social citizenship. The first was that these minimum social entitlements were a precondition of individuals being able to exercise their other rights of citizenship effectively. Chronic ill health, poverty, a rudimentary level of education, etc., all prevented individuals from functioning as full citizens. Secondly, he argued that there was a need to balance the amoral logic of capitalism and the social inequalities it generated, with the moral or 'normative' logic which he felt was inherent in the development of the citizenship ideal. This normative logic, based upon principles of equality and social justice, pointed to the progressive extension of welfare provision as an entitlement. Citizenship, he said:

> is an urge towards a fuller measure of equality, an enrichment of the stuff of which the status (of citizen) is made, and an increase in the number on whom that status is bestowed. (Marshall 1964, p. 92)

The third reason Marshall advocated social citizenship relates to social cohesion. Citizenship, he argued, could be a 'common possession', a common *status* which conferred dignity on all members of society. Referring to the National Health Service as an example of social citizenship, he argued that 'the common experience offered by a general health service embraces all but a small minority at the top and spreads across the important class barriers in the middle ranks of the [class] hierarchy' (Marshall and Bottomore 1992, p. 34). In this way, social citizenship counter-balanced the socially divisive inequalities of class and the resentments these can cause.

Neo-liberal citizenship's challenge to social citizenship

Marshall's ideas had considerable resonance and plausibility in Britain in the decades following the Second World War. The expansion of 'the welfare state' coincided with a period during which most Western European economies enjoyed thirty years of full employment and growing prosperity. This was linked to the growth of 'consensus politics', meaning that both the main political parties promoted the expansion of the State's role in the provision of education, welfare, social security, etc. In Britain, this period of consensus came to an end in the mid-1970s, when the country's economic weakness was exposed by a period of severe recession triggered by a fourfold increase in the world oil price. This, as well as other more fundamental tensions associated with rising inflation and problems of controlling levels of public spending, helped to promote a process of political reassessment and polarization, in which Conservative thinking shifted markedly to the right, while certain sections of the Labour Party moved leftward. Margaret Thatcher's election victory in 1979 both symbolized and consolidated the victory of these more right-wing doctrines, notably policies aiming to 'roll back' the state, to curtail the power of trade unions and the professions, and to embrace privatization and market forces in the provision of public services, including education and health.

Under these changed conditions, strongly right-wing 'neo-liberal' conceptions of citizenship began to be vigorously promoted. Through the 1980s and into the 1990s, the New Right, especially in the USA and the UK, articulated an increasingly influential critique of welfarism. This claimed that notions of welfare *rights* had engendered a 'dependency culture' which took away the incentive for individuals to seek work and to support themselves and their dependants, that welfarism had weakened self-respect and moral fibre, that it had undermined family values, and that the productive members of society were being unfairly taxed to support the unproductive. The unemployed needed to be compelled to 'price themselves back into jobs' and 'get on their bikes' to seek work. In sum, the claim was that the idea of social *rights* as rights of citizenship was misguided and harmful. What needed emphasizing instead was the *duty* of citizens to be law-abiding, to respect other citizens' liberties and property, and to be self-supporting.

Voluntary effort, civil society, social capital and active citizens

Another approach to citizenship is one which focuses on encouraging *voluntary* activities within 'civil society' i.e. the informal non-State sometimes to replace tasks performed by the State, and sometimes to supplement them. Ideas of this kind have been promoted both by some within the Conservative Party and by New Labour.

One advocate of this approach was the former Conservative Foreign Secretary, Douglas Hurd. Alarmed by what he and many other neo-Conservatives saw as the culture of greed and selfishness of some of the new rich during the Thatcher years, Hurd harked back to an older Conservative tradition in which the values of self-help, thrift, and hard work *were* emphasized, but were *complemented* by individuals feeling an obligation to be involved in voluntary service to the 'community'.

> The Conservative Party is moving forward from its justified concern with the motor of wealth creation towards a redefinition of how the individual citizen, business, or voluntary group can use resources and leisure to help the community. The English tradition of voluntary service is, of course, not new. What *is* new is the rediscovery that schemes based on this tradition are often more flexible and more effective than bureaucratic plans drawn up on the Fabian principle. A social policy founded upon ideals of responsible and active citizenship is compatible with free market economic policies. (Hurd 1988)

More recently, influential New Labour voices have supported similar ideas, though here the problem is often diagnosed in terms of the fashionable concept of 'social capital', popularized by the American writer Robert Putnam (1993). Putnam defined social capital in terms of 'three features of social life – networks, norms and trust – that enable participants to act together more effectively to pursue shared objectives' (Putnam 1996, p. 56). New Labour writers have endorsed Putnam's claim that there has been a worrying decline in civic engagement and community involvement in societies like Britain and the USA, and that this is closely linked to problems of rising crime, family breakdown and 'social exclusion'. One remedy, therefore, is to foster active citizenship and voluntary participation as a key to community regeneration. As Tony Blair put it in 1997:

> Individuals prosper in a strong and active community of citizens. But Britain cannot be a strong community, cannot be one nation, when society is falling apart. Social exclusion is more damaging to self-esteem, more corrosive for society as a whole, more likely to be passed down from generation to generation, than material poverty. (Blair 1997, p. 3)

The wider vision was spelled out in a later speech:

> We can only realise ourselves as individuals in a thriving civil society, comprising families and civic institutions buttressed by intelligent government 'Enabling' government strengthens civil society and helps families and communities improve their own performance. This is the Third Way – a modernised social democracy for a changing world which will build its prosperity on human and social capital.
> (Blair 1998, pp. 3, 14, 20 quoted in Gamarnikow and Green 2000, p. 96)

Critics of these neo-Conservative and New Labour visions of 'active citizenship', however, point out that they run the risk (or have the intention) of diminishing welfare *entitlements* as rights of citizenship. The poorer sections of society are increasingly pressurized to act to improve their *own* situations, to take responsibility for regenerating their own run-down communities, etc. Meanwhile, the better off can salve their consciences by engaging in somewhat tokenistic efforts to 'put something back into society' while remaining resistant to the tax increases which would be necessary to pay for better funded public services available as of right to all citizens.

ACTIVE CITIZENSHIP, CITIZENSHIP EDUCATION AND POLITICAL IMPARTIALITY

In view of such criticisms, it is worth distinguishing here between two different interpretations of the idea of 'active citizenship'. One is as sketched out above and is located within a specific political stance supportive of what might crudely be called 'late capitalism with a social conscience'. Another, and importantly different, interpretation of 'active citizenship', is located within the tradition of 'civic republicanism'. This seeks to promote more active involvement by ordinary citizens in the political process. In this case, there is *no* specific political or ideological agenda. The aim is to encourage active engagement in political life and in democratic processes because these things are held to be worthwhile in themselves, as well as being collectively beneficial. Two people with strongly opposed political beliefs could both be active citizens in this second sense – but not in the first.

Clearly, both these kinds of active citizenship stress individual involvement and participation. Yet it is just because there *is* this overlap that some have seen a problem for citizenship *education*. There is a risk that the two kinds of active citizenship could become entangled in such a way that schools might end up inadvertently promoting a specific political stance. The Crick Report itself has been criticized on these grounds. For example, paragraph 2.5 begins, relatively uncontroversially:

> We firmly believe that volunteering and community involvement are necessary conditions of civil society and democracy. Preparation for these, at the very least, should be an explicit part of education

However, it continues by appearing to directly endorse current government policy:

> This is especially important at a time when government is attempting a shift of emphasis between, on the one hand, state welfare provision and responsibility, and, on the other, community and individual responsibility. (Advisory Group on Citizenship 1998, p. 10)

Sociologists Gamarnikow and Green contend that the effect of such statements could be that:

> Marshall's social citizenship as a site for welfare *rights* disappears, and its place is now occupied by duties of volunteering and community development. The Crick Report constructs the Third Way citizen whose individual and civic responsibility enables the Third Way state to provide opportunities rather than services (2000, p. 106).

Even if this judgement is somewhat unfair to the Crick himself and the Report as a whole,[3] it illustrates very clearly how difficult it may prove to develop forms of citizenship education which are genuinely politically impartial. Community involvement and community service can so easily be seen as politically innocent – and very often they are. But a basically apolitical approach to citizenship education, or an approach which merely emphasizes information (in the style of old-fashioned 'civics'), arguably runs the risk of implicitly endorsing just those kinds of political agendas which deceptively claim to have transcended ideology or to have gone 'beyond left and right' (Fukuyama 1992, Giddens 1994).[4]

Moreover, issues that are *politically* controversial are not the only areas of controversy which impinge on citizenship education. In the final section, we examine the wider issue of value diversity in pluralistic societies.

CITIZENSHIP AND VALUE DIVERSITY IN PLURALISTIC SOCIETIES

The issue of value diversity in modern societies and the problems such diversity may pose for social cohesion have recently become another key focus of debate among writers (and politicians) interested in citizenship.

Most modern liberal democracies are highly *pluralistic* and for a number of reasons:

- the legacy of colonialism and/or the effects of mass migration have brought about increased ethnic diversity and the greater cultural diversity that goes with it; this often includes the co-existence of several different religious faith communities within a single society
- in some societies, which were settled by Europeans and subsequently became independent nations, there are communities of indigenous peoples
- the effects of globalization, in both its economic and cultural aspects, are deeply invasive of localised and traditional ways of life: to an unprecedented extent, people across the world have no alternative but to become aware of alternative ways of life, alternative values, alternative beliefs (see Beck 1998, chapter 2, Giddens 1990).

All these developments create a situation in which not only individuals but communities – sometimes with very different outlooks and values – must co-exist within the framework of a single polity and society.

What is more, these developments do not exhaust the sources of value diversity. No less significant has been the steady advance in modern societies of those rationalistic and scientific forms of knowledge and understanding of ourselves and of the world, which are sometimes, rather misleadingly, described as 'Western'. It is this kind of *knowledge* which is one of the key sources of the 'openness' which modern democratic societies exhibit. An 'open' society is, perhaps, above all else, one that permits (and even encourages) wide-ranging rational interrogation of claims to the possession of truth, however authoritative the source of such 'truths' may claim to be. Such sceptical, critical reason is, of course, profoundly corrosive of what Descartes called 'custom and example'. It undermines established 'certainties', dethrones religious and other dogmas, and encourages ordinary people as well as philosophers and scientists to ask 'why?' In Ernest Gellner's words:

> there are no privileged knowers, no organisation is allowed to claim cognitive monopoly, there are no privileged events or objects. Logical cogency and evidence are king. (Gellner 1992, p. 146)

Much recent debate in liberal political theory has focused upon the question of how social integration and stability can be maintained in the face of such increasing diversity, as well as the increased *consciousness* of diversity that is such a feature of modern life. Ironically, liberal politics is itself part of the *problem* here. The Western tradition of citizenship is built around discourses of *rights* – most significantly rights protecting the freedoms of individuals and groups from unwarranted interference by others – whether from more powerful fellow citizens, dominant social groups, or the state itself. Historically, freedom of *religious* belief was a key issue around which struggles to achieve such protection were fought out. The point of these struggles was precisely to establish protected freedom of conscience as well as the right to worship as individual conscience dictated. In the Reformation, for example, what was being fought for was the *right* to be a 'dissenter' or 'Protestant' in relation to the previously prevailing conceptions of truth upheld by the Catholic church. The eventual victory of dissenters in these respects was an early and key step in the protection of pluralism even if such dissenting groups were often themselves deeply intolerant of deviation among their own members!

A fundamental problem for liberal politics and liberal conceptions of citizenship, therefore, is this: how far and in what ways is a liberal democratic state *justified* in infringing the freedoms of individuals and groups whose beliefs and values may differ from one another? Perhaps the first point to notice here is that 'democracy' *per se* does not provide anything like a complete answer. Superficially, it might seem that once a democratic system of government has been established, then decisions taken by the elected political representatives of the majority are *ipso facto* legitimate, and that is the end of the matter. But a moment's reflection reveals a basic problem with this simplistic view. This is that it can result in quite unacceptable forms of 'majoritarianism' – the tyranny of the majority over minorities. (This has, of course, been a potent cause of chronic social division between majorities and minorities in areas such as Northern Ireland and the former Yugoslavia, to mention only two topical and tragic instances.) Majoritarianism of such kinds is clearly incompatible with certain fundamental principles of protective liberal citizenship notably the recognition of the rights of individuals to be self-determining so long as their actions are not demonstrably harmful to others. A genuinely liberal interpretation of democracy, therefore, must have built into it principles and mechanisms to protect the autonomy, interests and ways of life of legitimate minorities.

But recognizing this still leaves a great deal of room for reasoned debate about the extent to which, and the respects in which, it is justifiable for governments in liberal democracies to interfere in and restrict the freedoms of their citizens. There is little argument that in most circumstances the state is entitled to prohibit and 'police' actions that are demonstrably injurious to others and/or to society as a whole. Prohibition of murder, rape, domestic violence against women or children, drunk-driving, burglary, etc. are all obvious examples. But a feature of liberal pluralism is that individuals and groups are attached to significantly different conceptions of the good life. And their attachment to these different 'comprehensive theories of the good' as the philosopher John Rawls calls them (Rawls 1993), can result in deep differences of belief about, say, the acceptability of homosexuality or of abortion, about when it is legitimate to engage in warfare, or whether within certain communities it is legitimate to limit women's liberties if women themselves in these communities accept such restrictions, etc.

Once such differences are recognized, a further set of problems arises relating to the question of how such liberal societies should *educate* their future citizens. For example, should parents, by virtue of *being* parents, be free to bring up their children in conformity with their own beliefs and values and to insulate them as far as possible from competing viewpoints? Or, alternatively, is the state justified in intervening so as to try to ensure that the education of all young people introduces a wide-ranging examination of *competing* arguments and evidence about matters which are, in the society as a whole, controversial? An underlying question here concerns the extent to which a liberal society has a duty to promote ethical autonomy as well as political autonomy in young people. (Democratic liberal institutions, after all, *presuppose* an ideal of political autonomy: reasoned public deliberation about complex and controversial issues is the very stuff of political argument and decision-making in a democracy.) These questions are also related to the scope of the sphere of '*public values*' in relation to '*non-public*' values, an issue which is discussed in more detail in Chapter 13.[5]

CONCLUSION

In a brief introductory chapter such as this, it is not possible to discuss the different positions within these debates in any detail. What may be worthwhile, in conclusion, is to highlight just how diverse are the responses that now exist to the shared recognition of the fact of pluralism in modern societies. Three such 'responses' will be very briefly outlined.

1. Liberal theorists of protective citizenship

Writers of this persuasion tend to support, albeit with significant modifications, John Rawls's idea that the stability of liberal polities in the face of extensive value pluralism is most likely to be sustained by serious efforts on the part of all citizens of goodwill to reason together to construct an 'overlapping consensus' on common public values. Citizens are called upon to seek the common ground between the otherwise very diverse comprehensive theories of the good life to which they are attached. This area of overlap is the sphere of 'public values' which all reasonable citizens are seen as having a duty to support. The values in question constitute a kind of minimum basis for the reproduction of a stable liberal polity: they centre on the ideals of justice, of free and equal citizenship, of mutual respect and the rights and duties derived from these ideals. The overlapping consensus builds support for and thus protects liberal politics itself, as well as the legitimate liberties of citizens. Followers of Rawls disagree with one another about many matters. Perhaps the most significant area of disagreement continues to be the extent to which, and the grounds upon which, the liberal state is justified in restricting the liberties of individual citizens.

2. Communitarian theorists

Most communitarian theorists distrust the strong emphasis which liberalism accords to the *individual* and to the supposed rights of individuals. As Charles Taylor has summarized the situation, there is a continuum of positions here which 'at one end give primacy to individual rights and freedom, and at the other give higher priority to community life and the good of collectivities' (Taylor 1989, pp. 159–60). Politically, communitarians may be inclined to the left or to the right, but all of them tend to think that liberal theories promote an 'excess' of individualism which renders collective life precarious and danger-ously weakens people's attachment to the society of which they are part. Communitarians tend to stress the *particularity* of given societies, their shared culture and history, and the need of individuals for a strong and specific cultural grounding of their sense of identity. For these reasons, most communitarians tend to regard the Rawlsian 'overlapping consensus' as something altogether too 'thin' and artificial to command allegiance and commitment, or to function as a viable basis of social solidarity (or even integration). Consequently, most communitarians would support forms of citizenship *education* which, in David Hogan's words, would 'focus not so much on the protection of individual interests as on social integration and the common good' (Hogan 1997, p. 50). Critics of communitarian positions, however, suggest that communitarians are nostalgic for a pre-modern world of culturally homogeneous societies, that they have not developed an adequate response to legitimate cultural diversity within any one society, and that their proposals to educate for stronger 'community' values risk becoming indoctrinatory.

3. Postmodernism and citizenship

Postmodernism is even harder to characterize succinctly than liberalism or communitarianism. Perhaps the most important tenet of postmodern thinking is the subversive idea of 'deconstruction'. This includes the claim that 'grand narratives' of ordered progression towards a better future (like Marshall's account of the development of citizenship) are to be radically distrusted. Another candidate for radical deconstruction is the 'integrated self' – i.e. the idea that our 'selves' have an ordered coherence and stability, and that we are the authors of our own actions. Postmodernism instead stresses incoherence, discontinuity and the contradictions that fragment supposedly unitary, cohesive and purposeful wholes. Postmodernism's responses to pluralism are various. One is a tendency to *celebrate* cultural and value diversity, to welcome 'polyculturalism' – not least *because* of the unpredictability of its consequences. Another element of the response is a radical *cultural relativism* which validates the great diversity of previously suppressed cultural 'voices' silenced by various kinds of oppression – the voices of the dispossessed, of women, of indigenous peoples, etc. As far as citizenship is concerned, postmodernists suggest that the preoccupation of most citizenship discourse with the nation state is anachronistic and that it is perceived, especially by the young, as increasingly irrelevant. Postmodernists point instead to the vitality of *other* kinds of politics as constituting new spheres of action which have greater appeal and relevance. These include the 'new social movements' around issues like the environment, transnational concerns with 'human rights', concern about the global power and predatory activities of multi-national corporations, etc. Critics of postmodernism, however, highlight what they see as its *own* incoherence: for example its simultaneous celebration of consumerist lifestyles and cultural globalization alongside its enthusiasm for environmentalism. An even deeper source of incoherence, they suggest, lies in the apparent insouciance of some postmodernists about criteria of *truth*. If all 'voices' speak truly because they speak from authentic experience, then when they disagree, are there *any* objective grounds for testing the validity of competing claims? Postmodernism may have its finger on the pulse of many contemporary developments that are radically changing our lives, but it may also be too loose and incoherent an intellectual framework to offer really satisfactory answers.

NOTES

1. Despite this neglect of explicit civic education within the formally prescribed curriculum, British schools *have*, nevertheless, been potent agents of political socialization through both the taught and the hidden curriculum. The hierarchical character of the education system, long organized on lines of explicit social class divisions (see Chapter 1), played a key role in perpetuating both deference and class antagonism in British political culture. Also, for many decades, the teaching of subjects like history and geography was imbued with strong assumptions about the national and racial superiority of the British, particularly in relation to 'the peoples of the commonwealth and Empire'. As John Ahier has shown in his study of school textbooks:

    > regional geography both established a national confidence and at the same time, a set of assumptions about other races. It located 'them' firmly in their climates and in lands which inhibited their growth towards civilisation ….
    > In the so-called 'hot lands' of the Caribbean and Africa, life was thought to be too easy, there being no necessity to work hard and save …
    >
    > In the books, there is a clear implication of a natural hierarchy by which the British are given their place in the world. It is a place that demands hard work and delayed gratification but it offers superiority. (Ahier 1988, pp. 163–4)

2. A fuller discussion of these matters can be found in Ahier, Beck and Moore 2003, especially chapter 1.

3. Crick has himself stated that the report as a whole is centrally located within the civic republican tradition:

> there is a philosophy behind the Report, of course: what scholars used to call civic republicanism, and pluralism. (Crick and Green 2002, p. 120)

Crick's own commitment to 'political literacy', i.e. educating future citizens to be not merely politically informed but equipped to make up their own minds about controversial issues, is consistent and central throughout his writings on political education. His commitment to active citizenship in the civic republican sense is equally evident. However, public documents like the Crick Report are the products of committees – and as such they almost always involve compromise among the members as well as reflecting external political influences.

4. Crick explained his own thinking about the relationship between a civic republican approach to active citizenship and 'volunteering', in a debate with Damian Green, Conservative shadow Secretary of State for Education:

> I am an Aristotelian. I believe, with him, that preparation for political life in its broadest sense is part of education, and that freedom depends on widespread participation, not just good leadership. Some politicians are fond of praising volunteering among the young. But not all volunteering involves active citizenship. Some volunteers are just cannon fodder, and are never given the chance to influence the activity. (Crick and Green 2002, p. 18)

5. These issues are examined at length in Callan (1997). A fuller discussion of 'public' and 'non-public' values in relation to citizenship is contained in McLaughlin (1992).

Chapter 16

Sex and Relationships Education

MICHAEL J. REISS

BACKGROUND

The teaching of sex education in schools raises a number of contentious issues. For one thing, whether sex education should even be taught in schools is questioned by some. Then, the precise aims of sex education vary greatly. Other issues include the age at which school sex education should start, the teaching approaches to be used, the framework(s) of values within which it should take place, whether or not parents have the right to withdraw their children from school sex education, whether classes should (sometimes) be single sex, who should teach it, the training which teachers of sex education should receive, and where within the school curriculum it should be taught. In addition, there are conceptual difficulties in deciding how best to evaluate sex education. This chapter cannot deal with all these issues but focuses on questions of especial importance for those training to be school teachers or early in their teaching careers.

SHOULD SEX EDUCATION TAKE PLACE IN SCHOOLS?

UK surveys consistently show that the majority of parents and pupils want sex education to be provided in schools (Stone and Ingham 1998). Those who believe that it should not take place in schools generally hold that sex education is the responsibility of parents, and that schools have neither the right nor the competence to teach about it. In particular, those who argue that schools should not teach sex education are frequently unhappy about what they perceive as the amoral, or even immoral, framework adopted by many schools when they do teach sex education.

However, it can be argued that all schools inevitably engage in sex education, simply by their being a community of sexual people each with attitudes and behaviours shaped by their own personal history, by the ethos and composition of the school in which they find themselves and, more generally, by the collective values of the societies in which they grew up and presently exist. What is at debate, if this point of view is accepted, is not whether school sex education should occur, but what sort of sex education should take place.

THE HISTORY OF THE AIMS OF SEX EDUCATION IN THE UK

The history of sex education remains under-researched (Reiss 1998). We know little of school sex education in the UK before the outbreak of the Second World War in 1939, though some work has been done on the oral accounts of adults looking back to their school days as pupils (Humphries 1988). It seems likely that many pupils before the Second World War received little formal school sex education. What there was was probably largely aimed at the prevention of illegitimacy, and sex education at this time seems mainly to have been targeted at girls.

The Second World War had, of course, huge consequences for the lives of most of the population of Europe and a considerable number of countries beyond. It is often the case that the mass movement of people, particularly soldiers, results in an increase in the incidence of sexually transmitted infections. As one might expect, then, the outbreak of the war seems to have resulted in a shift in the main aim of sex education towards the prevention of syphilis and gonorrhoea.

Anecdotal accounts of innumerable lessons on the reproductive systems of rabbits or the pollination habits of flowering plants suggest that much school sex education in the 1950s and 1960s (as must often also have been the case for up to a hundred years previously) was largely carried out vicariously through the descriptions, though not the observations, of the reproductive habits of plants and non-human animals. It seems likely that boys, especially if educated in the public school (i.e. private education) boarding system, may also have received warnings about the dangers believed to follow from masturbation.

By the start of the 1970s, school sex education was beginning to change significantly (Went 1995). Biology textbooks started to provide fuller accounts of the human reproductive systems while methods of contraception began to be taught more widely. The emphasis was mostly on the provision of accurate information, and aims of sex education programmes included a decrease in ignorance, guilt, embarrassment and anxiety. Issues to do with relationships were probably more often discussed in programmes of personal and social education or their equivalents rather than in biology lessons.

The 1980s continued to see an increase in the aims of sex education. The growing acceptance of feminist thinking led to an increase in the number of programmes that encouraged pupils to examine the roles played by women and men in society. The aim was typically for students to realize the existence and extent of sexual inequality. Feminist critiques of sex education programmes pointed out how such programmes may simply reinforce gender inequalities (e.g. Wolpe 1987). It began more widely to be appreciated just how gendered was the discourse of sex education, which typically served to perpetuate the belief that male self-control, though possible, could not be relied on and that women by their behaviours should help men to act responsibly (Thomson 1994).

At the same time, sex education programmes increasingly began to have such aims as 'the acquisition of skills for decision-making, communicating, personal relationships, parenting and coping strategies' (Surrey County Council 1987, p. 3). Similar statements are evident in many publications of that time.

As the importance of skills became stressed, so sex education programmes increasingly talked about enabling young people to think for themselves and make their own informed decisions about issues that concerned their sexuality. It was this sort of language that so alarmed many on account of what was perceived as the increasing liberalization of school sex education.

The post-Second World War advent of antibiotics meant that for several decades a fear of sexually transmitted infections played only a minor role in the thinking behind most school sex education programmes. This situation changed suddenly in the late 1980s when it was realized that a new sexually transmitted agent – human immunodeficiency virus (HIV) – was rapidly spreading in many countries of the world. Near panic set in in some quarters as it became appreciated that many, perhaps most, people infected with HIV would go on to develop AIDS and subsequently die, that a person could be infected with HIV, and thus infectious, for many years without realizing it or having any symptoms of infection, and that there was no treatment either for HIV infection or for AIDS itself.

HIV and AIDS became a health issue in the UK at just the time that sex education became a political football. A number of circumstances, including the controversy over the 1985 Gillick case – which focused on whether parents always have the right to know if their children are being issued with contraceptives when under the age of 16 – and the growing strength of the lesbian and gay movement, led to a polarization of views on sex education among politicians at local and national level. A flurry of legislation and government education circulars, which continues to this day, resulted and it increasingly became acknowledged that a values-less sex education programme cannot exist.

Recent school sex education programmes have varied considerably in their aims (Reiss 1993). At one extreme (rarely found in the UK but well-funded and widespread in the USA), abstinence education aims to ensure that young people do not engage in heavy petting or sexual intercourse before marriage. At the other end of the spectrum, some sex education programmes challenge sexist and homophobic attitudes, try to help young people make their own decisions about their sexual behaviour, and discuss issues of sexual pleasure. Although a plurality of aims in almost any branch of education may be healthy, too great a range of possible aims can confuse both teachers and learners, and in this case is perhaps indicative partly of a lack of clarity about the precise functions of sex education and partly of the great range of firmly held views about the subject.

WHERE IN THE CURRICULUM SHOULD SCHOOL SEX EDUCATION BE TAUGHT AND HOW?

Most sex educators agree that the best provision for sex education occurs when schools teach it across the curriculum, in a number of traditional subjects (including science, English, religious studies, history and geography), in PSE, PSHE or PSHCE (personal, social, health and citizenship education) lessons and in tutor groups or form periods. Accordingly, all teachers in a school have a role to play in sex education.

Materials used in schools vary greatly in terms of how they treat human sexuality. Some are sensitively written, comprehensive and helpful. Others, though, are sexist, fail to tackle personal issues to do with menstruation, ignore lesbian and gay issues and either omit or fail adequately to deal with cultural issues. If you do use published materials to help you teach sex education in a secondary school, the most useful approach is probably to ensure that as well as picking and choosing carefully from them, you get your pupils to critique the materials by discussing among themselves and with you such questions as:

- What useful things do these materials contain?
- What angle do the authors seem to be taking? (e.g. 'Don't engage in sexual intercourse until you are ready for it' or 'There is more to sex than sexual intercourse'.)
- Are there any ways the material could be better? Are there other things which it would have been good for the authors to have included?

Published materials can be useful but they shouldn't dominate teaching about sex education. One of the great things about school lessons, when they go well, is that they provide an opportunity for pupils to discuss and reflect on important issues more deeply than they often can outside of school. If you find it difficult to get discussions going, try bringing into school a ten-minute (no longer!) video extract from almost any soap opera and get pupils to discuss various sex-related topics that crop up.

If you are comfortable with role plays these can work wonderfully well, especially if pupils are encouraged to play roles different from those that they normally occupy. For instance, pupils (both boys and girls) could role play being young mothers. Often some of the most important learning takes place when pupils are given the chance to talk subsequently about what it felt like to be in role.

A final technique which works well is to get pupils to write anonymous questions which they put into a box at the end of a lesson. This gives you time to think about which ones you want to deal with next lesson and, if needs be, to find someone who can help you answer some of them.

The golden rule for any beginning teacher when teaching sex education is to discuss it with an appropriate established member of staff (e.g. Head of Department or Head of Year) first. Team teaching may be a possibility if you think that would be helpful. For more extensive guidance about the practicalities of teaching sex education see Massey (1991), Ray and Went (1995), Harrison (2000) and Ofsted (2002).

STATUTORY ISSUES SURROUNDING SEX EDUCATION IN UK SCHOOLS

There is, though, much more to successful sex education teaching than following the suggestions in the previous section. You should know about the statutory issues surrounding sex education (this section) and have thought about a values framework for your teaching (next section).

Unfortunately the recent history about the legislation concerning sex education in the UK means that there has been considerable confusion among teachers about what is or is not permitted. A classic instance of this arose in relation to The Local Government Act (50/1) 1988, Section 28 of which states that:

> A local authority shall not – (a) intentionally promote homosexuality or publish material with the intention of promoting homosexuality; (b) promote the teaching in any maintained school of the acceptability of homosexuality as a pretended family relationship by the publication of such material or otherwise.

Many teachers became concerned that they might fall foul of the law simply by referring to issues of sexual orientation; other teachers reacted with fury both at the perceived injustice and prejudice and at the crude assumptions implicit in phraseologies about 'a pretended family relationship'; a minority of teachers welcomed the Circular. However, it then transpired that this part of the Local Government Act (generally referred to as 'Section 28') did not apply to schools as Section 18 of the Education Act (No. 2) 1986 – which gave school governors responsibility for decisions on sex education in schools – took precedence. Despite several attempts to repeal Section 28 it remains, at the time of writing (November 2002) on the statute books.

In England and Wales, the changes to the National Curriculum that were introduced into schools from September 2000 included a shift in language from 'sex education' to 'sex and relationship' education. At Key Stage 3 (for 11 to 14 year-olds), for example, the framework for personal, social and health education stipulates:

Developing Good Relationships and Respecting the Differences between People

3 Pupils should be taught
   a about the effects of all types of stereotyping, prejudice, bullying, racism and discrimination and how to challenge them assertively
   b how to empathise with people different from themselves

c   about the nature of friendship and how to make and keep friends

d   to recognise some of the cultural norms in society, including the range of lifestyles and relationships

e   the changing nature of, and pressure on, relationships with friends and family, and when and how to seek help

f   about the role and importance of marriage in family relationships

g   about the role and feelings of parents and carers and the value of family life

h   to recognise that goodwill is essential to positive and constructive relationships

i   to negotiate within relationships, recognising that actions have consequences, and when and how to make compromises

j   to resist pressure to do wrong, to recognise when others need help and how to support them

k   to communicate confidently with their peers and adults

(Qualifications and Curriculum Authority 1999, p. 190)

The move from sex education to sex and relationship education came about, according to the Department for Education and Employment, partly because of criticisms by young people of 'the lack of any meaningful discussion about feelings, relationships and values' (Department for Education and Employment 2000a, p. 11). It was noteworthy that the paragraph in the draft consultation from the Department for Education and Employment on relationships came in for a huge amount of comment and feedback:

Relationships

1.21. Young people, when asked about their experiences of sex education at school, often complain about the focus on the physical aspects of reproduction and the lack of any meaningful discussion about feelings, relationships and values. Sex and relationship education set within the framework for PSHE across the four key stages will significantly redress that balance. It will help young people to respect themselves and others, and understand difference. Within the context of talking about relationships children should be taught about the nature of marriage and its importance for family life and for the bringing up children. The Government recognises that there are strong and mutually supportive relationships outside marriage. Therefore, children should learn the significance of marriage and stable relationships as key building blocks of community and society. Teaching in this area needs to be sensitive so as not to stigmatise children on the basis of their home circumstances.

(Department for Education and Employment 2000b, p. 8)

Conservative commentators felt strongly that this down-graded marriage; liberal commentators felt equally strongly that to put any greater stress on marriage would be unacceptable. In the event, the only changes that were made in the published version were to improve punctuation and grammar (see Department for Education and Employment 2000a, p. 11). Although there are certain contemporary societies where marriage is almost universally regarded as the norm (e.g. Islamic societies and, to a certain extent, secular Japan), in most societies this is no longer the case. Research among young people in the UK shows a very wide range of views about marriage (Sharpe 2001).

A VALUES FRAMEWORK FOR SEX EDUCATION

It is difficult to produce a single classification or typology which manages validly to map the various positions that exist with respect to what should be the values or moral framework for sex education. Two widely used, and useful, classifications are the conservative/liberal one and the religious/secular one (see Halstead and Reiss 2003 for a much fuller discussion of values in sex education).

The conservative position can be characterized by its belief that what is best can generally be discovered by learning from history. It maintains that traditional values have much in them that is of value, and that if changes are to be made, they should be made slowly and with a high degree of consensus. Further, the conservative position suspects that too high a value can be placed on autonomy, suspecting that one person's autonomy can lead to costly mistakes and much suffering.

The liberal position stands in opposition to the conservative one. A liberal is scornful of too great a respect for tradition, holding that a perpetuation of yesterday's values may serve merely to maintain inequalities of power and knowledge. With particular regard to school sex education, a liberal is likely to press for a greater emphasis on individual rights and for more open discussion on such issues as contraception, sexual orientation and the roles of men and women.

The secular position (which can be either conservative or liberal) holds that religious values are of little relevance in modern societies. The way forward comes from rational debate unencumbered by religious views which are frequently old-fashioned and unintelligible to most people. An atheist involved in sex education may react with exasperation to theological arguments which are likely to be perceived as being of, at most, marginal relevance for the great majority of people. For example, Roman Catholic agonizings over natural theology and the acceptability of contraception may be considered bizarre and irrelevant.

The religious position (which is often conservative but can be liberal) also holds that rational debate is essential but is less confident about the power of human reason. It maintains that there are other sources of wisdom and knowledge including those revealed in the scriptures and those discerned by communities of believers and their leaders down the years.

Until recently, little was written on school sex education in the UK from a religious point of view and what there was was largely generated within a mindframe and for an audience which presumed the validity of the religious position. In recent years, though, there has been an increasing acknowledgement from all sex educators, whether or not they themselves are members of any particular religious faith, that religious points of view need to be taken into account, if only because a significant number of children and their parents have moral values at least partly informed by religious traditions (Thomson 1993; Reiss and Mabud 1998; Blake and Katrak 2002). Further, it has been argued that religion is increasingly becoming a means through which identities are articulated on the public stage.

TEACHING ABOUT SEXUAL ORIENTATION

Finally, I would like to examine one of the more controversial aspects of teaching about sex education, namely whether schools should provide teaching about sexual orientation.

There are a number of reasons that can be put forward in favour of schools teaching explicitly about homosexuality as well as about heterosexuality. First is the argument that the absence of such teaching is deeply hurtful to homosexuals. Adult gays and lesbians, when asked, often tell of the pain that they felt by their apparent non-existence at school – in the structured silence that surrounded their sexual identity. Often, even explicit teacher-controlled discussions on sexuality omit any reference to gay and lesbian orientation and behaviour. There is also evidence that lesbian and gay teenagers are more likely both to attempt and to commit suicide than their heterosexual counterparts (Khayatt 1994; Bagley and Tremblay 1997), even though lesbian and gay adults probably score at least as well as their heterosexual counterparts on psychological measures of self-esteem (Ruse 1988). It has been suggested that sex education that explicitly addresses issues of sexual orientation may help to reduce the incidence of teenage suicide.

It is difficult to be certain, but a conservative estimate would suggest that at least 4 per cent of adult males and 2 per cent of adult females are exclusively or predominantly homosexual (Johnson *et al.* 2001). In other words, while homosexuals are undeniably a minority, they are a sizeable one – comparable, in the UK, to the number of Muslims or Roman Catholics. As such they deserve the attention and curriculum space when teaching sex education that should be accorded to religious minorities when teaching religious education.

A second argument in favour of teaching about homosexuality is that even if the percentage of people who are exclusively or predominantly homosexual is not large, several times this number have at least some homosexual tendencies and this may be especially true of teenagers.

A third argument is that all of us, whether or not we are homosexual, need to know about homosexuality in order, as citizens, to understand and be able to make an informed contribution to such questions as 'Should homosexuals be permitted in the Armed Forces?', 'Should the age of consent be the same for homosexuals and heterosexuals?' and 'Should marriage be an option for homosexuals?'

A fourth argument is that such teaching may help to prevent homophobia and reduce the incidence of physical violence experienced by gays and lesbians. A 1994 survey of over 4,200 lesbians, bisexuals and gay men from all over the UK found that 34 per cent of men and 24 per cent of women who took part had experienced violence in the last five years on account of their sexuality (Mason and Palmer 1996). Teenagers were especially at risk: 48 per cent of respondents under the age of 18 had experienced violence, 61 per cent had been harassed and 90 per cent called names because of their sexuality. While one cannot extrapolate quantitatively from the results of such a survey (over 50,000 copies of the survey were distributed via *Gay Times* and other lesbian and gay publications and databases with only 8 per cent being returned), the detailed personal accounts make harrowing reading. Bullying of any sort, including homophobic bullying, is unacceptable, particularly in schools and teachers need to take steps to prevent it:

> in too many secondary schools homophobic attitudes among pupils often go unchallenged. The problem is compounded when derogatory terms about homosexuality are used in everyday language in school and their use passes unchallenged by staff. Where problems arise, staff have often had insufficient guidance on the interpretation of school values and what constitutes unacceptable language or behaviour. (Ofsted 2002, p. 10)

On the other hand, there are arguments against teaching about homosexuality. One is the belief that such teaching cannot be balanced. Just as peace studies and environmental education promote peace and the sustainable use of the environment, so, it is believed, teaching about homosexuality is likely to lead to its advocacy.

A related fear is that teaching about homosexuality, unless simply to condemn it, results in its implicit legitimization. We do not teach at school in an even-handed way about slavery, murder or child abuse. Indeed to teach about such issues in a 'balanced' way would be wrong, precisely because we hold such behaviours to lie outside the moral pale. Similarly, it can be argued, we should not even help students to consider the arguments in favour of homosexuality.

Further objections are that a significant number of parents do not want their children to be taught about homosexuality, even though other aspects of sex education are widely supported (Stone and Ingham 1998) and that many teachers feel uncomfortable teaching about homosexuality.

A different objection is that teaching in this area might even increase homophobia and prejudice. Halstead (1992) argues that three types of controversial issue can be distinguished: (a) situations where there is agreement over the existence of a particular moral imperative, but disagreement over how to interpret it; (b) situations where there are conflicting moral imperatives and uncertainty over which should take priority; (c) situations where disagreement arises because groups do not share the same fundamental moral principles. Now it isn't always easy to place any particular instance of controversiality into one of these three categories, but it is clear that the issue of homosexuality falls, at least for some people, into type (c). The significance of this is that discussion about type (c) controversies are especially likely to inflame the situation rather than inform the participants. Such discussions may be counterproductive.

While these objections to teaching about homosexuality should not be dismissed, I doubt that they are sufficient, always, to outweigh the arguments in favour of teaching about homosexuality. However, to be acceptable, teaching about homosexuality should (i) be balanced; (ii) be undertaken only by suitably trained teachers who wish to teach about it; and (iii) be part, where possible, of the explicit curriculum so that parents do not suddenly find that such teaching has been foisted on their children without their being aware of it. In addition, (iv), it should perhaps continue to be the case, as it currently is in England and Wales, that parents have the right to withdraw their children from school sex education; and (v), teaching in this area should be evaluated, particularly in terms of its acceptability to those receiving it. If a sex education programme of any sort proves highly divisive or unacceptable to a significant number, it needs amending.

For further discussion about the teaching of sexual orientation in schools see Reiss (1997), Halstead and Lewicka (1998), Beck (1999) and Halstead and Reiss (2003).

CONCLUSION

The above account may give too much of an impression of the problems that teaching sex education poses. This would be a pity. Most sex education in UK secondary schools still isn't very good though surveys suggest that pupils often find it of more value that one might suspect. Yet good sex education can be extremely valuable. You can provide pupils with accurate information that some of them would otherwise not receive and you can provide a safe framework in which pupils can develop their own views and learn from one another. Finally, don't worry if you feel embarrassed – you will probably find it a lot easier once you have taught the same topic within sex education a couple of times and, anyway, modesty is a perfectly appropriate virtue. And decline politely but firmly to answer any personal questions about your own sexual history!

Chapter 17

Drug Education

RUTH JOYCE

THE NATIONAL DRUG STRATEGY AND THE ROLE OF THE EDUCATION SERVICE

Drug use and misuse is part of the history of our civilization. It is a worldwide phenomenon and in the United Kingdom we live in a society where there is widespread use of illegal and legal drugs, both medically and socially. The same drug can kill or cure, depending on how it is used, who uses it and how much is used: alcohol, paracetamol, Temazepam and even amphetamines come into this category.

However, even with this long-term perspective in mind, recent studies indicate that there are significant changing patterns of behaviour around drug misuse, especially among young people. In particular:

- drug misuse is most common among people in their teens and early twenties, but the average age of first drug use is becoming younger
- almost half of young people are likely to take drugs at some time in their lives, but only about one fifth become regular users (i.e. at least once a month), with a tiny minority of that group taking drugs on a daily basis
- most young people who use drugs do so out of curiosity, boredom or peer pressure and continue using drugs through a combination of factors ranging from enjoyment to physical and psychological dependency
- cannabis is easily the most commonly used drug among the young, followed by amphetamines, poppers, LSD and ecstasy; while there are some identifiable groups such as cannabis users, dance drug users and addicts, the trend is towards more indiscriminate use, based on price and availability
- there is a very strong correlation between the use of illegal drugs and the use of volatile substances – tobacco and alcohol – among young people
- there is increasingly strong evidence that the earlier a young person starts taking the drugs, the greater the chance that he or she will develop serious drug problems over time

- from early to mid teens, there are strong links between drug problems, exclusion or truancy from school, break-up of the family and initiation into criminal activity
- for older teenagers and people in their twenties, there are strong links between drug problems and unemployment, homelessness, prostitution and other features of social exclusion
- whatever other influences affect young people, the role of parents throughout the process is vital

All this means that communities, including their schools, have a key role in addressing concerns about the effects of this growing use of legal and illegal drugs. No area in the UK is exempt and the potential and real consequences on the health of our communities, the crime in our communities and the effects it has on individuals and their families, affects us all. This means that we are all having to consider actions to prevent and manage the situations that the changing drug scene presents.

This changing scene led to both national and local responses, with the publication in May 1995 of the then Government's three-year strategy 'Tackling Drugs Together'. This first national drug strategy was superseded by the publication in 1998 of a ten-year strategy 'Tackling Drugs to Build a Better Britain'. Together, these initiatives develop a national framework for action through a series of national plans. These make clear that no single agency carries the responsibility for drug action, but that it is through co-ordinated and coherent action through multi-agency initiatives that we can begin to reduce both the demand and supply, particularly of illegal drugs. It is also acknowledged that a national strategy can only work if it is delivered effectively on the ground. The structure that allows this to happen requires each area to set up a Drugs Action Team (DAT) which includes senior representatives from the police, probation, prison, local authorities – including education – and health authorities. Their main task is to develop and co-ordinate a strategic local plan of action for all services to work together towards common goals.

KEY POLICY DOCUMENTS RELATING TO DRUG EDUCATION

The scope of drug education has been officially defined as including 'tobacco, alcohol, solvents and volatile substances, prescribed and non-prescribed medication and illegal drugs' (Department of Health Substance Misuse Team 2002 – Appendix 1). The role of the education service and schools has been clearly laid out through the following key documents:

1. *Tackling Drugs Together* (Government White Paper 1995) – which stated that schools have an important role in reducing the misuse of drugs and in minimizing their health risks.

The main objectives in these three areas related to young people are:

- to discourage young people from taking drugs
- to ensure that schools offer effective programmes of drug education
- to raise awareness among school staff, governors and parents
- to develop effective national and local educational strategies
- to ensure that young people at risk of drug misuse or who experiment with or become dependent on drugs have access to a range of advice, counselling, treatment, rehabilitation and aftercare services

2. *Circular 4/95 Drug Prevention and Schools* (DfEE 1995) which provides guidance to schools on the drug education curriculum, the principles which should inform it, advice on the policy framework, and advice on ways of handling drug-related incidents in schools. In this respect, it asks that schools should consider the welfare of their pupils and develop a range of appropriate responses to pupil behaviour. It includes the statement that, although some behaviour may break the law, it should not automatically lead to pupil exclusion.

3. *Drug Education – Curriculum Guidance for Schools* (DfEE and SCAA 1995) – which gives more details on the overall approach to drug education in schools. It reinforces the view that:

- drug education should begin early
- it should be delivered within a development framework
- it should involve the development of appropriate skills and attitudes as well as transmitting relevant information
- it should make use of active teaching and learning styles
- it should be developed within a broader whole-school policy on health education and promoting healthy living

4. *Drug Education and Schools* (Ofsted 1996). This document also comments on the development of appropriate action in schools. It identifies strengths and weaknesses of practice highlighted by the process of inspection by Ofsted. For the secondary sector, it points out that the poorest level of delivery is typically at Key Stage 3, especially when drug education work is delivered through tutorial sessions, or where it uses strategies which set out to shock or frighten young people. It suggests that the best approaches were those which approached drug education through well thought-out PSHE programmes. In-service training of teachers is similarly identified as a weak area in those schools where effective dissemination strategies were poorly developed.

5. *The Right Choice – choosing and developing drug education resources for schools* – this booklet, available free to all schools, helps teachers and other school staff decide which materials are most effective (SCODA 1997).

6. *Tackling Drugs to Build a Better Britain* (HMSO 1998b)
The new strategy outlined in this document involves a vision of a healthy and

confident society increasingly free from the harm caused to our citizens by the misuse of drugs. It recognizes four elements for action:

- *Young people* – to help them resist drug misuse in order to achieve their full potential in life
- *Communities* – to protect our communities from drug-related anti-social and criminal behaviour
- *Treatment* – to enable people with drug problems to overcome them and live healthy crime-free lives
- *Availability* – to restrict and control the availability of illegal drugs on our streets

The broader context of policies to reduce social exclusion and especially school exclusion is addressed, and the agenda for schools is set in the context of a whole range of actions to increase the quality of school delivery in the light of new evidence on effectiveness.

The specific targets for schools will:

- inform young people, parents and those who advise/work with them, about the risks and consequences of drug misuse – including alcohol, tobacco and solvents
- teach young people from the age of five upwards – in and out of formal education settings – the skills needed to resist pressures to misuse drugs, including a more integrated approach to Personal, Social and Health Education in schools
- promote healthy lifestyles
- ensure that young people most at risk have access to specific interventions
- build on what works best in prevention and education activity

7. *Protecting Young People: Good practice in drug education in schools and the youth service* (DfEE 1998)

This document supplemented the 1995 Circular, giving up-to-date guidelines in line with the ten-year strategy.

EFFECTIVE APPROACHES IN DRUG EDUCATION

The increased understanding about the effectiveness of drug education which has been developed as a result of these initiatives is of key importance to school staff. Research suggests that there are nine key factors in effective drug education in school. It should:

1. begin early – in Key Stage 1
2. include alcohol, tobacco, medicines, solvents as well as illegal drugs within the programme
3. develop a supportive school ethos – e.g. by appointing a co-ordinator, developing a clear and coherent whole-school policy

4. deliver drug education as part of a broad and developmental PSHE programme
5. identify and target the needs and understanding of individual young people
6. use teachers who are both competent and confident in the area as key deliverers
7. use teaching which focuses on the acquisition of knowledge, the development of skills and the development of appropriate attitudes and values
8. use interactive/experiential teaching methods
9. develop the support and commitment of parents and the local community

Although the strategy does specify what a competent and confident teacher is, there are indicators of competency which should be within all teachers – whether they deliver the curriculum entitlement in the area of drugs education or not.

CONCLUSION: CORE KNOWLEDGE AND SKILLS NEEDED BY SCHOOL STAFF WORKING WITH YOUNG PEOPLE

The following is a summary of the key requirements in this respect. Teachers and other school staff working in this area should have:

- a basic knowledge of the physical, psychological and social effects of drugs
- a knowledge of the impact on children of substance misuse by parents
- an awareness of their own attitudes towards and experiences of substance use and how this might affect their work with young people
- the ability to recognize substance misuse by young people
- assessment skills, particularly to distinguish between substances used and forms of use – e.g. experimental, recreational and problematic use
- a knowledge of basic life-support skills
- the capacity to deliver simple interventions, including relevant information and advice
- information on local agencies and when and how to refer young people appropriately

EDITORS' POSTCRIPT
DRUG EDUCATION AND THE HEALTH PROMOTING SCHOOL

Probably the most important development affecting drug education in Britain since the beginning of the twenty-first century has been its re-location within the wider framework of government policy to make every school a *health promoting school*. The concept of the health promoting school is not new: it was developed following a conference in Edinburgh in 1989 sponsored by the World Health Organization and disseminated more widely as a result of additional WHO conferences in the following years. A *European* conference in 1995 further developed the idea and provided the following definition:

The HPS sets out to create the means for all who live and work within it to take control over and improve their physical and emotional health. It does this through changes in its management structures, its internal and external relationships, the teaching and learning styles it adopts and the methods it uses to establish synergy with its social environment. (World Health Organization 1998 cited in Denman *et al.* 2002, p. 21)

A key feature of the HPS concept, clearly, is its holistic approach: it seeks to change not only the curriculum but the whole ethos of the school, including many aspects of the hidden curriculum, in an endeavour to achieve consistency in promoting healthy lifestyles. Some advocates of the HPS go even further and prefer the term 'eco-holistic' which emphasizes concern not only with human health but also responsibility for the *environment* locally, nationally and globally (*ibid.* p. 14).

In England and Wales, earlier government attempts to promote health education, such as the non-statutory *Curriculum Guidance 5: Health Education* (NCC 1990), were significantly narrower in scope focusing mainly on the overt curriculum and on imparting knowledge. This changed decisively, however, in 1997 when the incoming New Labour government announced a new Healthy Schools Programme. This was implemented chiefly via the introduction of *The National Healthy School Standard* (from 1999 onwards). This involved the creation of partnerships between local education authorities and departments of public health, backed by a government requirement that all LEAs should establish such partnerships by 2002. Denman *et al.* (2002) have pointed out that there is some tension, if not contradiction, between the 'bottom up or empowerment models' characteristic of earlier HPS projects and the 'compliance model of project delivery' adopted by the NHSS. But they observe that

It has to be acknowledged that the NHSS has served to successfully spread project activity across the country and brought the idea of the health promoting school into the consciousness of politicians and professionals, if not yet parents and children. It has also placed demands on local projects to reach all schools: a considerable challenge given that traditionally many projects have not targeted schools but have operated a system of working with interested schools. To observers, the tension is between the extent to which a national agenda can be steered for progress and change, and the degree to which the principles of the health promoting school can be adhered to at a local level by accommodating the processes needed to build ownership and commitment. (ibid., pp. 56–7)

The overall NHSS Guidance document contains a list of 'specific themes' which local programmes must observe and which are of two distinct kinds:

- *contextual issues*: local priorities, school priorities, PSHE, Citizenship
- *specific content issues*: drug education (including alcohol and tobacco), emotional health and well-being (including bullying), healthy eating, physical activity, safety, and sex and relationships education
(DfEE 1999, pp. 15–16)

Within this framework, the criteria for drug education are as follows:

- the school has a named member of staff and a governor who are responsible for drug education provision
- the school has a planned drug education programme involving development of skills, starting from early years, which identifies learning outcomes, appropriate to pupils' age, ability and level of maturity and which is based on pupils' needs assessment
- the school has a policy, owned and implemented by the whole school, including parents/carers, for managing drug-related incidents which includes identifying sources of support for pupils and alternatives to exclusion
- staff understand the role that schools can play in the national drug strategy and are confident to discuss drugs issues and services with pupils
- the school works with the police, youth service and local drug services in line with the Drug Action Team to develop its understanding of local issues and to inform its policy. (ibid., p. 15)

This approach clearly builds on previous good practice in the field of drug education but recontextualizes it within the wider NHSS framework. It is worth noting too that the non-statutory PSHE guidelines contained in the *Curriculum 2000* handbook for secondary teachers, similarly locate drug education within a section headed 'Developing a healthier, safer lifestyle' (DfEE and QCA 1999). Indeed, it is not unreasonable to think that one effect of the introduction of the NHSS may be to encourage both schools and LEAs to give greater prominence to the 'H' (for health) within PSHE.

In addition to the general support and funding for drug education in all schools, specific grants have been made available for more targeted initiatives, which, however, also operate through the nationally recognized local Healthy Schools Programme. One of the most significant examples of such initiatives is the Department of Health's Drug Prevention Funding, made available from 2001 onwards. This has been targeted in two specific areas:

- funding to allow primary health care professionals to participate in drug education activities in *primary schools* reflecting the belief that *early* intervention is increasingly necessary if drug education is to be effective

● funding to deliver early interventions 'targeted at people in vulnerable groups, including: young offenders, truants, looked-after children, children excluded from school, homeless people and children of drug users' (DoH Substance Misuse Team 2001)

In view of the wide range of agencies and departments of state now involved in matters affecting drug use and drug education, as well as the diversity of supporting documents and help available to schools, the issue of *co-ordination* to achieve effective delivery is clearly vital. In this respect, the over-arching framework set by the Government's 10-year National Drug Strategy is of key importance. Like the healthy schools initiative, the Strategy is holistic, placing equal emphasis on stifling the supply of drugs through enhanced enforcement and driving down the demand for drugs by using effective prevention, treatment and education. In terms of delivery of effective drug education programmes, co-ordination via local Drug Action Teams is proving crucial. Each DAT has responsibility for developing a 'Young Person's Substance Misuse Plan' which meets the Strategy's four-tier model of young people's needs, and which ensures that local problems are addressed in a holistic way involving all those concerned: schools, parents, the youth service, further education, the community and statutory agencies. Funding from various government departments will be pooled at the local level to finance the planned programmes, including work in schools.

Bibliography and Recommended Reading

Introduction

DfES and TTA (Department for Education and Skills and the Teacher Training Agency) (2002) *Qualifying to Teach: Professional Standards for Qualified Teacher Status and Requirements for Initial Teacher Training*, London: TTA.

University of Bristol Graduate School of Education (2002) *Teachers' Legal Liabilities and Responsibilities: The Bristol Guide*, Bristol: University of Bristol Graduate School of Education.

Chapter 1

Aldrich, R. (1990) 'The evolution of teacher training'. In Graves, N. J. (ed.) *Initial Teacher Education: Policies and Progress*, London: Kogan Page, pp. 12–24

Aldrich, R. (1996) *Education for the Nation*, London: Cassell.

Batho, G. (1989) *Political Issues in Education*, London: Cassell.

Benn, C. and Simon, B. (1970) *Halfway There*, Harmondsworth: Penguin.

Brooks, R. (1991) *Contemporary Debates in Education: An Historical Perspective*, London: Longman.

Chitty, C. (2002) *Understanding Schools and Schooling*, London: Routledge/Falmer.

DfEE (Department for Education and Employment) (1997) *Excellence in Schools*, London: Stationery Office.

DfEE (Department for Education and Employment) (1998) *News*, 584/98.

DfES (Department for Education and Skills (2002a) *Press Notice: 'David Miliband opens Unity City Academy in Middlesborough'*, 13 September.

DfES (Department for Education and Skills) (2002b) *Press Notice: 'Clarke pledges new freedoms for best schools to raise standards'*, 11 November.

Gordon, P., Aldrich, R. and Dean, D. (1991) *Education and Policy in England in the Twentieth Century*, London: Woburn Press.

Humphries, S., Mack, J., and Perks, R. (1988) *A Century of Childhood*, London: Sidgwick & Jackson.

Judge, H. (1984) *A Generation of Schooling: English Secondary Schools since 1944*, Oxford: Oxford University Press.

Lawrence, I. (1992) *Power and Politics at the Department of Education and Science*, London: Cassell.

Lowe, R. (1988) *Education in the Post-War Years: A Social History*, London: Routledge & Kegan Paul.

Maclure, S. (1970) *A History of Education in London 1870–1990*, Harmondsworth: Penguin.

Martin, C. (1979) *A Short History of English Schools*, London: Wayland Press.

Sanderson, M. (1999) *Education and Economic Decline in Britain: 1870 to the 1990s*, Cambridge: Cambridge University Press.

Sharp, P. and Dunford, J. (1990) *The Education System in England and Wales*, London: Longman.

Tawney, R. H. (1922) *Secondary Education for All*, London: Allen & Unwin.

Chapter 2

Ahier, J., Beck J. and Moore, R. (2003) *Graduate Citizens? Issues of Citizenship and Higher Education*, London: Routledge/Falmer.

Bailey, C. H. (1984) *Beyond the Present and the Particular: A Theory of Liberal Education*, London: Routledge & Kegan Paul.

Ball, S. J. (1999) 'Labour, learning and the economy: a "policy sociology" perspective', *Cambridge Journal of Education*, 29, 2, 195–206.

Barber, M. and Sebba, J. (1999) 'Reflections on progress towards a world class education system', *Cambridge Journal of Education*, 29, 2, 183–93.

Beck, J. (1999) 'Makeover or take-over? the strange death of educational autonomy in neo-liberal England', *British Journal of Sociology of Education*, 20, 2, 223–38.

Bernstein, B. (2000) Pedagogy, Symbolic Control and Identity: Theory, Research and Critique, (revised edn), Lanham, MD, Rowman & Littlefield.

Blair, T. (1998) *The Third Way: New Politics for the New Century*, Fabian Pamphlet 588, London: Fabian Society.

Blair, T. (2002) Speech to the Labour Party Conference, 1 October 2002, *Guardian*, 2 October, 9–10.

Bloom, A. (2002) 'Speculate to educate …', *Times Educational Supplement*, 13 September, 12.

Blunkett, D. (1998) *Speech to the Labour Party Conference*, London: The Labour Party.

Bolton, E. (1994) 'Divided we fall', *Times Educational Supplement*, 21 January, 7.

Carnoy, M. (2000) 'Globalization and educational reform'. In Stromquist, M. and Monkman, K. (eds) *Globalization and Education*, Lanham, MD: Rowman & Littlefield.

Cox, C.B. and Dyson, A.E. (eds) (1969) *Fight for Education: A Black Paper*, London: Critical Quarterly Society.

Dearing, Sir Ronald (1993) *The National Curriculum and its Assessment – Final Report*, London: School Curriculum and Assessment Authority.

DfEE (Department for Education and Employment) (1998) *The Learning Age: A Renaissance for a New Britain*, Cmnd. 3790, London: DfEE.

DfES (Department for Education and Skills) (2002) *14–19: Extending Opportunities, Raising Standards: Summary*, London: DfES.

DES (Department of Education and Science) (1977) *Education in Schools: A Consultative Document*, Cmnd. 6869, London: HMSO.

DES (Department of Education and Science (1987) *The National Curriculum 5–16: A Consultation Document*, London: DES and Welsh Office.

Deuchar, S. (1989) *The New History: A Critique*, York: Campaign for Real Education.

Hall, S. (1991) 'The local and the global: globalization and ethnicity'. In King, A.D. (ed.) *Culture, Globalization and the World System*, London: Macmillan.

Hargreaves, D.H. (1982) *The Challenge for the Comprehensive School: Culture, Curriculum and Community*, London: Routledge & Kegan Paul.

Hattersley, R. (2002) 'Read my lips: there will be selection', *Guardian*, 1 July, 18.

Hillgate Group (1986) *Whose Schools? A Radical Manifesto*, London: Hillgate Group.

Hirst, P.H. and Peters, R.S. (1970) *The Logic of Education*, London: Routledge & Kegan Paul.

Lawlor, S. (1994) 'This crazy National Curriculum', *Observer*, 20 February.

Marquand, D. (1995) 'Flagging fortunes', *Guardian*, 3 July, 13.

Morris, E. (2002) '*Professionalism and Trust: The Future of Teachers and Teaching*', Speech to the Social Market Foundation, June, London: Department for Education and Skills.

Norman, E. R. (1977) 'The threat to religion'. In Cox, C. B. and Boyson, R. (eds) *Black Paper 1977*, London: Temple Smith.

Phillips, R. (1998) *History Teaching, Nationhood And The State: A Study in Educational Politics*, London: Cassell.

Readings, B. (1996) *The University in Ruins*, Cambridge, MA: Harvard University Press.

Richards, C. (1999) 'The primary school curriculum: changes, challenges and questions'. In Richards, C. and Taylor, P. (eds) *How Shall We School Our Children?* London: Falmer.

Scruton, R. (1987) 'The myth of cultural relativism'. In Palmer, E. (ed.) *Anti-racism: The Assault on Education and Value*, London: The Sherwood Press.

Thatcher, M. (1993) *The Downing Street Years*, London: HarperCollins.

Tooley, J. (2000) *Reclaiming Education*, London: Cassell.

Whitty, G. (2002) *Making Sense of Education Policy*, London: Paul Chapman.

Chapter 3

Black, P. (1998) *Testing: Friend or Foe? Theory and Practice of Assessment and Testing*, London: Falmer Press.

Black, P., Harrison, C., Lee, C., Marshall, B. and Wiliam, D. (2002) *Working inside the Black Box: Assessment for Learning in the Classroom*, London: King's College.

Black, P. and Wiliam, D. (1998) *Inside the Black Box: Raising Standards through Classroom Assessment*, London: King's College.

Broadfoot, P. (1998) *Education, Assessment and Society*, Buckingham: Open University Press.

DES (Department of Education and Science) (1987) *Report of the National Curriculum Task Group On Assessment And Testing*, London: DES.

DfES (Department for Education and Skills) (2002) *Tomlinson Report on Outcomes of Review of A Level Grading*, http://www.dfes.gov.uk

DfES and TTA (Teacher Training Agency) (2002) *Qualifying to Teach: Professional Standards for Qualified Teacher Status and Requirements for Initial Teacher Training*, London: TTA.

Gipps, C. (1991) *Assessment: A Teachers' Guide to the Issues*, London: Hodder & Stoughton.

Gipps, C. (1994) *Beyond Testing: Towards a Theory of Educational Assessment*, London: Falmer Press.

Lambert, D. and Lines, D. (2000) *Understanding Assessment: Purposes, Perceptions, Practice*, London: Routledge/Falmer.

Ofsted (Office for Standards in Education) (1998) *How Teachers Assess the Core Subjects at Key Stage 3*, London: Ofsted.

Rowntree, D. (1977) *Assessing Students: How Shall We Know Them?* London: Harper & Row.

Sadler, R. (1998) 'Formative assessment: revisiting the territory', *Assessment in Education* 5, 1, 77–84.

Wood, R. (1991) *Assessment and Testing*, Cambridge: Cambridge University Press.

Wragg, E. (1997) *Assessment and Learning*, London: Routledge.

Chapter 4

Anderson, M. (ed.) (1999), *The Development of Intelligence*, Hove: Psychology Press.

Black, P. J. (1998) *Testing: Friend or Foe?*, London: Falmer Press.

Brown, A. L., Ash, D., Rutherford, M., Nakagawa, K., Gordon, A. and Campione, J. C. (1993) 'Distributed expertise in the classoom'. In Salomon, G. (ed.) *Distributed Cognitions: Psychological And Educational Considerations*, Cambridge: Cambridge University Press, pp. 188–228.

Bruner, J. (1996) *The Culture of Education*, Cambridge, MA: Harvard University Press.

Ceci, S. J. (1996) *On Intelligence: A Bioecological Treatise On Intellectual Development* (expanded edn), Cambridge, MA: Harvard University Press.

Cronbach, L. J. (1990) (5th edn), *Essentials of Psychological Testing*, New York: Harper & Row.

Davidson, J. E. and Downing, C. L. (2000) 'Contemporary models of intelligence'. In Sternberg, R. J. (ed.), *Handbook of Intelligence*, Cambridge: Cambridge University Press, pp. 34–49.

Feuerstein, R. in collaboration with Rand, Y., Hoffman, M. B. and Miller, R. (1980) *Instrumental Enrichment: An Intervention Program for Cognitive Modifiability*, Baltimore, MD: University Park Press.

Gardner, H. (1993) (2nd edn), *Frames of Mind: The Theory of Multiple Intelligences*, London: Fontana Press.

Gardner, H., Kornhaber, M. L. and Wake, W. K. (1996) *Intelligence: Multiple Perspectives*, Fort Worth, TX: Harcourt Brace.

Goleman, D. (1996) *Emotional Intelligence: Why It Can Matter More than IQ*, London: Bloomsbury Publishing.

Gould, S. J. (1996) (revised edition) *The Mismeasure of Man*, London: Penguin.

Grotzer, T. A. and Perkins, D. (2000) 'Teaching intelligence: a performance conception'. In Sternberg, R. J. (ed.), *Handbook of Intelligence*, Cambridge: Cambridge University Press, pp. 492–515.

Howe, M. J. A. (1997) *IQ in Question: The Truth about Intelligence*, London: Sage.

Huxley, A. (1932) *Brave New World*, London: Chatto & Windus.

Lidz, C. S. and Elliott, J. G. (eds) (2000) *Dynamic Assessment: Prevailing Models and Applications*, New York: JAI/Elsevier Science.

Mugny, G. and Carugati, F. (1989) *Social Representations of Intelligence*, trans. by I. Patterson, Cambridge: Cambridge University Press.

Pea, R. D. (1993) 'Practices of distributed intelligence and designs for education'. In Salomon, G. (ed.) *Distributed Cognitions: Psychological and Educational Considerations*, Cambridge: Cambridge University Press, pp. 47–87.

Richardson, K. (1998) *The Origins of Human Potential: Evolution, Development and Psychology*, London: Routledge.

Richardson, K. (1999) *The Making of Intelligence*, London: Weidenfeld & Nicolson.

Shayer, M. and Adey, P. (eds) (2002) *Learning Intelligence: Cognitive Acceleration across the Curriculum from 5 to 15 Years*, Buckingham: Open Unversity Press.

Smith, A. (1998) *Accelerated Learning in Practice: Brain-based Methods for Accelerating Motivation and Achievement*, Stafford: Network Educational Press.

Sternberg, R.J. (1997) *Thinking Styles*, Cambridge: Cambridge University Press.

Sternberg, R. J. (1985) *Beyond IQ: A Tiarchic Theory of Human Intelligence*, Cambridge: Cambridge University Press.

Sternberg, R. J. (ed.) (2000) *Handbook of Intelligence*, Cambridge: Cambridge University Press.

Styles, I. (1999) 'The study of intelligence – the interplay between theory and measurement'. In Anderson, M. (ed.) (1999), *The Development of Intelligence*, Hove: Psychology Press, pp. 19–42.

Thomas, G. and Loxley, A. (2001) *Deconstructing Special Education and Constructing Inclusion* (especially the section: 'The knowledge-roots of special education'), Buckingham: Open University Press, pp. 21–45.

Vygotsky, L. S. (1978/1935) *Mind in Society: The Development of Higher Psychological Processes*, Cambridge, MA: Harvard University Press.

Chapter 5

Bloom, B. (1976) *Human Characteristics and Social Learning*, New York: McGraw Hill.

Bruner J. S. (1960) *The Process of Education*, Cambridge, MA: Harvard University Press.

Bruner, J. S. (1966) *Towards a Theory of Instruction*, Cambridge, MA: Harvard University Press, paperback edn 1968, New York: Norton.

Bruner, J. S. (1986) *Actual Minds, Possible Worlds*, Cambridge, MA and London: Harvard University Press.

Cooper P. and McIntyre, D. (1996) *Effective Teaching and Learning: Teachers' and Students' Perspectives*, Milton Keynes: Open University Press.

de Bono, E. (1995) *Parallel Thinking: From Socrates to de Bono*, Harmondsworth: Penguin.

Donaldson, M. (1978) *Children's Minds*, London: Fontana.

Egan, K. (1984) *Educational Development*, Oxford: Oxford University Press.

Entwistle, N. J. (1991) *Styles of Learning and Teaching*, London: Wiley.

Fielding, M. (1996) 'How and why learning styles matter: valuing difference in teachers and learners'. In Hart, S. (ed.) *Differentiation and Equal Opportunities*, London: Routledge.

Holt, J. (1969) *How Children Fail*, New York: Pitman, UK paperback edn: Harmondsworth: Pelican.

Hunt, J. Mc.V. (1971) 'Using intrinsic motivation to teach young children', *Educational Technology*, 2, 2, 52–64.

Kolb, D. (1984) *Experiential Learning*, Englewood Cliffs, NJ: Prentice-Hall.

Kolb, D. (1985) (revised edn) *Learning Style Inventory*, Boston, MA: McBer.

Lister, I. (1974) *Deschooling: A Reader*, Cambridge: Cambridge University Press.

Neil, A.S. (1960) *Summerhill: A Radical Approach to Child-Rearing*, New York: Hart; UK paperback edn, 1968: Harmondsworth: Pelican.

Postman, N. and Weingartner, C. (1969) *Teaching as a Subversive Activity*, New York: Delacorte Press, UK paperback edn, 1971, Harmondsworth: Penguin.

Vygotsky, L. S. (1962) *Thought and Language*, Boston, MA: Massachusetts Institute of Techology Press.

Wertsch, J. V. (1985) (ed.) *Culture, Communication and Cognition; Vygotskian Perspectives*, Cambridge: Cambridge University Press.

Chapter 6

Bearne, E. (1998) *Use of Language across the Secondary Curriculum*, London: Routledge.

Carter, R. (1995) *Keywords in Language and Literacy*, London: Routledge.

Crystal, D. (1988) *Rediscover Grammar*, London: Longman.

Crystal, D. (1996) *Discover Grammar*, London: Longman.

DES (Department of Education and Science) (1975) *A Language for Life*, London: HMSO.

DES (Department of Education and Science) (1989) *English for ages 5–16*, London: HMSO.

DfEE (Department for Education and Employment) (1998) *The National Literacy Strategy Framework for Teaching*, London: HMSO.

DfEE (Department for Education and Employment) (2001) *Key Stage 3 National Strategy Framework for Teaching English: Years 7, 8 and 9*, London: DfEE.

DfEE/QCA (Department for Education and Employment and the Qualifications and Curriculum Authority) (1999a) *The National Curriculum Handbook for Secondary Teachers in England*, London: DfEE/QCA.

DfEE/QCA (Department for Education and Employment and the Qualifications and Curriculum Authority) (1999b) *Citizenship in the National Curriculum*, London: DfEE/QCA.

Hall, C. and Coles, M. (1999) *Children's Reading Choices*, London: Routledge.

Hall, D. (1995) *Assessing the Needs of Bilingual Learners*, London: David Fulton.

Kress, G. (1995) *Writing the Future: English and the Making of a Culture of Innovation*, Sheffield: National Association for the Teaching of English.

Lewis, M. and Wray, D. (eds) (2000) *Literacy in the Secondary School*, London: David Fulton.

Meek, M. (ed.) (1996) *Developing Pedagogies in The Multilingual Classroom: The Writings of Josie Levine*, Stoke-on-Trent: Trentham Books.

Mercer, N. (2000) *Words and Minds: How We Use Language to Think Together*, London: Routledge.

National Literacy Trust: http://www.literacytrust.org.uk/

Norman, K. (ed.) (1992) *Thinking Voices*, London: Hodder & Stoughton.

Perera, K. (1987) *Understanding Language*, London: NAAE.

Sampson, G. (1925) *English for the English*, Cambridge: Cambridge University Press.

Vygotsky, L.S. (1978) *Mind in Society*, Cambridge, MA and London: Harvard University Press.

Vygotsky, L.S. (1986) *Thought and Language*, Cambridge, MA and London: Massachusetts Institute of Technology.

Wray, D. and Lewis, M. (1997) *Extending Literacy*, London: Routledge.

Chapter 7

Adams, G. (ed.) (2000) *Adolescent Development*, Oxford: Blackwell.

Berthoud, J. (1996) *Pecking Order*, London: Gollanz.

Best, R., Lang, P., Lodge, C. and Watkins, C. (1995) *Pastoral Care and Personal-Social Education*, London: Cassell.

Birch, A. (1997) (2nd edn) *Development Psychology*, New York: Palgrave.

Blackburn K. (1975) *The Tutor*, London: Heinemann.

Bradley, J. and Dubinsky, H. (1994) *Understanding 15–17 Year Olds*, London: Rosendale Press.

Erikson, E., (1963) *Childhood and Society*, London: Paladin/Granada.

Erikson, E. H. (1984) 'Adolescence'. In Conger, J. J. and Petersen, A. C. (eds) *Adolescence and Youth*, New York: Harper & Row.

Fontana, D. (1981), *Psychology for Teachers*, London: Macmillan.

Francis, L. J . and Kay W. K., (1994) *Teenage Religion and Values*, London: Gracewing.

Frankel, R. (1998) *The Adolescent Psyche*, London: Routledge.

Goleman, D. (1996) *Emotional Intelligence*, London: Bloomsbury.

Janeway Conger, J. and Petersen, A. C. (1984) *Adolescence and Youth: Psychological Development in a Changing World*, London: Harper & Row.

McLaughlin, C., Clark, P. and Chisholm, M. (1996) *Counselling and Guidance in Schools*, London: David Fulton.

McLaughlin, T. H. (1994) 'Values, coherence and the school', *Cambridge Journal of Education*, 24, 3, 453–70.

Maslow, A. (1987) *Motivation and Personality*, New York: Harper & Row.

Marland, M. (1989) *The Tutor and the Tutor Group*, London: Longman.

Chapter 8

Ainscow, M. (1999) *Understanding the Development of Inclusive Schools*, London: Falmer Press

Audit Commission (2002) *Statutory Assessment and Statements of Special Educational Need: In Need of Review*? London: Audit Commission.

Black, P. (1996) 'Formative assessment and the improvement of learning', *British Journal of Special Education*, 23, 2, 51–5.

DES (Department of Education and Science) (1978) *Special Educational Needs: Report of the Committee of Enquiry into the Education of Handicapped Children and Young People* (The Warnock Report), London: HMSO.

DfEE (Department for Education and Employment) (2000) *Working with Teaching Assistants: A Good Practice Guide*, London: DfEE.

DfES (Department for Education and Skills) (2001a) *The Special Educational Needs Code of Practice*, London: DfES.

DfES (Department for Education and Skills) (2001b) *Inclusive Schooling: Children with Special Educational Needs*, London: DfES.

Florian, L. (2002) 'The more things change the more they stay the same? A response to the Audit Commission's report on statutory assessments and Statements of Special Education Needs', *British Journal of Special Education*, 29, 4, 164–69.

Florian, L. and Rouse, M. (2001a) 'Inclusive practice in secondary schools: lessons learned', *Cambridge Journal of Education*, 31, 3, 399–412.

Florian, L. and Rouse, M. (2001b) 'Inclusive practice in secondary schools'. In Rose, R. and Grosvenor, I. (eds) *Doing Research in Special Education*, London: David Fulton.

HM Government (1981) *Education Act 1981* (15 Statutes 300).

HM Government (2001) *Special Educational Needs and Disability Act 2001.*

McLaughlin, M. and Tilstone, C. (1999) 'Standards and the curriculum: the core of educational reform'. In McLaughlin, M. and Rouse, M. (eds) *Special Education and School Reform in the United States and Britain*, London: Routledge.

Norwich, B. (2002) *LEA Inclusion Trends in English LEAs 1997–2001*, Bristol: Centre for the Study of Inclusive Education.

QCA (Qualifications and Curriculum Authority) (2001) *Planning, Teaching and Assessing the Curriculum for Pupils with Learning Difficulties*, London: QCA.

Tilstone, C., Florian, L. and Rose, R. (1998) *Promoting Inclusive Practice*, London: Routledge.

Wedell, K. (1990) 'Overview: The 1988 Act and current principles of special educational needs'. In Daniels, H. and Ware, J. (eds) *Special Educational Needs and the National Curriculum*, London: Kogan Page.

Chapter 9

Abraham, J. (1995) *Divide and School: Gender and Class Dynamics in Comprehensive Education*, London: Falmer Press.

Arnot, M., David, M. and Weiner, G. (1996) *Educational Reforms and Gender Equality in Schools,* Manchester: Equal Opportunities Commission.

Arnot, M., David, M. and Weiner, G. (1999) *Closing the Gender Gap: Post-war Social and Educational Change,* Oxford: Polity Press.

Arnot, M., Gray. J., James, M. and Rudduck, J. (1998) *Recent Research on Gender and Educational Performance,* London: Ofsted/Stationery Office.

Arnot, M. and Gubb, J. (2001) *Adding Value to Boys' and Girls' Education: A Gender and Achievement Project in West Sussex,* Chichester: West Sussex County Council.

Bleach, K. (ed.) (1998) *Raising Boys' Achievement in Schools,* Stoke on Trent: Trentham Books.

Bray, R., Downes, P., Gardner, C., Hannan, G. and Parsons, N. (1997) *Can Boys Do Better?*, Leicester: Secondary Heads Association.

Chaplain, R. (1996) 'Making a strategic withdrawal: disengagement and self-worth protection in male pupils'. In Rudduck, J., Chaplain, R. and Wallace, G. (eds) *School Improvement; What Can Pupils Tell Us?* London: David Fulton.

David, M., West, A. and Ribbens, G. (1994) *Mothers' Intuition: Choosing Secondary Schools*, London: Falmer Press.

Department for Education and Skills (DfES) (2001) *Schools Achieving Success*, White Paper (*http://www.legislation*.hmso.gov.uk/acts.htm).

Epstein, D., Elwood, J., Hey, V. and Maw, J.(eds) (1998) *Failing Boys? Issues in Gender and Achievement*, Buckingham: Open University.

Equal Opportunities Commission (2001) Response to DfES White Paper, *Education and Skills: Schools Achieving Success, www.eoc.org.uk*

Francis, B. (2000) *Girls, Boys and Achievement: Addressing Classroom Issues*, London: Routledge.

Gerwitz, S., Ball, S. and Bowe, R. (1995) *Markets, Choice and Equity in Education*, Buckingham: Open University Press.

Gilbert, R. and Gilbert, P. (1998) *Masculinity Goes to School*, London: Routledge.

Gillborn, D. and Gipps, C. (1996) *Recent Research on the Achievements of Ethnic Minority Pupils*, London: Ofsted/HMSO.

Gillborn, D. and Mirza, H. (2000) *Educational Inequality: Mapping Race, Class and Gender*, London: Ofsted.

Gillborn, D. and Youdell, D. (2000) *Rationing Education: Policy, Practice, Reform and Equity*, Buckingham: Open University Press.

Hodgson, A. (1999) 'Analysing education and training policies for tackling social exclusion'. In Hayton, A. (ed.) *Tackling Disaffection and Social Exclusion: Education Perspectives and Policies*, London: Kogan Page.

Kenway, J. and Willis, S. (1998) *Answering Back: Girls, Boys and Feminism in Schools*, London: Routledge.

Mac an Ghaill, M. (1994) *The Making of Men: Masculinities, Sexualities and Schooling*, Buckingham: Open University Press.

MacDonald, A., Saunders, L. and Benfield, P. (1999) *Boys' Achievement: Progress, Motivation and Participation: Issues Raised by the Recent Literature*, Slough: NFER.

Martino, W. and Meyenn, B. (eds) (2001) *What about the Boys? Issues of Masculinity in Schools*, Buckingham: Open University Press.

National Commission on Education (1993) *Learning to Succeed: A Radical Look at Education Today and a Strategy for the Future*, London: Heinemann.

Plummer, G. (2000) *Failing Working-Class Girls*, London: Trentham.

Reay, D. (2000) 'Rethinking social class: qualitative perspectives on social class and gender', *Sociology*, 33, 2, 259–75.

Reay, D. and Ball, S. J. (1997) '"Spoilt for choice": the working classses and educational markets' *Oxford Review of Education*, 23, 1, 89–101.

Reay, D., Ball, S., David, M. and Davies, J. (2001) 'Choices of degree or degrees of choice? Social class, race and the higher education choice process', *Sociology*, 35, 4, 855–74.

Robertson, S. and Lauder, H. (2001) 'Restructuring the education/social class relation: a class choice?' In Phillips, R. and Furlong, J. (eds) *Education, Reform and the State: Twenty-Five Years of Politics, Policy and Practice*, London: Routledge/Falmer.

Rolfe, H. (1999) *Gender Equality and the Careers Service*, Manchester: Equal Opportunities Commission.

Sewell, T. (1997) *Black Masculinities and Schooling*, Stoke on Trent: Trentham Books.

Skelton, C. (2001) 'Typical boys? theorising masculinity in educational settings'. In Francis, B. and Skelton, C. (eds) *Investigating Gender: Contemporary Perspectives in Education*, Buckingham: Open University Press.

Teese, R., Davies, M., Charlton, M. and Polesel, J. (1995) *Who Wins at School? Boys and Girls in Australian Secondary Education*, Melbourne: Department of Education, Policy and Management, University of Melbourne.

Willis, P. (1977) *Learning to Labour: How Working-class Kids get Working-class Jobs*, Westmead: Saxon House.

Wright, C., Weekes, D., McLaughlin, A. and Webb, D. (1998) 'Masculinised discourses within education and the construction of black male identities amongst African-Caribbean youths', *British Journal of Sociology of Education*, 19, 1, 75–87.

Chapter 10

Blair, M. (2001) *Why Pick on Me? School Exclusion and Black Youth*, Stoke-on-Trent: Trentham Books.

Blair, M., and Bourne, J. with Coffin, C. (1998) *Making a Difference: Teaching and Learning Strategies in Successful Multi-ethnic Schools*, Sudbury: DFEE.

Coard, B. (1971) *How the West Indian Child Is Made Educationally Subnormal in the British Education System*, London: New Beacon Books.

Cohen, P. (1988) 'The perversions of inheritance: studies in the making of multiracist Britain'. In Cohen, P. and Bains, H. S. (eds) *Multiracist Britain*, Basingstoke: Macmillan.

DES (Department for Education and Science) (1985) *Education for All: The Report of the Committee of Inquiry into the Education of Children from Ethnic Minority Groups* (Chairman: Lord Swann), London: HMSO.

DfEE (Department for Education and Employment) (1999) *The Stephen Lawrence Inquiry Report: Action Plan*, Memorandum by the Department for Education and Employment, London: DfEE.

Fryer, P. (1984) *Staying Power: The History of Black People in Britain*, London: Pluto Press.

Fuller, M. (1984) 'Gender, race and education'. In The Open University, *Unit 27: Inequality, Gender, Race and Class*, Milton Keynes: The Open University Press.

Gillborn, D. and Gipps, C. (1996) *Recent Research on the Achievements of Ethnic Minority Pupils*, London: HMSO.

Gilroy, P. (1987) *There Ain't No Black in the Union Jack: The Cultural Politics of Race And Nation*, London: Hutchinson.

Hall, S. (1978) 'Racism and reaction'. In Commission for Racial Equality, *Five Views of Multiracial Britain: Talks on Race Relations Broadcast by BBC TV*, London: Commission for Racial Equality.

Home Office (1999) *The Stephen Lawrence Report: Home Secretary's Action Plan*, London: Home Office.

Home Office (2002) *Community Cohesion: A Report of the Independent Review Team, Chaired by Ted Cantle*, London: Home Office, *http://homeoffice.gov.uk/reu/community_cohesion.pdf*.

Macphearson, Sir William (1999) *The Stephen Lawrence Inquiry: Report of an Inquiry by Sir William Macphearson of Cluny Advised by Tom Cook, The Right Reverend Dr John Sentamu, Dr Richard Stone*, London: Stationery Office.

Nehaul, K. (1996) *The Schooling of Children of Caribbean Heritage*, Stoke-on-Trent: Trentham Books.

Osler, A. and Morrison, M. (2000) *Inspecting Schools for Race Equality: Ofsted's Strengths and Weaknesses, A Report for the Commission for Racial Equality*, Stoke-on-Trent: Trentham Books.

Ouseley, H. (2001) *Community Pride not Prejudice: Making Diversity Work in Bradford*, Bradford: Bradford Vision.

Parekh, B. (1986) 'The New Right and the politics of nationhood'. In Cohen, G., Bosanquet, N., Ryan, A. and Parekh, B. (eds) *The New Right: Image and Reality*, London: Runnymede Trust.

Ramdin, R. (1999) *Reimaging Britain: 500 Years of Black and Asian History*, London: Pluto Press.

Rashid, M. (2002) 'Director's report: an overview'. In Oldham Race Equality Partnership, *Working with Oldham's Communities for a Just Society: Annual Report 2002/2020*, Oldham: Victoria House.

Richardson, R. and Wood, A. (2000) *Inclusive Schools, Inclusive Society: Race and Identity on the Agenda*, Stoke-on-Trent: Trentham Books.

Runnymede Trust (2000) *The Future of Multi-Ethnic Britain: Report of the Commission on the Future of Multi-Ethnic Britain* (Chair: Bhiku Parekh), London: Profile books.

Solomos, J. (1992) 'The politics of immigration since 1945'. In Braham, P. Rattansi, A. and Skellington, R. (eds) *Racism and Antiracism: Inequalities, Opportunities, and Policies*, London: Sage.

Stanford, J. (2001a) 'Race, labour and the Archbishop, or the currency of race', *Race, Ethnicity and Education*, 4, 1, 81–97.

Stanford, J. (2001b) 'Identities in transition: Theorising race and multicultural success in school contexts in Britain', unpublished PhD thesis, University of Cambridge, Cambridge, England.

Troyna, B. (1992) 'Can you see the join? A historical analysis of multicultural and antiracist education policies.' In Gill, D., Mayor, B. and Blair, M. (eds) *Racism and Education: Structures and Strategies*, London: Sage.

Chapter 11

Bailey, C. (1984) *Beyond the Present and the Particular. A Theory of Liberal Education*, London: Routledge & Kegan Paul.

Bridges, D. and McLaughlin, T. H. (eds) (1994) *Education and the Market Place*, London: Falmer Press.

Feinberg, J. (1980) 'The child's right to an open future'. In Aiken, W. and LaFollette, H. (eds) *Whose Child? Children's Rights, Parental Authority, and State Power*, Totowa, NJ: Littlefield Adams.

Jonathan, R. (1997) *Illusory Freedoms. Liberalism, Education and the Market*, Oxford: Blackwell.

McLaughlin, T. H. (1992) 'The ethics of separate schools'. In Leicester, M. and Taylor, M. (eds) *Ethics, Ethnicity and Education*, London: Kogan Page.

McLaughlin, T. H. (1994a) 'The scope of parents' educational rights'. In Halstead, J. M. (ed.) *Parental Choice and Education: Principles, Policy and Practice*, London: Kogan Page.

McLaughlin, T. H. (1994b) 'Politics, markets and schools: the central issues'. In Bridges, D. and McLaughlin, T. H. (eds) *Education and the Market Place*, London: Falmer Press.

Midwinter, E. (1975) *Education and the Community*, London: Unwin.

Ree, H. (1973) *Educator Extraordinary: The Life and Achievement of Henry Morris*, London: Longman.

Tooley, J. (1996) *Education without the State*, London: Education and Training Unit, Institute of Economic Affairs.

White, J. (1990) *Education and the Good Life. Beyond the National Curriculum*, London: Kogan Page.

Chapter 12

Bonnett, M. (1997) 'Environmental education and beyond', *Journal of Philosophy of Education*, 31, 249–66.

Bonnett, M. (2002) 'Education for sustainability as a frame of mind', *Environmental Education Research*, 8, 1, 9–20.

Corney, G. (1998) 'Learning to teach environmental issues', *International Research in Geographical and Environmental Education*, 7, 2, 90–105.

Corney, G. and Middleton, N. (1996) 'Teaching environmental issues in schools and higher education'. In Rawling, E. M. and Daugherty, R. A. (eds) *Geography into the Twenty-First Century*, Chichester: Wiley, pp. 321–38.

Dove, J. (1996) 'Student teacher understanding of the greenhouse effect, ozone layer depletion and acid rain', *Environmental Education Research*, 2, 10, 89–100.

Fien, J. (1995) 'Teaching for a sustainable world: the environmental and development education project for teacher education', *Environmental Education Research*, 1, 1, 21–33.

Fien, J. and Slater, F. (1985) 'Four strategies for values education in geography'. In Boardman, D. (ed.) *New Directions in Geographical Education*, Lewes: Falmer Press.

Gayford, C. (1991) 'Environmental education: a question of emphasis in the school curriculum', *Cambridge Journal of Education*, 21, 1, 73–93.

Greig, S., Pike, G. and Selby, D. (1987) *Earthrights : Education as if the Planet Really Mattered*, London: Worldwide Fund for Nature/Kogan Page.

Hicks, D. (1994) *Education for the Future: A Practical Classroom Guide*, Godalming: Worldwide Fund for Nature.

Hicks, D. and Bord, A. (2001) 'Learning about global issues: why most educators make things worse', *Environmental Education Research*, 7, 4, 413–25.

Hicks, D. and Holden, C. (1995) 'Exploring the future: a missing dimension in environmental education', *Environmental Education Research*, 1, 2, 185–93.

Huckle, J. (1990) 'Environmental education: teaching for a sustainable future', in Dufour, B. (ed.) *The New Social Curriculum: A Guide to Cross-Curricular Issues*, Cambridge: Cambridge University Press.

Huckle, J. (1993a) 'Environmental education and sustainability: a view from critical theory', in Fien, J. (ed.) *Environmental Education : A Pathway to Sustainability*, Geelong: Deakin University Press.

Huckle, J. (1993b) 'Environmental education and the National Curriculum in the United Kingdom', *International Research in Environmental and Geographical Education*, 2, 2, 101–4.

Huckle, J., Allen, E., Edwards, P., Symons, G. and Webster, K. (1995) *Reaching Out: Education for Sustainability*, Godalming: Worldwide Fund for Nature.

Huckle, J. and Sterling, S. (eds) (1996) *Education for Sustainability*, London: Earthscan.

Naish, M., Rawling, E. M. and Hart, C. (1987) *Geography 16–19: The Contribution of a Curriculum Development Project to 16–19 Education*, Harlow: Longman.

National Curriculum Council (1990) *Curriculum Guidance 7: Environmental Education*, York: NCC.

Pike, G. and Selby, D. (1988) *Global Teacher, Global Learner*, London: Hodder & Stoughton.

Rickinson, M. (2001) 'Learners and learning in environmental education: a critical review of the evidence', *Environmental Education Research*, 7, 3, 207–320.

Stables, A. and Bishop, K . (2001) 'Conceptions of educational literacy', *Environmental Education Research*, 7, 1, 89–97.

Stenhouse, L. (1970) *The Humanities Project: An Introduction*, London: Heinemann.

Sterling, S. (1993) 'Environmental education and sustainability: a view from holistic ethics', in Fien, J. (ed.) *Environmental Education: A Pathway to Sustainability*, Geelong: Deakin University Press.

Sterling, S. and the Edet Group (1992) *Good Earth-Keeping: Education, Training and Awareness for a sustainable Future*, London: Environment and Development Education and Training Group, UNEP-UK.

Stoltman, J. P. and Lidstone, J. (2001) 'Citizenship education: a necessary perspective for geography and environmental education', *International Review in Geographical and Environmental Education*, 10, 3, 215–17.

Summers, M., Kruger, K., Childs, A. and Mant, J. (2000) 'Primary school teachers' understanding of environmental issues: an interview study', *Environmental Education Research*, 6, 4, 293–312.

Tilbury, D. (1995) 'Environmental education for sustainability: defining the new focus of environmental education in the 1990s', *Environmental Education Research*, 1, 2, 195–212.

United Nations Conference on Environment and Development (1992) *Earth Summit 92*, Conches: UNCED, Chapter 36.

Ward, C. and Fyson, A. (1973) *Streetwork: The Exploding School*, London: Routledge & Kegan Paul.

World Commission on Environment and Development (1987) *Our Common Future*, Oxford: Oxford University Press.

Chapter 13

Advisory Group on Citizenship (1998) *Education for Citizenship and the Teaching of Democracy in Schools. Final Report of the Advisory Group on Citizenship*, London: Qualifications and Curriculum Authority.

Bottery, M. (1990) *The Morality of the School: The Theory and Practice of Values in Education*, London: Cassell.

Bridges, D. (1986) 'Dealing with controversy in the school curriculum: a philosophical perspective'. In Wellington, J. J. (ed.) *Controverial Issues in the Curriculum*, Oxford: Basil Blackwell.

Commission on the Future of Multi-Ethnic Britain (2000) *The Future of Multi-Ethnic Britain: The Parekh Report*, London: Runnymede Trust in association with Profile Books.

Committee of Enquiry into the Education of Children from Ethnic Minority Groups (Swann Committee) (1985) *Education for All*, Cmnd. 9453, London: HMSO.

Halstead, J. M. and Taylor, M. J. (eds) (1996) *Values in Education and Education in Values*, London: Falmer Press.

Haydon, G. (1997) *Teaching about Values: A New Approach*, London: Cassell.

McLaughlin, T. H. (1992) 'The ethics of separate schools'. In Leicester, M. and Taylor, M. J. (eds) *Ethics, Ethnicity and Education*, London: Kogan Page.

McLaughlin, T. H. (1995a) 'Public values, private values and educational responsibility', in Pybus, E. and McLaughlin, T. H., *Values, Education and Responsibility*, St Andrews: Centre for Philosophy and Public Affairs, University of St Andrews.

McLaughlin, T. H. (1995b) 'Liberalism, education and the common school', *Journal of Philosophy of Education*, 29, 239–55.

Qualifications and Curriculum Authority (2000) *Citizenship at Key Stages 3 and 4: Initial Guidance for Schools*, London: QCA.

Sacks, J. (1991) *The Persistence of Faith. Religion, Morality and Society in a Secular Age (The Reith Lectures 1990)*, London: Weidenfeld & Nicolson.

White, J. (1990) *Education and the Good Life. Beyond the National Curriculum*, London: Kogan Page.

Chapter 14

Best, R. and Lang, P. (1997) 'Introduction'. In Haydon, G. *Teaching about Values*, London: Cassell.

Cohen, B. (1969) 'The problem of bias'. In Heater, D. (ed.) *The Teaching of Politics*, London: Methuen.

DfEE and QCA (Department for Education and Employment and Qualifications and Curriculum Authority (1999) *The National Curriculum Handbook for Secondary Teachers in England – Key Stages 3 and 4*, London: DfEE and QCA.

Gilligan, C. (1982 *In a Different Voice: Psychological Theory and Women's Development*, Cambridge, MA: Harvard University Press.

Haydon, G. (1997) *Teaching about Values*, London: Cassell.

Haydon, G. (1999) *Values, Virtues and Violence: Education and the Public Understanding of Morality*, Oxford: Blackwell.

Hirst, P. (1973) 'The foundations of moral judgement'. In Lord, E. and Bailey, C. (eds) *A Reader in Religious and Moral Education*, London: Student Christian Movement.

Kohlberg, L. (1966) 'Moral education in the schools: a developmental view', *School Review*, 1, 1–30.

Kohlberg, L. (1969) 'Stage and sequence: the cognitive developmental approach to socialization'. In Goslin, D. (ed.) *Handbook of Socialization Theory and Practice*, Chicago: Rand McNally.

National Forum for Values in Education and the Community (1996) *Consultation on Values in Education and the Community*, London: School Curriculum and Assessment Authority.

Noddings, N. (1984) *Caring: A Feminist Approach to Ethics*, Berkeley: University of California Press.

Pring, R. (1987) *Personal and Social Education in the Curriculum*, London, Hodder & Stoughton.

Spiecker, B. (1988) 'Education and the moral emotions'. In Spiecker, B. and Straughan, R. (eds) *Philosophical Issues in Moral Education and Development*, Milton Keynes: Open University Press.

Straughan, R. (1982) *Can We Teach Children to be Good?*, London: Allen & Unwin.

Talbot, M. and Tate, N. (1997) 'Shared values in a pluralist society'. In Smith, R. and Standish, P. (eds) *Teaching Right and Wrong*, Stoke on Trent: Trentham Books.

Warnock, M. (1996) 'Moral values'. In Halstead, J. M. and Taylor, M. J. (eds) *Values in Education and Education in Values*, London: Falmer Press.

White, J. (1994) 'Instead of Ofsted', *Cambridge Journal of Education*, 24, 3, 369–377.

Wringe, C. (1998) 'Reasons, rules and virtues in moral education', *Journal of Philosophy of Education*, 32, 225–37.

Chapter 15

Advisory Group on Citizenship (1998) *Education for Citizenship and the Teaching of Democracy in Schools: Final Report of the Advisory Group on Citizenship*, (Crick Report), London: Department for Education and Employment and the Qualifications and Curriculum Authority.

Ahier, J. (1988) *Industry, Children and the Nation: An Analysis of National Identity in School Textbooks*, London: Falmer Press.

Ahier, J., Beck, J. and Moore, R. (2003) *Graduate Citizens? Issues of Citizenship and Higher Education*, London: Routledge/Falmer.

Arnot, M. (1997) 'Gendered citizenry: new feminist perspectives on education and citizenship', *British Educational Research Journal*, 23, 3, 275–95.

Beck, J. (1998) *Morality and Citizenship in Education,* London: Cassell.

Blair, T. (1997) *Bring Britain Together*, Speech by the Prime Minister, The Right Honourable Tony Blair MP, for the launch of the Social Exclusion Unit, London: Social Exclusion Unit.

Blair, T. (1998) *The Third Way: New Politics for the New Century,* Fabian Pamphlet 588, London: Fabian Society.

Callan, E. (1997) *Creating Citizens: Political Education and Liberal Democracy*, Oxford, Clarendon Press.

Commission on Citizenship (1990) *Encouraging Citizenship (Report of the House of Commons Commission on Citizenship)*, London: HMSO.

Crick, B. (2000) *Essays on Citizenship*, London: Continuum.

Crick, B. and Green, D. (2002) 'Should citizenship be taught in British schools?, *Prospect*, September, 16–19.

Crick, B. and Porter, A. (eds) (1978) *Political Education and Political Literacy*, London: Longman.

Dahrendorf, R. (1996) 'Citizenship and social class'. In Bulmer, M. and Rees, A. M. (eds) *Citizenship Today: The Contemporary Relevance of T. H. Marshall*, London: University College London Press.

Davis, I., Gregory, I. and Riley, S. C. (1999) *Good Citizenship and Educational Provision*, London: Falmer Press.

Fukuyama, F. (1992) *The End of History and the Last Man*, New York: Free Press.

Gamarnikow, E. and Green, A. (2000) 'Citizenship, education and cultural capital'. In Lawton, D., Cairns, J. and Gardner, R. (eds) *Education for Citizenship*, London: Continuum.

Gellner, E. (1992) *Reason and Culture: The Historic Role of Rationality and Rationalism*, Oxford, Blackwell.

Giddens, A. (1990) *The Consequences of Modernity*, Cambridge: Polity Press.

Giddens, A. (1994) *Beyond Left and Right*, Cambridge: Polity Press.

Hogan, D. (1997) 'The logic of protection: citizenship, justice and political community'. In Kennedy, K. (ed.) *Citizenship, Education and the Modern State*, London: Falmer Press.

Hurd, D. (1988) 'Citizenship in the Tory democracy', *New Statesman*, 29 April.

McLaughlin, T. H. (1992) 'Citizenship, diversity and education: a philosophical perspective', *Journal of Philosophy of Education*, 29, 2, 239–50.

Marshall, T. H. (1950) *Citizenship and Social Class*, Cambridge: Cambridge University Press.

Marshall, T. H. (1964) 'Citizenship and social class'. In Marshall, T. H. *Class, Citizenship and Social Development*, Chicago: Chicago University Press.

Marshall, T.H. and Bottomore, T. (1992) *Citizenship and Social Class,* London: Pluto Press.

Ministry of Education (1949) *Citizens Growing Up*, Pamphlet No. 16, London: Ministry of Education.

NCC (National Curriculum Council) (1990) *Curriculum Guidance 8: Education for Citizenship*, London: National Curriculum Council.

Putnam, R. D. (1993) *Making Democracy Work: Civic Traditions in Modern Italy*, Princeton, NJ: Princeton University Press.

Putnam, R. D. (1996) 'Who killed civic America?', *Prospect*, March, 66–72.

QCA (2000) *Citizenship at Key Stages 3 and 4: Initial Guidance for Schools*, London: QCA Publications.

QCA (2001) *Citizenship: A Scheme of Work for Key Stage 3*, (Circular No. 128/01), London: QCA Publications.

QCA and DfEE (Qualifications and Assessment Authority and Department for Education and Employment) (1999) *The National Curriculum Handbook For Secondary Teachers In England*, London: QCA Publications.

Rawls, J. (1993) *Political Liberalism*, New York: Columbia University Press.

Taylor, C. (1989) 'Cross purposes: the liberal-communitarian debate', in Rosenblum, N. (ed.) *Liberalism and the Moral Life*, Cambridge, MA: Harvard University Press.

Chapter 16

Bagley, C. and Tremblay, P. (1997) 'Suicidal behaviors in homosexual and bisexual males', *Crisis*, 18, 24–34.

Beck, J. (1999) 'Should homosexuality be taught as an acceptable alternative lifestyle? A Muslim perspective: a response to Halstead and Lewicka', *Cambridge Journal of Education*, 29, 121–30.

Blake, S. and Katrak, Z. (2002) *Faith, Values and Sex and Relationships Education*, London: National Children' Bureau.

DfEE (Department for Education and Employment) (2000a) *Sex and Relationship Education Guidance, DfEE 0116/2000*, London: Department for Education and Employment.

DfEE (Department for Education and Employment) (2000b) *Sex and Relationship Education Guidance: Draft for Consultation 16 March 2000*, London: Department for Education and Employment.

Halstead, J. M. (1992) 'Ethical dimensions of controversial events in multicultural education'. In Leicester, M. and Taylor, M. (eds), *Ethics, Ethnicity and Education*, London, Kogan Page, pp. 39–56.

Halstead, J. M. and Lewicka, K. (1998) 'Should homosexuality be taught as an acceptable alternative lifestyle? A Muslim perspective', *Cambridge Journal of Education*, 28, 49–64.

Halstead J. M. and Reiss, M. J. (2003) *Values in Sex Education: From Principles to Practice*, London: Routledge/Falmer.

Harrison, J. K. (2000) *Sex Education in Secondary Schools*, Buckingham: Open University Press.

Humphries, S. (1988) *A Secret World Of Sex*, London: Sidgwick & Jackson.

Johnson, A. M., Mercer, C. H., Erens, B., Copas, A. J., McManus, S., Wellings, K., Fenton, K.A., Korovessis, C., Macdowell, W., Nanchahal, K., Purdon, S. and Field, J. (2001) 'Sexual behaviour in Britain: partnerships, practices, and HIV risk behaviours', *The Lancet*, 358, 1835–42.

Khayatt, D. (1994) 'Surviving school as a lesbian student', *Gender and Education*, 6, 47–61.

Mason, A. and Palmer, A. (1996) *Queerbashing: A National Survey of Hate Crimes against Lesbians and Gay Men*, London: Stonewall.

Massey, D. (1991) (2nd edn) *School Sex Education: Why, What and How*, London: Family Planning Association.

Ofsted (Office For Standards in Education) (2002) *Sex and Relationships HMI 433*, London: Office for Standards in Education. Available at *www.ofsted.gov.uk*

QCA (Qualifications and Curriculum Authority) (1999) *The National Curriculum: Handbook for Secondary Teachers in England*, London: Department for Education and Employment and Qualifications and Curriculum Authority. Available at *www.nc.uk.net*

Ray, C. and Went, D. (1995) *Good Practice in Sex Education: A Sourcebook for Schools*, London: Sex Education Forum/National Children's Bureau.

Reiss, M. (1993) 'What are the aims of school sex education?', *Cambridge Journal of Education*, 23, 125–36.

Reiss, M. J. (1997) 'Teaching about homosexuality and heterosexuality', *Journal of Moral Education*, 26, 343–52.

Reiss, M. J. (1998) 'The history of school sex education', *Muslim Education Quarterly*, 15, 2, 4–13.

Reiss, M. J. and Mabud, S. A. (eds) (1998) *Sex Education and Religion*, Cambridge: The Islamic Academy.

Ruse, M. (1988) *Homosexuality: A Philosophical Inquiry*, Oxford: Basil Blackwell.

Sharpe, S. (2001) *More Than Just a Piece of Paper? Young People's Views on Marriage and Relationships*, London: National Children's Bureau.

Stone, N. and Ingham, R. (1998) *Exploration of the Factors that Affect the Delivery of Sex and Sexuality Education and Support in Schools: Final Report*, Southampton: Centre for Sexual Health Research, Faculty of Social Sciences, University of Southampton.

Surrey County Council (1987) *Sex Education: A Guide for Schools/Colleges*, Woking: Surrey County Council.

Thomson, R. (ed.) (1993) *Religion, Ethnicity and Sex Education: Exploring The Issues*, London: National Children's Bureau.

Thomson, R. (1994) 'Moral rhetoric and public health pragmatism: the recent politics of sex education', *Feminist Review*, 48, 40–59.

Went, D (1995) 'From biology to empowerment: how notions of good practice have changed', paper presented on 11 July, Copthorne Tara Hotel, London at the 'Sex Education in Schools: Working towards Good Practice' Conference.

Wolpe, A.-M. (1987) 'Sex in schools: back to the future', *Feminist Review*, 27, 37–47.

Chapter 17

Davies, J. and Coggens, N. (1991) *The Facts about Adolescent Drug Abuse*, London: Cassell.

Denman, S., Moon, A., Parsons, C. and Stears, D. (2002) *The Health Promoting School: Policy, Research and Practice*, London: Routledge Falmer.

DfEE (Department for Education and Employment) (1995) *Circular 4/95 – Drug Prevention and Schools*, London: DfEE.

DfEE (1998) *Protecting Young People: Good practice in drug education in schools and the youth service*, London: DfEE.

DfEE (Department for Education and Employment) (1999) *National Health School Standard Guidance*, London: DfEE.

DfEE and QCA (Department for Education and Employment and the Qualifications and Curriculum Authority (1999) *The National Curriculum: Handbook for Secondary Teachers in England*, London: DfEE and QCA.

DfEE and SCAA (Department for Education and Employment and the School

Curriculum and Assessment Authority) (1995) *Drug Education – Curriculum Guidance For Schools*, London: DfEE.

Department of Health Substance Misuse Team (2002) *Health Authority Drugs Education and Prevention Funding 2002/3*, London: DoH.

Drug and Alcohol Prevention Team (2001) *Opportunities for Drug and Alcohol Education in the School Curriculum*, London: Alcohol Concern and Drugscope.

HEA (Health Education Authority) (1995) *A Parents' Guide to Drugs and Solvents*, London: Health Education Authority.

HMSO (Her Majesty's Stationery Office) (1990) *The Need for a New Impetus – Drug Education and Schools*, London: HMSO.

HMSO (Her Majesty's Stationery Office) (1998a) *Drug Misuse and the Environment*, London: HMSO.

HMSO (Her Majesty's Stationery Office) (1998b) *Tackling Drugs to Build a Better Britain*, London: HMSO.

ISDD (Institute for the Study of Drug Dependence) (1997a) *Drug Abuse Briefing – 6*, London: ISDD.

ISDD (Institute for the Study of Drug Dependence) (1997b) *Drug Misuse in the UK*, London: ISDD.

Joyce, R. and Grant, R. (1997) *Smack or Sympathy – Exploring Drug Issues in Schools*, London, Forbes.

NCC (National Curriculum Council) (1990) *Curriculum Guidance 5: Health Education*, London: NCC.

Ofsted (Office for Standards in Education) (1996) *Drug Education and Schools*, London: Ofsted.

SCODA (Standing Conference on Drug Abuse (1997) *The Right Choice – Choosing and Developing Drug Education Resources for Schools*,London: SCODA.

WHO (World Health Organization) (1998) *The Health Promoting School – Report for the First Conference of European Health Promoting Schools*, The Saloniki-Haldiki, Greece, 1–5 May 1997, Copenhagen: WHO.

Index